PEARLS
BEFORE
POPPIES

PEARLS BEFORE POPPIES

THE TRUE STORY OF THE RED CROSS PEARLS

RACHEL TRETHEWEY

For Mum,

for inspiring me.

First published 2018
This paperback edition first published 2019

The History Press
97 St Georges Place
Cheltenham, GL50 3QB
www.thehistorypress.co.uk

British Library Cataloguing in Publication Data.
A catalogue record for this book is available from the British Library.

ISBN 978 0 7509 9209 1

Typesetting and origination by The History Press
Printed and bound in Great Britain by TJ International Ltd

CONTENTS

ACKNOWLEDGEMENTS

Like the Red Cross Pearl Appeal itself, writing this book has only been possible thanks to the support of many people. When I first started my research, Jane High for the British Red Cross and Lynda McLeod at Christie's welcomed me into their archives and were so generous with both their time and knowledge, their continuing interest in the project has been a great boost.

I am also particularly grateful to the many descendants of the women who gave pearls. Without access to their papers it would have been impossible to get a real insight into what motivated the donations. It was thanks to the Great War Exhibition at Port Eliot that I first had the idea for this book and when I told Lady St Germans my idea she was very supportive, providing me with colourful details about the family. Other relatives of Blanche and Mousie St Germans have also shared their memories with me; David Seyfried, Lord Herbert and Sir Michael and Lady Ferguson Davie sent me photographs and Blanche's diary of her flying adventure, which showed just what a resilient woman she was.

The Wemyss/Elcho family tragedy lies at the heart of my story and so one of the most special times was visiting their timeless home, Stanway, in the Cotswolds. As I looked through the dusty files of letters and diaries in the muniment room, Mary Wemyss and Letty Elcho really came alive for me. Being shown around the house, sitting in Mary's drawing room, looking at her photo albums and at the sketches of Letty and Ego Elcho by John

Singer Sargent in one of the bedrooms made me even more aware of how the war destroyed their way of life. I cannot thank Lord Wemyss enough for his hospitality and for allowing me to use the family papers and pictures in my book. Mary Wemyss' story is closely intertwined with her friend Ettie Desborough's, and I would like to thank Viscount Gage and the British Library for allowing me to quote from her writing and photographs in her *Pages from a Family Journal*, which is a heart-rending memoir of a mother's experience of the First World War. Similarly, I am grateful to the Trustees of the Bowood Collection for permitting me to use the papers of the 5th Marquess of Lansdowne and a photograph of him with his grandson, George Mercer Nairne, which so poignantly illustrate a father's grief for his lost son. Bowood's archivist Jo Johnston has been a sounding board for my ideas and has pointed me in the right direction for the material I needed.

Another highlight of my research was spending a stimulating afternoon with Philip Astor discussing his grandmother, Violet Astor. I am most grateful to him for allowing me to quote from the letters written to her about her remarriage and for the stunning photograph of her in her pearls which he sent to me. I would also like to thank Lady Emma Kitchener for a wonderful lunch and for showing me the photographs and belongings of her ancestor Lord Kitchener. Her enthusiasm for the human stories behind the great moments of history made her immediately understand what I was trying to do in my book. She provided me with just the information I wanted and, by telling me about her family's love of animals, she helped me to crack the meaning of a donation which would otherwise have remained an enigma.

Noël, Countess of Rothes' granddaughter, Angela Young, kindly provided me with information about her grandmother and the Leslie family. The Duchess of Westminster's grandson, Dominic Filmer Sankey, was also very helpful, telling me about the complex dynamics of the Grosvenor family after his grandparents' divorce. I was given an insight into life in the wards at the Duchess of Westminster's Hospital through reading Nurse Martha Frost's scrapbook and I am grateful to her nephew, Ian Broad, who has agreed to me quoting from it.

With the Duke of Rutland's permission, Peter Foden, the archivist at Belvoir Castle, gave up his time to try to find out the history of the pearls which the Duchess of Rutland gave to the Red Cross appeal. Lord Rowallan and his aunt, Fiona Patterson, also tried to discover what had happened to the pearl necklace bought by their family at the Red Cross Auction. Emma Clarke at Mikimoto, London, provided me with additional information on Kokichi Mikimoto and the history of cultured pearls. Otley Museum and Archive Trust's Margaret Hornby sent me *Legacies of War: Untold Otley Stories* and Barbara Winfield looked into Ada Bey's role in Otley during the First World War.

I am also indebted to the many archives and museums which have granted me permission to quote from letters and reproduce illustrations in their collections:

The Canadian War Museum, for the letters of Katherine MacDonald, her family and friends, the photographs associated with her and the painting of No. 3 Canadian Stationary Hospital at Doullens by Gerald Moira; the Hertfordshire Archives and Local Studies for the Desborough Papers; the Somerset Archives and Local Studies Service (South West Heritage Trust) for the de Vesci Papers; the Devon Archive and Local Studies Service for information on the Kekewich family; the Imperial War Museum for a letter from Lord Kitchener's sister and one from his cousin written in 1916 – we have been unable to find the current copyright holders of these letters but every reasonable effort has been made to seek permission. Thank you to the British Red Cross Society for the letters between Sir Robert Hudson and Lord Northcliffe, which are held at the British Library, and the Grafton Galleries Red Cross Pearl Exhibition poster which is held at the Imperial War Museum; the Record Office for Leicestershire, Leicester and Rutland, for Arthur Percival Marsh's letter about the Duchess of Westminster's Hospital; the Parliamentary Archive for letters to Andrew Bonar Law, David Lloyd George and Hansard. My thanks also to Her Majesty the Queen and the Royal Collection Trust for their photographs of Princess Victoria wearing pearls, and Queen Mary and Queen Alexandra's visit to the Pearl Exhibition at the Grafton Galleries; the Lafayette Negative Collection at the Victoria and Albert Museum for photographs of Lady Northcliffe and the Duchess of Westminster; the National Portrait Gallery for a portrait of Blanche St Germans.

The Mary Evans Picture Library kindly supplied photographs of many of the people written about in the book, and Christie's Archive provided two cartoons, one entitled 'For the Wounded' and the other by Max Beerbohm of the Red Cross auctions. The British Library supplied a photograph of the Countess of Cromer which appeared on the cover of *The Queen* newspaper.

As well as manuscript sources, I am also grateful to have been allowed to quote from printed sources. My thanks go to Rosalind Asquith and Tom Atkins at Random House for the use of Cynthia Asquith's books, her writing evocatively captured the experience of her society. To Sophie Scard of United Agents who, on behalf of Jane Ridley, agreed that I could quote from Jane Ridley and Clayre Percy's book, *The Letters of Arthur Balfour and Lady Elcho 1885–1917*. My understanding of what it was like to live through the war has also been enhanced by reading many contemporary newspapers. The accessibility of online sources including *The Times*, the *Daily Mail* and *The Spectator* archives, the Illustrated First World War and the British Newspaper Archives made my task much faster and easier.

I would also particularly like to thank the people who shared my belief that this was a story worth telling. My agent, Heather Holden-Brown at hhb agency, has been immensely supportive from when I first came to her with the embryonic idea. Her assistant, Jack Munnelly, has also been a great help. My publisher at The History Press, Sophie Bradshaw, has had the same vision for the book as I have and this has made it an exciting project to work on together. I would also like to thank Lucy Keating at the British Red Cross, whose enthusiasm for the idea in the initial stages was energising.

Finally, I want to thank my friends and family who have patiently put up with my obsession with the Red Cross Pearls for several years. Christopher Wilson, Andrew Wilson, Marcus Field, Kay Dunbar and Stephen Bristow have helped me with their experience of the literary world. My husband, John Kiddey, joined me on my research trips, photographed countless letters and discussed what we found – he has been the perfect person to share those experiences with. My son, Christopher, helped me with technical challenges or any computer related problems, while my sister, Rebecca Trethewey, was a great proofreader. My last thanks, which should really come first, go to my mother, Bridget Day, who inspired me in so many ways to write this book.

INTRODUCTION

I have always been a pearl lover. For me, their natural lustre is more alluring than the glitter of diamonds. Worn next to the skin every day, not just for special occasions, they are the most intimate of jewels. My grandmother told me that pearls reflect the health of the woman who wears them and that, when my great-grandmother was dying of cancer, all her pearls turned black. It was just one of the stories she shared with me when, as a child, I spent many spellbound hours sitting on her bed looking through her jewellery box with her. For me, a string of pearls has always represented the links between one generation of women and another, as mother to daughter, grandmother to granddaughter, they pass on stories of family celebrations, happiness and sorrow, love and loss. When my grandmother died, she left me her two-strand pearl necklace with a sapphire and diamond clasp. It is my most precious piece of jewellery and I wore it on my wedding day as a tangible connection between my old and new life.

I am still attracted by the subtle seductiveness of pearls, so when I went to Port Eliot Festival in the summer of 2014 it was not the eclectic mix of bands, books and bohemians that stuck in my memory but a story about those jewels. As I went around the exhibition about the effects of the First World War on the St Germans family and the tenants on the Port Eliot Estate, one line on the large storyboards particularly fascinated me: In 1918, Emily, Countess of St Germans gave a pearl, which had belonged to the

Empress Josephine, to the Red Cross Pearl Necklace Appeal. Intrigued, I wanted to know more.

Emily had a special reason for donating one of her most precious jewels to the British Red Cross. At the beginning of the war, her son John Cornwallis Eliot, 6th Earl of St Germans, known as 'Mousie', became a captain in the Scots Greys. Tall, athletic and handsome, he was 'an amateur comedian of no mean ability', who often entertained his friends. After fighting in the Battle of the Somme and at Ypres, he was awarded the Military Cross in recognition of several acts of gallantry. He was severely wounded and sent home. Fortunately, unlike so many of his comrades, he survived. When the countess gave her pearl, she was giving thanks for her son's survival while also remembering the loss of so many other men from the estate who had died in the war. In March 1918, as she sent her gift, Emily had another cause to celebrate. 'Mousie' had got engaged to Blanche 'Linnie' Somerset, daughter of the Duke of Beaufort. With their wedding planned for June, Lady St Germans could at last look forward to the future with hope.

Discovering Emily's story made me want to find out which other women gave pearls to the Red Cross and what were the stories behind their gifts? As celebrations of the centenary of the Great War reached a crescendo with the Poppy Appeal at the Tower of London, I thought more about the pearls. I discovered that before the sea of poppies there was an ocean of pearls. I also found out that using these jewels to commemorate the sacrifice made in the First World War pre-dated selling artificial poppies as a symbol of remembrance for charity. A French woman, Anna Guerin, originally had the idea, which was then adopted by the British Legion, who held their first poppy appeal in 1921.[1]

The Red Cross Pearl Appeal had been launched three years earlier, in 1918, to raise funds for the wounded while paying tribute to the brave servicemen who had fought for king and country. Each pearl represented a life. No jewel could have been more appropriate. For thousands of years pearls had been symbolically linked to mourning. In Greek and Roman mythology it was believed that pearls were formed from teardrops of the gods falling into oysters. The link between these miracles of nature and grief was expressed by Shakespeare in *Richard III*, 'The liquid drops of tears that you have shed, Shall come again, transform'd to orient pearl'.[2] However, although associated with loss, pearls also represent hope and resurrection. In the *Epic of Gilgamesh*, which dates back to 2100 BC, pearls were described as 'a flower of immortality'. In the Bible, they symbolise purity and perfection and are associated with Christ, the Virgin Mary and the Kingdom of Heaven. In Matthew 13, Jesus compared the Kingdom of Heaven to a 'pearl of great price'.[3] Pearls also feature in the description of the new Jerusalem in Revelations, 'The twelve gates were pearls, each gate was made from a single pearl.'[4]

Like the 2014 Poppy Appeal, the 1918 pearl necklace collection developed a momentum all its own. At first, the Red Cross had wanted to gather enough pearls to make one necklace, but the appeal captured the public imagination and jewels poured in from around the world until there were nearly 4,000, enough to make forty-one necklaces.

This book interweaves the story of the Pearl Necklace Campaign with the personal stories behind individual pearls. Like the pearls that make up a string, each story is complete in itself but when joined together with the other wartime experiences it creates a wider picture. Through the pearls we gain an insight into a world that was changing forever. The pre-war certainties of the pleasure-seeking Edwardian era were shattered by the Great War. Heroic young men, who saw themselves as riding into battle like medieval knights in a Christian Crusade, lost their lives in the industrial-scale carnage of modern warfare. Although this book describes their valour, rather than being about the battlefields of the Great War it is primarily about the home front. It does not aim to provide a social history of all sections of society, since only women from the higher strata of society could afford to give pearls. However, bereavement was a great leveller, and the grief experienced by a mother, wife or lover cut through class barriers.

The pearls were a uniquely feminine way of paying tribute to the fallen. Some mothers who donated had lost two or even three sons in the war. Many of the young widows who gave were left with small children who would never remember their fathers. Their grief was often overwhelming, but so was their courage in facing bereavement. Instead of surrendering, they showed an indomitable spirit worthy of their men and carried on. The pearls provided an evocative outlet for their grief. Amidst the horror and devastation of war, these very personal gems represented more than just jewels; their beauty was a reminder of gentler pre-war days and they showed that civilisation would not be destroyed by the barbarism of the Great War. Using them to raise funds for the Red Cross emphasised that humanitarian values would not be beaten.

In this book there are many tragic stories, but there are also tales of joy, new love and transformed lives. For centuries, pearls have been associated with female empowerment, both Cleopatra and Elizabeth I used pearls to symbolise their power and status. The Red Cross Pearls also reflect dauntless female strength of character and they remind us of what women can achieve when faced with the most extreme circumstances. The Countess of Rothes rowed a lifeboat to safety from the *Titanic* and went on to donate one of the pearls she was wearing on that fateful night to the appeal. The selfless sacrifice of the young Canadian nurse Katherine MacDonald, who lost her life while caring for the wounded, was also commemorated by a pearl.

Although the Red Cross Pearls have been largely forgotten by history, in 1918 they were the talk of society. They were discussed over candlelit dinners in country houses, in the senior common rooms of universities and in newspaper newsrooms. By the summer, their fate was even debated in Parliament. What began as a collection among an interconnected elite spread across the country, and eventually the world, to touch the hearts of women from many different backgrounds. Pearls poured in from Egypt, South America and Singapore. They were given in memory of soldiers and nurses, not only from Britain but from Canada, New Zealand and Australia. In the final necklaces each pearl became anonymous, a gem from the queen could be next to a jewel from a poor widow, but each one was of equal sentimental value.

Although the Pearl Appeal was predominantly a tribute from women, it was supported by powerful men. Tracing the history of the pearls takes us behind the public façade of some of the most influential men in the war to reveal their human side. It shows the newspaper proprietor Lord Northcliffe mourning for his nephews, the politician Lord Lansdowne grief-stricken about the loss of his favourite son, and the icon of the army, Lord Kitchener, devastated by the death of his protégé Julian Grenfell. Examining this intimate history gives an additional dimension to understanding their attitudes to the war.

The full story of the Red Cross Pearls has never been told before. Using research from the Red Cross and Christie's archives, and the extensive contemporary coverage of the Pearl Appeal in *The Times*, the *Daily Mail*, *The Sketch*, the *Illustrated London News*, *The Queen* and provincial newspapers, this book pieces together its inspiring story. Drawing on diaries, journals and letters of the people who gave pearls, it explores the emotions and experiences that motivated so many women to donate.

Through these contemporary records, we are able to enter the mindset of some of the women going through this tragedy. We get an insight into the complex emotions of Letty Elcho and Violet Astor, the young widows who had lost their soulmates, and Mary Wemyss and Ettie Desborough, the mothers who had to come to terms with the deaths of two of their sons. Reading how they reacted is often a heart-breaking experience and, for our generation, with its different attitudes to duty, faith and patriotism, it is sometimes hard to understand. It shows that their individual responses were as unique as each pearl and even women who were the closest friends reacted in very different ways. Whether it was the Duchess of Rutland doing everything in her power to prevent her son going to war or Ettie Desborough glorifying the sacrifice of her sons, what becomes clear is that they did what they needed to survive. Before judging them, we should consider what we would do if we were faced with a similar situation.

Remembering the sacrifices made by the women who donated pearls is deeply moving. The Red Cross Pearls are a tribute to them as much as to their men. Ultimately, their generosity reflected their faith in a selfless love which could transcend tragedy. As *The Times* wrote:

> And so one is brought back in the end to look with reverence, upon the heart of this gift of pearls […] It is the memories and the tears of mothers, wives and lovers. Of these thousands of pearls not one is merely a pearl. It is a proud memory of one who proudly died for freedom; it is a tear shed in secret over an irreparable loss; a shining tribute to a man or to a band of men […] who gave their all to win all for those whom they loved.[5]

ONE

TEARS TRANSFORMED TO PEARLS

Last night – we went off to bed about 11.30 and no one spoke of sitting up to see the New Year in and poor 1917 slunk away in silence, shame and sorrow. I kept the window open and I heard bells ringing in my ears and fell sadly asleep, feeling too dull and apathetic to cry.[1]

These were the despondent words written by Mary, Countess of Wemyss in her red leather diary on New Year's Day, 1918. She was not alone in her depression – after three and a half long years of fighting, Britain was war-weary. Mary, and thousands of women like her, had waved off their loved ones to fight for king and country, to see many of them never return, slaughtered in the fields of Flanders, on the cliffs of Gallipoli or in the deserts of the Middle East. One loss followed another so relentlessly that families were left dazed. So many tears had been shed that the bereaved were almost beyond crying.

As well as the emotional exhaustion, there were practical problems that added to the demoralising atmosphere in Britain. With shortages of supplies, exacerbated by the heavy demands over Christmas when large numbers of soldiers had come home on leave, food became a national obsession.[2] The winter of 1917–18 was the winter of the queue; at first this affected the working class most, but soon middle-class women who could no longer get servants joined them. In freezing weather, sometimes standing in inches of thick snow, they spent hours in the long lines that snaked outside the shops where small amounts of tea, sugar, margarine or meat were still available.[3] In many parts of the country there was no butter or margarine to be had; butchers had to close for several days a week because they had no meat, while fish and chip shops shut because they had run out of fat.[4] Concerned by the appearance of food queues, from January 1918 the government issued ration cards and began to build up a system of regional and local food distribution centres.[5] With no end to the war in sight, morale was at such low ebb that the army feared people at home would fail them by losing heart to see the war through to victory.[6]

In the first months of 1918 Britain's prospects of winning the war had never looked bleaker. Once Russia withdrew from the war, following the Bolshevik Revolution, the Germans were able to concentrate their best troops on the Western Front. The British forces were in a poor state to fight back because, after the casualties of the previous year, their army was dangerously under strength. The master of German strategy, General Erich Ludendorff, knew that he had a brief window of opportunity during which his enemies were weak; his aim was to defeat Britain and France quickly before the Americans arrived in large numbers to support the Allies.[7] For civilians there was no escape from thinking about the war. The Germans' intensive night-bombing of London and the south-east added a new dimension of terror at home. For many women, it was only the desire to find some meaning in their losses that made them continue to stand firm.[8]

Nearly every family had been touched by bereavement; if they had not suffered it personally they had friends who had lost a loved one. It was clear that a deep well of grief existed, which needed to be expressed. In an age of stoicism there was no room for hysteria, instead the women of the country needed a dignified way to remember their loss with pride. These patriotic and practical women wanted to help the soldiers who were still fighting. Hospitals at home and abroad needed staff and equipment to give the wounded the best chance of survival, while those who had been maimed in the conflict deserved the highest quality of care once they returned home.

The British Red Cross was at the heart of providing this vital support. Following the outbreak of the war, the Red Cross had formed the Joint War

Committee with the Order of St John of Jerusalem. The two organisations worked together and pooled their fundraising activities and resources for the duration of the war.[9] However, by 1918 they needed £3 million a year – or £10,000 a day – to keep going.[10] Women across the country had already given so much to the cause; they had run flag days, held bazaars, put on concerts and donated whatever they could afford. Yet their generosity was not exhausted and, when provided with an innovative idea that recognised the extent of their sacrifice, they were ready to give again.

It was at this critical moment that Mary (known as Molly) Northcliffe, wife of the press baron Alfred Harmsworth, Lord Northcliffe, stepped in with the perfect plan to reinvigorate the women of Britain and the Empire. She would ask them to give a pearl from their precious necklaces to make a new string of pearls, which would be sold in aid of the British Red Cross. Each jewel would represent a life changed forever by the war. The appeal was very much a reflection of Molly Northcliffe, and without her inspirational leadership it would not have become such a resounding success.

By 1918, Lady Northcliffe was at the peak of her powers. In her late forties and recently made Dame Grand Cross of the Order of the British Empire for her charitable work during the war, on 9 January 1918 a full-page photograph of her graced *The Sketch*. Looking like the modern incarnation of Britannia, her steady gaze engaged readers. Fashionably dressed in a toque and velvet opera coat, with her hands placed on her hips opening her coat to reveal a cascade of pearls, she exuded confidence. Looking poised and uncompromising, she embodied all the women who had found a new sense of purpose through their war work. Recognising their role, in the summer of 1917 the government had introduced this new order of chivalry. The Order of the British Empire (OBE) was used to honour civilians for their contribution to the war. It was soon known as 'Democracy's Own Order', reflecting just how much women had done for their country, it was the first order of chivalry to admit them on equal terms with men.[11]

However, although the majority of new OBEs had shown real commitment to the war effort or bravery – for instance, saving the lives of fellow workers in munitions factory fires – the new honour soon gained a bad reputation. The public impression was that it was a tawdry bauble awarded to society hostesses, time-servers and war profiteers for trivial acts. It became known as the 'Order of the Bad Egg', 'Other Buggers' Efforts' or the 'Order of Bloody Everybody'.[12] Reflecting this critical perception, in a column in *Tatler*, 'Eve' commented on the unprecedented number of women honoured in the recent list. Expressing ambivalence to the new awards, in her usual tongue-in-cheek tone, 'Eve' explained that 'our grandmothers' would have fainted with surprise to see as many women as men in the honours list, particularly as the majority of them were 'honoured' for doing jobs which were once seen as exclusively masculine. The columnist joked that if there were more lists like this 'the chief distinction, if not honour, will be <u>not</u> to have letters after your name'. She added, 'I've already heard of one Wicked Woman who appends DNWW to her well-known name – which, being interpreted, means Done No War Work.'[13]

Lady Northcliffe was too self-assured to be put down by such mocking comments. *The Sketch* picture of her shows a woman ready to launch the most ambitious charitable campaign of her career. Molly had the experience, connections and imagination to make the appeal take off. After founding a newspaper empire which, from 1908, included the establishment's 'Thunderer', *The Times*, as well as the *Daily Mail*, her husband, Lord Northcliffe, was one of the richest and most influential men in British life. At the beginning of the war Northcliffe controlled four out of every ten morning newspapers.[14] Politicians feared and courted him, knowing that his newspapers could help to make or break governments.

Molly had been a true partner in her husband's meteoric rise. In the Pearl Appeal, as in their life together, she drew on her husband's considerable resources while distancing herself from his sometimes socially embarrassing vendettas. In her Red Cross campaign, Molly used the skills she had honed while advancing her husband's career.

When they married in 1888, Alfred and Molly had little money but endless dreams set out in the groom's '*Schemo Magnifico*', a brown paper folder containing his ideas for building a newspaper empire. With no inherited money to rely on, as he was the son of an impoverished barrister while she was the daughter of a West Indies sugar importer, the young couple were determined to make their own fortune. On their wedding day, Alfred borrowed the money from a friend to pay for the engagement ring and appeared at the church with a 'dummy' copy of his planned penny weekly, *Answers to Correspondents*, sticking out of his jacket pocket. His domineering mother predicted that the couple would have many children and no money – she could not have been more wrong.

Later, Lord Northcliffe attributed much of his success to his wife's sure judgement and quick brain. She knew what made a story that would appeal to women, and she used this knowledge first in her husband's newspapers and then in the pearl campaign. In the first years of their marriage, she worked side by side with Alfred in the little front room of their terraced house in Pandora Road, West Hampstead, writing articles and collecting interesting material from American newspapers for *Answers to Correspondents*. Across the floor were strewn newspaper clippings, papers, scissors and paste, while proofs were draped over the armchairs. Both husband and wife looked back on this time as a period of great happiness, as they were working together with a common purpose.

Molly's influence was important again when Alfred founded the *Daily Mail* in 1896. Wanting to attract women readers whose interests had previously been largely ignored by the press, he made it the first newspaper with a dedicated women's page, known as the 'Women's Realm'. Molly gave him hints about the type of stories which would interest women readers. No doubt thinking of his socially aspirational wife, when giving advice to his young colleague, Tom Clarke, Alfred explained that women readers were most interested in other people, their failures and successes, their joys and sorrows and their peccadilloes. He told him that the more aristocratic names he got in the paper the better, because the public was 'more interested in duchesses than servant girls [...]. Everyone likes reading about people in better circumstances than his or her own.'[15] Two decades later, Lady Northcliffe applied the same principles to reach the same female audience with the Pearl Appeal; it combined the glamour of the aristocracy humanised by the pathos of the war.

Unlike many of the women who were to donate pearls, Molly had not lost a son in the war. Instead, the great sadness in her life was to be childless. Both husband and wife had longed for children, and when Molly did not conceive naturally, the most skilled doctors in England and on the Continent were consulted, but none could find a medical explanation. In April 1893 Molly underwent surgery but it was unsuccessful. Their childlessness remained a permanent disappointment to them both.

Alfred did have illegitimate children, but he never had the heir he could publicly acknowledge to the world. When sympathy was offered, Alfred would brush it aside, simply saying that in every life 'there is always a crumpled rose leaf'.[16] Described as boyish, he had a natural affinity with children and built a strong relationship with his many nieces, nephews and godchildren. He kept a cupboard of toys in his newspaper office and would sit on the floor playing with his young guests on their regular visits. He also gave generous gifts to employees for their children.

Molly's unhappiness was reflected in her poor health. In the early years of their marriage she suffered from double pneumonia which affected her heart. The psychological effect of infertility on her mood is plain to see in a photograph taken at this time. While Alfred dominates the photo, staring into the distance with one foot resting on a stone mounting block, one hand on his hip, the other proprietorially placed on Molly's shoulder, she looks desperate. Her eyes are downcast, her shoulders hunched, her whole demeanour is as fragile as the delicate lace on her cream blouse.

However, being fundamentally feisty, Molly did not sit back and wallow in self-pity for long; instead, she carved a new and independent life for herself. Called by her husband 'my little lion-heart', she was known for her fearlessness. She would ride the most spirited horses, drive as fast as possible in early motorcars and was one of the first women to go up in an aeroplane.[17] When her husband started having affairs, she also took lovers, including one of Alfred's most trusted colleagues, Reggie Nicholson.

Educated at Charterhouse, Reggie first helped to run the Northcliffes' household finances, but later held important newspaper posts. He often travelled abroad with the couple; his easy charm and tact made him invaluable to them both. It seems that Lord Northcliffe knew of the affair and accepted it because he valued and respected his wife too much to divorce her. Although he became increasingly irritable and volatile in private, he remained courtly in his outward devotion to her. Resting on an easel in his office at Carmelite House was a regal portrait of Molly surrounded by flowers. In his diaries, he called her 'the little wife', 'wifie' and 'wifelet', but while the diminutives suited her 'dainty' physique, he knew that she was no little woman, instead she was his equal.[18]

Importantly for Molly, Alfred gave her a generous allowance to fund her opulent lifestyle. In return, she tolerated his infidelities and publicly played the role of a loyal wife to perfection. While he spent time with his mistress Kathleen Wrohan and their three illegitimate children at Elmwood, his country house at Broadstairs in Kent, Molly stayed for extended periods in their London town house or at Sutton Place, a Tudor mansion near Guildford. Sutton Place became the ideal show home for Molly to demonstrate her impeccable taste and skill as a society hostess. Lavishly spending her husband's growing fortune, she made sure that every aspect of the house was finished to her exacting standards. Sutton Place was described rhapsodically in *The Sketch* as a place where guests could wander in the famous rose gardens cultivated by Lady Northcliffe, or walk by the stream where 'yellow and blue lilies gaze at themselves' and which was 'so full of charm and serenity that Ophelia would have changed her resolve when nearing it'.[19] For the more energetic there were tennis courts and the first private golf course in England to enjoy. The less sporty could relax in the many nooks of the historic house or view relics of Lord Northcliffe's hero, Napoleon, in the panelled gallery.

The contacts Molly made helped to make the Pearl Appeal one of the most fashionable fundraising campaigns of the war. At their house parties, the Northcliffes entertained an eclectic mix of politicians, journalists, society figures, actors and actresses from Britain and abroad. While Molly was known for her fascination with the aristocracy, Alfred was not motivated by snobbery so much as the desire to make contact with other people of exceptional achievement. As a newspaper tycoon, he wanted to know exactly what was going on in the world. During dinners he would listen attentively to what was said but often retired early to bed, leaving his wife to entertain their guests. While Alfred was never totally at ease in social settings, Molly moved with grace to the heart of pre-war society. She was able to charm not only her husband's friends but also his enemies.

Although Northcliffe always remained an outsider, never quite accepted by the landed aristocracy, he could not be ignored by the ruling elite. His mass-market newspapers reflected the growth of democracy. In exchange for his services to the Conservative Party, Alfred was made a baronet in 1904, and a year later he became the youngest peer ever created. The culmination of his career came just months before the launch of the Pearl Appeal in November 1917 when David Lloyd George made him a viscount. A social mountaineer, Molly relished each elevation and saw it as her triumph as much as his. When Alfred became a baronet, she congratulated him, adding that her happiest thought was that they began life together and she had been with him through all the years of hard work that had earned him his distinction and fortune so young.

Without children to distract her, Molly threw her considerable energy into philanthropy. During the war she became a doyenne of charity fundraising.

She served on countless committees, ran her own private hospital and took a prominent part in the control of Red Cross finances and operations. Lord Northcliffe also worked hard for the charity, collaborating closely with Sir Robert Hudson, the chairman of the Red Cross and St John's Ambulance Joint Finance Committee. Northcliffe used his newspapers to promote the work of the Red Cross through *The Times* Fund. Since the war began, *The Times* had donated significant advertising space to the organisation almost daily and free of charge. It was a generous gesture at a time when newspapers had been forced to reduce the number of pages they produced due to a drop in advertising revenue and paper shortages. By 1918, the situation became even worse when paper rationing was introduced and the allocations to newspapers were reduced by 50 per cent.[20]

Throughout the war years, the paper informed its readership about what the Red Cross was doing. In November 1915, *The Times* produced free with every copy a Red Cross supplement of thirty-two pages containing full descriptions of the charity's work with illustrations and maps. Determined to use his journalistic skills for the war effort, Alfred went to France to see for himself how the war was being conducted. In 1916, he published his *At the War* book about the work of the Red Cross and life at the Front. All royalties from the sales were donated to the charity. Fifty-six thousand copies of the book were sold in the English edition alone and the Red Cross received over £5,000 in the first six months of sales.[21]

During the war, Northcliffe was one of the most powerful propagandists in Britain. In 1918 Lloyd George made him Director of Propaganda in Enemy Countries, but he had been using his newspapers to undermine enemy morale throughout the war. He was one of the Germans' greatest hate figures. In 1914, a medal was struck in Germany showing Northcliffe on one side, sharpening a quill pen, and on the other a devil stoking flames, with the caption, 'The architect of the English people's soul'. Similarly, a 1918 German cartoon showed the devil in an inquisitor's robe with one arm around a rotund Lord Northcliffe, who was dressed in a vulgar checked suit and had a threatening look on his face, holding a copy of *The Times* in one hand and the *Daily Mail* in the other. In the caption, Satan said to Lord Northcliffe, 'Welcome, Great Master! From you we shall at last learn the science of lying.'[22]

Northcliffe was perceived as such a threat by the Germans that they launched a direct attack on his country home, Elmwood, which was on the Kent coast. On a cold night in February 1917 the house came under a barrage of shells from a German destroyer. Shrapnel burst around the house, with some hitting the library. Alfred survived unharmed but his gardener's wife, who was with her baby 50 yards from the house, was killed and two others were badly wounded.

Like so many families in Britain the Northcliffes lost loved ones in the war. Four Harmsworth nephews, who had been like sons to the couple, were killed in action. Vere Harmsworth, the son of Alfred's brother, Harold, wrote home in October 1916 warning that he might be killed. Aged just 21, he explained that he could not imagine himself growing old. If he fell, he asked his family not to mourn but to be glad and proud. He believed that his death was the price that had to be paid for the freedom of the world and that they should see his life as not wasted but gloriously fulfilled.[23] Vere was killed shortly after writing this letter. His self-sacrificing sentiments reflected the attitude of so many young men who were to be immortalised through the Pearl Appeal.

Another nephew, and son of Harold Vyvyan Harmsworth, who had joined the Irish Guards a few days after the outbreak of war, was wounded for the third time and died on 12 February 1918. When the news was broken to him at his desk, Lord Northcliffe cried out, 'They are murdering my nephews!'[24] Yet another family death just as the Red Cross appeal was launched gave a very personal impetus to Molly's crusade. The determined society hostess called on all her contacts and ran the Pearl Appeal like a military campaign.

On 27 February it was announced that a committee had been formed with Lady Northcliffe as its chairman. Giving the royal seal of approval, Princess Victoria, the spinster sister of King George V, agreed to be president of the appeal. Tall and elegant with large expressive eyes, the princess was the right person to encourage other royalty to donate. Although she could sometimes be sharp-tongued, she was seen as 'the good angel' of the family, the unmarried daughter, sister and aunt, who sacrificed her own needs for others. After her father, Edward VII's death she lived with her elderly, stone deaf mother, Queen Alexandra. Although she had little in common with her sister-in-law, Queen Mary, who she described as 'deadly dull', she was particularly close to her brother, the king. Sharing a sense of humour and a similar outlook, they spoke daily on the telephone.[25] As president of the Pearl Appeal she took her role seriously and was to be an active member of the committee, not just a figurehead.

Reflecting the interconnections and intricate morality of the Edwardian era, also on the steering committee was Alice Keppel, the mistress of Princess Victoria's father, Edward VII. Evidently Lady Northcliffe had no qualms about drawing on both women's talents. As a woman of the world herself, Molly understood the subtle rules of the game; affairs were acceptable providing appearances were kept up and everyone behaved with tact. Sitting around a committee table with her father's '*La Favorita*' was much less highly charged for Princess Victoria than an earlier occasion where both women were thrown together. When Edward VII was dying, Mrs Keppel sent the queen a letter the king had written to her in 1901 when he had appendicitis. In it he explained that if he were to die he wanted to say goodbye to her. Queen Alexandra agreed to her husband's wish and both wife and mistress met by the deathbed. According to Mrs Keppel, the queen shook hands with her and said she was sure that she had always been a good influence on her husband. Alexandra then turned away and walked to the window. The king had a series of heart attacks and kept falling forward in his chair, by this time he was so ill that he did not recognise his mistress. When the usually poised Mrs Keppel became distraught, it was Princess Victoria who gently escorted her father's great love from the room and tried to calm her.[26]

Kind and generous, Alice Keppel was a popular member of society. She was ready to use her charm to encourage her friends to give pearls. She was also an expert on jewellery, having received a priceless collection of love tokens from the king. One of the couple's favourite jewellers was Fabergé. At Christmas 1900, she had a gold cigarette case designed for her lover by the jeweller, enamelled in royal blue with a coiled serpent studded in diamonds. Showing the magnanimity expected of her, another year she advised the king on a gift for his wife. Queen Alexandra also collected works by Fabergé and, thanks to Mrs Keppel, the king commissioned gold models of all their Sandringham animals for her. Habitually dressed in gowns by Worth and diamond and pearl chokers, Alice was renowned for her jewellery. Her daughter Violet wrote that she always imagined her wearing a tiara. She added that her mother had a goddess-like quality, but any pedestal she was placed on would have to be made by Fabergé.[27]

Also in the inner circle on the executive committee was Lady Sarah Wilson, the sister of the Duke of Marlborough and aunt of Winston Churchill. She was a close friend of Mrs Keppel, and as they were so often at the same house parties Lady Sarah became known as her 'lady-in-waiting'. Both women had sat together at Edward VII's coronation at Westminster Abbey in a special pew reserved for the king's girlfriends, past and present, humorously referred to as 'the king's loose box'.

Lady Sarah had also known the Northcliffes for many years. During the Boer War, Alfred had made her the *Daily Mail*'s first female war correspondent, sending back stories which were aimed at women readers. During the winter of 1899, trapped in the besieged garrison of Mafeking with her husband Lieutenant Colonel Gordon Chesney Wilson, she kept a diary for the *Daily Mail*. She gained a huge following of readers, who liked her down-to-earth writing style and optimistic attitude. Although the situation at times seemed desperate, she did not dwell on the horror. Despite food shortages meaning they had to eat horse sausages, minced mule and curried locusts, she also described the more positive side, including cycling events and the celebrations for Baden-Powell's birthday. When the siege finally ended after 217 days in May 1900, there were widespread celebrations back in Britain. Spirited Lady Sarah was treated as a heroine. The *Daily Mail* published a picture of their 'lady correspondent' wearing a large black hat topped with plumes and bows and her bravery was lauded as a symbol of the British 'bulldog spirit'.

During the First World War she called on that spirit once again. Within days of the war being declared she posed for a photograph with a bulldog and a resolute expression on her face, appealing for funds for a hospital. After her husband was killed in action in November 1914, she dedicated all her energy to the war effort. With her sister-in-law, Lady Randolph Churchill, she raised money for free buffets for soldiers and sailors at railway stations. Rather daringly she also sold lingerie in a shop in Piccadilly to raise funds for the Women's Army Auxiliary Corps. She was a useful member of the Pearl Committee because of her journalistic ability and her experience in asking her friends to donate heirlooms. Earlier in the war she had appealed for art and furniture to sell to raise money for the hospital she was setting up for the Belgian Army.[28]

Soon, nearly every society woman in London wanted to be involved in the pearl gathering. Lending their names to the cause were nine duchesses, twenty-seven countesses and dozens of viscountesses. The wife of the American ambassador, Mrs Page, and even the glamorous Princess of Monaco appeared on the list of patrons. Demonstrating her ability to distance herself from her husband when necessary and run the appeal as a formidable woman in her own right, Molly pulled off the considerable coup of persuading both the present and previous prime ministers' wives, Margaret Lloyd George and Margot Asquith, to serve on the appeal's general committee.

Margot Asquith loathed Lord Northcliffe with a passion, believing he represented a force of evil in public life because he very publicly criticised her husband's running of the war. Using the full force of his newspapers, Northcliffe had attacked Asquith's government for the high-explosive shell shortage, which he blamed for the death of many British soldiers. Under increasing pressure, Asquith's Liberal government fell in May 1915 and was replaced with a coalition government with Asquith still as prime minister but David Lloyd George as the Minister of Munitions. At this time, Northcliffe admired Lloyd George, seeing him as another self-made man of outstanding ability, he called him 'the little wizard from Wales'.[29]

In the following months, Northcliffe's unrelenting attacks on Asquith continued. By this point Margot Asquith became increasingly hysterical, writing in her diary that she would like to see the press baron arrested and claiming that because he encouraged the generals and politicians to quarrel, Germany had no better friend than him.[30] In the political crisis of December 1916, which brought the Asquith government down, Alfred gave his support to Lloyd George becoming the new prime minister. Historians debate the extent of Northcliffe's role in events; most agree that he helped to create a hostile atmosphere for the government, but his direct involvement in the final manoeuvring was limited. However, Northcliffe liked to see himself as a powerbroker. When the government collapsed, he phoned his brother Cecil and asked, 'Who killed cock robin?' Cecil replied with the answer he wanted, 'You did.'[31]

The fact that the wives of the men at the centre of these bitter political struggles could put aside their differences for the sake of the cause illustrates the strength of the Red Cross appeal and how it was fast becoming the most fashionable charity fundraiser of the era. At a meeting to launch the campaign at the Automobile Club, Lady Northcliffe rallied her troops. Emphasising that this was women's special tribute to the men who fought, while joking about the new right of some women aged over 30 to vote (which became law on 6 February 1918), she began:

> Your Royal Highness, ladies and gentlemen – You observe that I have put man in what is now regarded as his proper place. We are not concerned, however, to-day with women's rights, it is women's duty which brings us here. Our plan is to collect from willing givers pearls which shall make an historic necklace to be sold eventually for the benefit of the sick and wounded.[32]

She called on the owners of beautiful pearls to give from their strings and to persuade others to donate. A little laugh went around the crowded room when she remarked that no one would miss one pearl from her necklace. *The Queen*, the society lady's newspaper, agreed with her, adding:

> [Probably not] a woman in the land would mind missing just one of her gems for such a cause. It seems so little to give to those who give so much, and yet the price of one pearl may save a life; indeed the price of some of the pearls already given will save many lives.[33]

Like her husband's newspaper success which relied on reaching all sections of society, not just a limited elite, Lady Northcliffe wanted her appeal to extend beyond the upper classes to include all women who wanted to give. She reminded her audience that it was not only the most perfect pearls that could hope to find a place in the necklace, there was room for smaller ones too, so that no one need hold back fearing her gift would be deemed unworthy.

Soon the Pearl Appeal was reaching far beyond the drawing rooms of Mayfair. Across the country, committees were set up to collect pearls; in the counties, the high sheriffs' wives headed the appeal, in the cities the lady mayoresses took on the role. In Birmingham, the lady mayoress, Mrs Brooke, announced in the local paper that she was 'at home' at the Council House to receive pearls.

Although word of mouth was vitally important, what really made the difference was publicity. Thanks to Lady Northcliffe's press connections, the Pearl Appeal reached a mass audience. Her husband threw the full weight of his newspapers behind her fundraising and over subsequent months stories about the pearls appeared in *The Times* and the *Daily Mail* several times a week. With *The Times* selling 131,000 copies a day and the *Daily Mail* being bought by 973,000 in 1918, public awareness of the Red Cross appeal soon spread across the country.[34]

Women from all walks of life, who were not part of high society, wanted to do their bit for the cause. Those who did not have pearl necklaces or could not afford to give a pearl individually were urged to give collectively. In response, one gem came 'from a few ladies in County Galway'. It was suggested that collections for the purchase of a pearl should be organised among workers in munitions and aeroplane factories or in the mining districts. Soon, a fine orient pearl weighing 8.2 grains was sent in by the crew of an airship. The original idea had been to form a single rope of pearls, but the owners of the gems had other views and soon jewels were pouring in from across the country.

TWO

FAMOUS PEARLS

A picture of a society beauty, with her hair knotted in a simple chignon, her eyes cast down and wistfully looking away from the camera graced the cover of a March edition of *The Queen*. However, the focus of the photograph was not on the cover girl but on her large, luminous pearls which were perfectly set off by a gauzy white wrap draped discreetly across her shoulders. Under the chaste image, the caption read, 'The Countess of Cromer, who is on the Committee of the Historical Pearl Necklace which will be sold for the Benefit of the Red Cross Funds.'[1]

The countess was a particularly appropriate figure to represent the appeal. Before her marriage known as Lady Ruby Elliot, one of the three daughters of the Earl of Minto, she had been made a Lady of Grace of the Order of St John of Jerusalem for her war work. The Pearl Appeal had become a family affair for Ruby, as her mother, the Countess of Minto, and her sister, Violet Astor, were also involved. The Minto family, like so many others, had paid a high price during the war. Both Violet's husband, Charles Mercer Nairne, and the Minto girls' brother, Esmond Elliot, had been killed. However, reflecting the idea that the pearls represented hope as well as loss, the countess' serenity in the photograph was partly because she was pregnant. Already the mother of two daughters, in July she gave birth to her first son.

The cover was the ultimate endorsement from fashionable society. Inside this edition, *The Queen* captured the evocative element of the Pearl Appeal and the excitement it was creating:

> If all pearls come to us with the moving mystery of romance about them, how immensely greater is this quality in the case of that wonderful Red Cross necklace – that necklace which is growing, pearl by pearl by pearl, in the service of those who are wounded in the fight for Britain, for Liberty, for Right. Strangely suitable are pearls to be the vehicle of mercy and of healing with their tender beauty, their mystic meaning, their almost spiritual loveliness: and how great is the need which these treasures will supply.[2]

The article was illustrated by a necklace made up of pearls interspersed with seed pearl-framed miniatures of royal donors and the symbols of the Red Cross and the Order of St John.

The royal family had led the way by giving the first pearls. Three generations offered their support: on 4 March, Queen Mary donated a fine jewel, and on subsequent days Queen Alexandra and Princess Mary also gave gems. Each of the royal ladies wore a different style of pearls.

Alexandra was the 'Queen of Pearls', from the moment the Danish princess married Bertie, Prince of Wales, in 1863 she became closely identified with the jewels. For her wedding, her family gave her the 'Dagmar necklace'. Designed by the Copenhagen court jeweller Julius Dideriksen, the necklace was Byzantine in style, with pearl and diamond medallions set in ornate gold and diamond scrolls and swags. It was made from 118 pearls and 2,000 diamonds. The two large drop pearls came from the Danish royal collection and had been exhibited at the Great Exhibition of 1851.[3] The necklace's name came from the Dagmar Cross pendant, which is attached to it.

In the eleventh century, Queen Dagmar was the much-loved wife of the King of Denmark. When she died she was buried with a Byzantine cross on her breast and when her tomb was opened in 1690 the cross was removed and treated as a relic. It depicts Christ on one side and his crucifixion on the other. It became a tradition to give Danish princesses a copy of the cross when they were married. The replica, which was given to Alexandra, included within the pendant a piece of silk from the grave of King Canute and a sliver of wood which reputedly came from the True Cross. Weighted with history, the necklace was difficult to wear and Alexandra soon had it altered by Garrard. The jewellers made parts of the necklace detachable so that the cross could be worn separately, attached to a single strand of pearls, and the whole necklace could be worn as a stomacher.

The Prince of Wales also gave his bride pearls, selecting a necklace, earrings and a brooch set with diamonds which she wore on her wedding day. However, Alexandra became best known for her pearl chokers. As Princess of Wales, she had first worn a choker to conceal a scar on her neck but, because she was a fashion icon, soon high society women across Europe were copying her. Alexandra's signature style was sometimes taken to extremes, and at Edward VII's coronation in 1902, Consuelo, Duchess of Marlborough wore a choker of nineteen rows, causing herself considerable discomfort.[4] Perhaps she was trying to compete with the queen, who on that occasion seemed to don all the pearls in her collection, wearing the Dagmar necklace as well as the choker and swags of long pearls.

Opting for a different style to her mother-in-law, Queen Mary favoured a fashion created by Cartier, known as a '*draperie de decollete*' of forty-one strands of pearls worn around the neck and shoulders.[5] Following the more practical fashions of the modern era, Queen Mary's daughter, Princess Mary, chose a simpler style for her pearls. Until she was 18, the only jewellery her mother allowed the princess to wear was a single row of pearls or a small pendant of gold and pearls that was given to her by her brothers for her birthday. Even when she came of age Princess Mary kept ornamentation to a minimum, favouring a more severe style than her mother and grandmother.[6]

The royal family's different taste in pearls reflected the changing fashions. During the Edwardian era, elaborate jewellery and clothes were used to display a woman's wealth and emphasise her decorative role. However, during the war, as people lived simpler lives ostentatious jewellery seemed inappropriate. A new simplicity in jewels and dress became the fashion and pearls perfectly suited this wartime austerity. A simple string of pearls, whether real or imitation, became an essential part of a patriotic woman's wardrobe.[7]

As the weeks went by, the Red Cross appeal developed a momentum of its own; dozens of pearls soon increased to several hundred. An added impetus was given to donations by events in France. During the spring and early summer of 1918 the Germans launched their most threatening offensive yet in a do-or-die final attempt to put Britain out of the war before the German economy collapsed and the number of American troops was massively increased to support the Allies. The German General Erich Ludendorff knew that it was now or never; his aim was to crush the British Army in the belief that once Britain was defeated the French would surrender. At 4.40 a.m. on 21 March, an artillery barrage of unprecedented ferocity was unleashed by the Germans along the Front between Arras and the River Somme. Out of the early morning mist came an inferno created by more than a million shells being fired in five hours. The British troops were outnumbered; they were blinded and dazed by the fumes and the gas which turned the mist into a suffocating fog. They suffered 38,500 casualties, of which 21,000 were taken prisoner and around 7,500 were killed.[8] They were forced to retreat back across the old Somme Battlefield.[9] It was one of the worst reverses for the British Army of the whole war.[10] After the fighting, the Kaiser jubilantly shouted to his soldiers awaiting him at a station, 'The battle is won! The English have been utterly defeated!'[11]

However, neither the British soldiers at the Front nor their wives, mothers and daughters at home were willing to give up so easily. While the men fought doggedly on, the women needed a positive outlet for their anxiety; many found what they were looking for in helping the Red Cross Pearl Appeal. So rapidly did the enterprise grow that in March Lady Northcliffe set up an office at 10 Dover Street, Piccadilly, to run the campaign. It was an efficient operation; a committee of the top society jewellers including Cartier, Boucheron, Carrington & Co, Tiffany and Garrard agreed to be involved, and donors were told to send their pearls directly to them. As *The Sketch* wrote, 'When Tiffany and Mrs George Keppel, Garrard and Lady Northcliffe, with all the other ladies and gentlemen concerned, put their heads together, something pretty should come of it.'[12]

There was a frisson of excitement as, every day, small cardboard boxes arrived from across the country at the Bond Street jewellers. Inside were precious pearls and poignant messages about why they had been given. Each donor was treated the same. First she received a receipt from the jewellers and then a hand signed thank-you letter from Princess Victoria.

Soon the stories behind the gems were fascinating the public. Particularly memorable was the gift from Noël, Countess of Rothes. In April 1912, the 33-year-old set sail on the *Titanic's* maiden voyage to meet her husband who was abroad on business. Her parents, Thomas and Clementina

Dyer-Edwardes, her husband's cousin, Gladys Cherry, and her maid, Roberta Maioni, boarded with her. Noël was looking forward to the trip and before leaving Southampton she gave an interview to the *New York Herald* saying that she was full of joyful expectation.

Fortunately, her parents left the ship at Cherbourg on the evening of 10 April, because if her father had stayed on board it is likely he would have drowned with many of the other men. On the night of the disaster, Noël was in her cabin on C-deck when the *Titanic* collided with an iceberg just before midnight. Awakened by the crash she went up three decks to the boat deck to investigate. She was instructed to return to her cabin and be dressed and have a lifebelt on in ten minutes.

After pouring out some brandy for Gladys, Roberta and herself, she put on one of her warmest fur coats, her pearl necklace and a lifejacket. There were only sixteen lifeboats and as women and children were first to be rescued she was assigned to lifeboat eight. Able Seaman Jones was in charge of her boat and, because her husband owned a yacht, Noël explained to him that she knew how to take a tiller and row. As the other two men on the boat were not seamen but one a steward, the other a cook, Able Seaman Jones valued her expertise.[13] He later said, 'When I saw the way she was carrying herself and heard the quiet, determined way she spoke to others, I knew she was more of a man than any we had on board.'[14]

Taking charge of the tiller, Noël manoeuvred the lifeboat clear of the sinking liner. As the lights went out on the *Titanic* and the ship began to sink, a heated argument broke out on the lifeboat. As their boat was not full, Noël, Able Seaman Jones and several other passengers tried to persuade the others that they should go back and pick up people who would otherwise drown in the freezing sea. Unable to persuade her fellow passengers because they were afraid their lifeboat would be overturned as drowning people fought to get on board, Noël had no choice but to continue rowing away. During that traumatic night, not only did she display incredible physical courage, she also had a calming effect on her terrified fellow passengers. Particularly distraught was a young Spanish newlywed, 17-year-old, Josefa de Sato de Peñasco, whose 18-year-old husband Victor had been lost in the sinking. Noël comforted her like a mother and encouraged her not to give up hope.

For the rest of that freezing Atlantic night, Noël rowed the lifeboat and also taught other passengers to row. To keep morale up they sang hymns:

first 'Pull for the Shore', later 'Lead Kindly Light'. The familiar words were reassuring, 'Lead Kindly light amid the encircling gloom/ Lead thou me on!/ The night is dark, and I'm far from home/ Lead me on!' As the rescue ship RMS *Carpathia* came into sight they stopped singing and began to pray. Once on board the ship, Noël continued to help others, sewing children's clothes from blankets, assisting the doctor and soothing the bereaved.

As news spread of her courage, she became a heroine overnight and was soon known as 'the plucky little countess'. Although she rarely talked about the tragedy, the experience was to affect her for the rest of her life. Haunted by what she had witnessed, she found it hard to get the screams of the drowning out of her head. While dining out with friends a year after the disaster, she suddenly experienced the intense feeling of cold and horror that she associated with that night. For a moment, she could not understand why, then she realised that the orchestra was playing 'The Tales of Hoffmann', the last piece of after-dinner music she remembered hearing aboard the ship.[15]

In contrast to the negative effects, Noël was also left with a profound sense of gratitude for her survival. In 1915 she visited Fraserburgh to launch the motor lifeboat *Lady Rothes*, which had been given by her family as a thank-you offering for her escape.[16]

Three years later, her donation of pearls served a similar purpose. As Noël escaped from the *Titanic* she had only managed to save one piece of jewellery – her 300-year-old pearl necklace. In April 1918, she gave a pair of pearls from the string she had worn on that fateful night to the Red Cross appeal. A pearl that had survived the *Titanic* was an apt gift, as the earlier tragedy was seen as a harbinger of the First World War. It shook the hubristic Edwardians out of their complacency and showed them that there were forces beyond their control that threatened even the most civilised society. It was also a typically generous donation from a woman who was one of the most popular figures in London society. Blonde, petite and energetic, Noël was often photographed in the London illustrated weeklies.

Even before her lucky escape, Noël had shown a well-developed social conscience. Her husband inherited one of the oldest peerages in Britain and a large estate at Leslie in Fife, Scotland. Spending much of their time at Leslie House, the couple won the love and respect of the local community. Every Christmas, the countess celebrated her birthday on 25 December by treating all the children in the parish to an entertainment in Leslie town hall. After the performance, each child was presented with a Christmas gift.[17]

In 1911, Noël began her work for the Red Cross, setting up a branch in Leslie and endowing it with three ambulances. This grew into a larger ambulance corps which served Fife and was known as the Countess of Rothes Voluntary Aid Detachment (VAD). During the war, she was keen to help the war effort in as many ways as possible. Leslie House was used to entertain Belgian refugees and in September 1915 a garden party was held in its grounds to raise money for the Serbians. It was reminiscent of gracious pre-war days, as visitors strolled on the lawn or enjoyed tea in the marquee, while listening to music provided by the new army recruiting band from Kirkcaldy. Local Red Cross ladies organised a miniature flower show, field sports and a flag day, while Lady Rothes ran a stall which raised £21 for wounded soldiers and sailors. Drawing on her acting and dancing skills, Noël also put on a series of variety shows in the Fife towns of Cupar, Anstruther, Lochgelly and Newport-on-Tay to raise money for local war funds. Her female friends, army officers and even the local doctor were persuaded by her to take part in the entertainment.[18]

Noël had trained as a nurse before the war and so she ran nursing and first aid courses at Leslie. During the war, when not needed in Scotland, she worked at the Coulter Hospital in London. The 100-bed hospital had opened in September 1915, in a house in Grosvenor Square. The medical staff were mainly consultants from Guy's Hospital and the Middlesex Hospital but there was also an Australian resident surgeon.

A bizarre story lay behind the founding of the Coulter. Charlotte Herbine, an American psychic from Indianapolis, first established the hospital, naming it after Dr Coulter, the spirit of her family physician with whom she had communicated since she was a child. Apparently, Dr Coulter had told her to go to England and contact the Earl of Sandwich. Once at the earl's Hinchingbrooke estate, Dr Coulter communicated with him using Mrs Herbine as a medium. On the dead physician's instructions, the earl took up spiritual healing which he hoped to be able practise at the Coulter Hospital, but he was prevented by the objections of the medical staff.

The Coulter Hospital attracted many society ladies who wanted to do their bit for the war effort. When Lord Rothes, who was in the Highland Cyclist Battalion, was wounded in the face and leg in action in France in 1916, he was sent to recover at the hospital. Once there he was nursed back to health by his wife before returning to the Front. Noël found the work fulfilling and stayed at the Coulter for two years. It seems the countess gave her pearls in thanksgiving that both she and her husband had survived against the odds.

Another famous donation used to publicise the appeal was the gift of a pearl scarf pin which had belonged to the champion tennis player Anthony Wilding. Of the great sportsmen who lost their lives in the war, Anthony was arguably the greatest of them all. Born in New Zealand, before the war Anthony had been the ultimate sportsman. He won four successive men's singles titles at Wimbledon between 1910 and 1913, and also triumphed in four men's doubles titles there. He seemed unbeatable when, in 1913, he won the World Championships triple at Wimbledon, Paris and Stockholm.

However, Wilding was more than just a sportsman, he personified the godlike young men who lived life to the full before going to war. As his friend and biographer, A. Wallis Myers wrote, he had that 'rare, elusive quality called personal magnetism'.[19] Tall and blond with matinee idol looks, crowds flocked to see him on the base line of the Centre Court at Wimbledon. At the peak of fitness, he seemed absolutely ready as he waited to serve, swinging his racket with just a hint of impatience. In 1913 Wilding mania hit the All England Tennis Club as his fans literally swooned at his feet. Overcome by seeing their heartthrob, many women in the crowd of 7,000 fainted and had to be laid out on the court beside the roller until they could be removed. He became the darling of Edwardian society, welcomed by the Marlboroughs at Blenheim, the Westminsters at Eaton Hall and the Desboroughs at Taplow Court. After becoming friends with Bendor, the Duke of Westminster, they spent three weeks together in Cannes playing tennis all day long. Anthony described the duke as an irresponsible schoolboy who was great fun.[20] Following a meeting at a house party, a more unlikely friendship developed between the young athlete and the veteran politician, Arthur Balfour. They also played tennis together, staying in a villa while competing in a tennis tournament in Nice.

A performer himself, Anthony also enjoyed mixing in theatrical circles. In 1910, he fell in love with the American Broadway star Maxine Elliott. A statuesque beauty with ivory skin, waist-length black hair and enormous eyes that changed from blue to brown to purple, she was in the crowd watching him win at Wimbledon. Always keen to know the man of the moment, Maxine could not resist going to Centre Court to meet him. With her usual directness, she asked him if he would come to her country estate and give her some advice on her tennis courts. He readily agreed, recognising that Maxine was a force to be reckoned with. She was an independent woman who had fought her way to the top, leaving two ex-husbands and a string of lovers in her wake. Her first husband was an alcoholic, her second, the much-married American actor and comedian Nat Goodwin, also had a drink problem. However, Maxine was never a victim and although it was not a romantic success her second marriage served its purpose by advancing her career. Nat claimed that she used him as a ladder to reach her goal of having her name in lights over New York theatres. He added that she had 'the ambition of Cleopatra [...] She was one of the cleverest women I ever met, her dignity that of Joan of Arc, her demeanour Nero-like in its assertive qualities, and yet with channels of emotion that manifested womanhood in the truest sense of the word.'[21] By the age of 35, she was a star in her own right, but that was not enough for her, she was also determined to make her own money and use her formidable financial brain. In 1908, she opened her own theatre in New York called Maxine Elliott's Theatre, that same year she was divorced by Nat on the grounds of desertion.

Although an American by birth, Maxine preferred life in England. Introduced into society by Mrs Keppel's husband, George, she was an immediate hit. As George had suspected, his wife liked Maxine as much as he did and welcomed her into her circle. Needing her own base, Maxine bought Hartsbourne Manor in Hertfordshire where she became known for giving the most relaxed house parties. She brought with her a level of American comfort rare in many of the more spartan English country houses, she insisted on plenty of bathrooms and central heating for her guests. Called 'the Queen of Harts' by her friends, the actor and theatre manager Sir Herbert Beerbohm Tree said that she was 'one of those rare women who make everybody they come in contact with happy. A blessed thing in woman!'[22]

Maxine inspired myths and her name was linked with many famous men. By her early forties, she was totally sure of herself and she amused her admirers with her frank comments. According to gossip, both the Duke of Rutland and Edward VII tried to seduce her; it seems the duke succeeded and for several years Maxine was his mistress.[23] His wife, Violet, turned a blind eye to the affair and became friends with Maxine, often inviting her to Belvoir Castle because she found the actress a useful ally in managing her sometimes difficult husband. Once the affair was over, Maxine remained close friends with both husband and wife.[24] Apparently both the former prime minister, Lord Rosebery, and the former Viceroy of India, Lord Curzon, wanted to marry her but Maxine wanted to remain independent. When her sister Gertrude asked if the Curzon rumour was true, Maxine replied, 'I would not marry God,' while she told a journalist who enquired, 'I have honourable intentions towards no man.'[25]

Fifteen years younger than her, Tony Wilding was very different from the other men Maxine had known. The actor and theatre manager Gerald du Maurier described him as one of the most attractive men he had ever met because he was so healthy, clean-minded and unconventional.[26] This unconventionality suited Maxine; it gave her the freedom she needed to be herself. Although they did not formalise their relationship, her niece believed that Anthony was the love of Maxine's life.[27] He was good for her physical and psychological health. As he was so often at her house parties, he had his own room at Hartsbourne Manor near to a secret staircase leading to Maxine's bedroom and boudoir. Always health conscious himself, he discouraged her from smoking and encouraged her to stay slim by playing tennis. On the court he would say, 'Max, you must *run*.'[28] They also supported each other in their careers. When in 1913 Maxine returned to acting in Sir Herbert Beerbohm Tree's production of *Joseph and His Brethren*, Tony rushed back from playing tennis in Sweden to be there for her opening night. Dressed in a sensuous shimmering costume, her portrayal of the vengeful Zuleika was a huge success. Maxine was equally proud of Tony's achievements. She was more upset than he was when he was beaten in the men's singles at Wimbledon in 1914. She sat throughout the match clutching the hand of her friend, Lady Drogheda, and burst into tears when Tony lost to Norman Brookes. Apparently the only calm person on the court was Tony. He walked back with his arm round his opponent's shoulder, laughing with him before meeting the tear-stained Maxine and his friend Arthur Balfour for tea in the pavilion.[29]

Newspapers claimed that Tony and Maxine had been secretly married in Nice, but they both declared the rumour was nonsense. Although they spent as much time as possible together, they also enjoyed their freedom, and loving the adrenaline rush of danger, Anthony drove fast cars and travelled around Europe to tennis championships on his motorcycle. Sometimes riding for 500 miles, he got to know France, Belgium, Holland, Germany, Austria–Hungary, Scandinavia and Switzerland well. In France, in 1910, he took his first trip in an aeroplane – although the engine misfired and the plane almost crashed as it hurtled at great speed towards the earth, he found the experience particularly exhilarating.

When the call came for volunteers at the beginning of the war Anthony soon signed up. He hated the idea of war in the abstract and had no quarrel against the Germans, but he believed that it was his duty as a New Zealander to serve the motherland. He was also spurred on by a spirit of adventure. His friend, Winston Churchill, who was First Lord of the Admiralty, suggested that he should apply for a temporary commission in the Royal Marines.

In early October 1914, Wilding was gazetted second lieutenant, however, he was only a marine for a few days because his detailed knowledge of Europe and his skill as a driver were needed at the headquarters of the Intelligence Corps. His job was to drive his chief, Major Baird, from one place to another along the Allied Front, often under shellfire. Although he told his parents that he abhorred the slaughter of war, he described his job as the most intensely interesting work he had ever done.[30]

On leave from the Front in February 1915, the Duke of Westminster invited Wilding to stay at Grosvenor House where he saw his friends and played tennis. Back in France, on 16 March 1915 he was attached to the new squadron of Rolls-Royce armoured cars that was commanded by the duke. In May the squadron was moved near the Front. In his last letter, written on 8 May, he wrote:

> For really the first time in seven and a half months I have a job on hand which is likely to end in gun, I, and the whole outfit being blown to hell. However, it is a sporting chance, and if we succeed we will help our infantry no end.[31]

He was killed the following day during the Battle of Aubers Ridge at Neuve Chapelle in France. Shortly after 4 a.m., he met up with a colleague, who described him as looking totally relaxed – as though he was about to pop down in his car to Wimbledon. Instead of putting on the regulation breeches and puttees, he strolled up in 'slacks' and low shoes.[32] At 4.50 a.m. Anthony's gun crew opened fire and continued firing for more than ten hours. Firing was occasionally interrupted because of shrapnel bursting over the gun, which ignited the sandbags. Anthony directed the fire from the gun platform and the trench. Although constantly under intense counter-shelling, throughout the action he was, as usual, very cool and his example influenced his men.

At 4.30 p.m. several officers warned him not to go into the dugout as it was directly in the danger zone and more exposed to enemy fire, but Anthony, relying on his own judgement, crawled in. Shells came hurtling down in one of the greatest trench bombardments of the war. A quarter of an hour later there came a loud burst of laughter from the dugout, and immediately afterwards a heavy shell exploded on the roof. Digging through the debris of earth, iron and sandbags, his colleagues first removed the bodies of two privates then another soldier who was still breathing, finally they found the remains of Captain Wilding. Lying intact amidst the wreckage, blown out of his pocket, was a gold cigarette case, a souvenir of his Riviera lawn tennis triumphs in 1914.[33]

Wilding was 31 years old when he died. He was one of more than 18,000 New Zealanders to lose their lives in the war. His acting commander wrote to his father that his loss would be greatly felt from a technical point of view as he was carrying out experiments of great importance. He added that, on every occasion, Anthony had displayed the greatest bravery in exposing himself to every risk.[34] Voicing the attitude of so many parents, his father replied that it was better his son died in the 'manful discharge of his clear duty' than that he should have stayed safely in England.[35] The Duke of Westminster's mother, the Countess Grosvenor, reinforced this ethos, using the words which were to become the mantra of many grieving parents. She wrote to Anthony's mother:

> You will find comfort in knowing that he was fighting *so* bravely, and giving all for his King and Country, and was so loved and had such happy days in England with his friends. I saw him not long before he left – and now he is among the band of heroes who have made the great sacrifice, and that will be your comfort dear Mrs Wilding.[36]

In October 1915, Anthony's mother gave two of his trophies, a smoker's companion and scarf pin to the Red Cross Committee at Christchurch, New Zealand. They were put up for auction and made £300.[37] It is possible that this scarf pin was the one donated to the Pearl Appeal, or perhaps it was a different one from Maxine, who was friends with many of the women involved in the collection. Alice Keppel, Sir Herbert Beerbohm Tree's actress wife, Helen, the Duchess of Rutland and Lady Sarah Wilson all served on the Pearl Committee, while Maxine's fellow actress, Ellen Terry, was one of the patrons.

Before Anthony died, Maxine had already shown her commitment to war work but it became an even more important *raison d'être* after her bereavement. From the outbreak of war, she was determined to take a hands-on role. She dedicated much of her time and fortune to Belgian war relief, supporting families who had been displaced by the fighting.

In the first weeks of the war about 4,000 Belgian civilians were killed by the Germans. Although the vast majority of them were men, and most were probably of military age, women and children were also murdered. On 8 August 1914, a German infantry regiment took the seventy-two villagers of Meten out into a meadow and executed them. Among the dead were eight women and four girls under the age of 13.[38]

In response to the German advance, a large refugee movement began as thousands of Belgian refugees escaped the atrocities being carried out by Germans in their country and came to Britain. However, despite the wholesale burning of houses and shooting of any civilians suspected of being partisans, some Belgians refused to leave their homeland. Maxine was determined to help them. Using much of her own money, she converted a 300-ton, 150ft barge named *Julia* into a large storage unit with living quarters for herself and her helpers. Lord Northcliffe supported her mission using his newspapers to print an appeal for salt pork, bully beef, tinned butter, potatoes, rice, jam, chocolate, candles, matches, warm clothes and shoes for the Belgians.

Since August 1914 Northcliffe's *Daily Mail* had been commenting on the destruction of Belgian villages as monstrous crimes against the law of nations. He had been personally touched by the plight of the Belgians when he visited a hospital in the Belgian town of Furness. He was deeply moved by meeting a white-haired old lady of 80 who had been wounded by the splinter of a shell. Sitting on her bed he asked his companions, 'What has she done that War should punish her?'[39]

Maxine set off on her adventure with her maid, her butler, her sister's chauffeur, a Belgian skipper and a barge dog called Dinah. She also invited her feisty friend, the 'flying countess', Lady Drogheda. The story intrigued the public, *The Sketch* published a photograph of Maxine standing beside a Red Cross ambulance and captioned it, 'The Beauty of the Red Cross Barge: Miss Maxine Elliott, who is playing Lady Bountiful.'[40] 'Eve' in *Tatler* suggested that going up canals in a barge seemed to be 'the last word in war jobs for women', although she feared that it would be 'awful chilly work' and exhausting. However, she reminded readers that Lady Drogheda and Maxine were used to plenty of exercise as they played lawn tennis all year on their own and other people's courts and 'one must keep fit, war or no war, mustn't we'.[41]

The 'Queen of Harts' now became 'Lord High Admiral of the Barges'. After working hard during the day, Maxine made sure that her barge offered the degree of luxury to which she was accustomed. *Julia* was turned into a miniature Hartsbourne Manor. There were attractive cabins with baths and lavatories, and in the main sitting room a card table was set up for baccarat or bridge while delicious meals were rustled up by a Belgian chef. The barge even smelt like Hartsbourne with the familiar combination of cigarette smoke and Maxine's heady scent. It attracted many visitors, the Dukes of Sutherland and Westminster called in and Lady Sarah Wilson came to stay. Most importantly for Maxine, she was near enough for Anthony to visit her. He came for the last time the day before he died. For some reason, they quarrelled and this was to haunt Maxine for the rest of her life.

She was on her barge when she heard of his death and, although she never spoke of her bereavement, her friends and family believed that the essential light went out of her after losing him.[42] Needing to grieve away from the limelight, she stayed on the barge until the early months of 1916. During her time in Belgium she had fed and clothed about 350,000 people.

On her return, her aim was to make up the money she had spent on her war work. In the following years, she made two films for Samuel Goldwyn: she was paid \$100,000 for appearing in *Fighting Odds* and *The Eternal Magdalene*. When asked to discuss her wartime experiences for publicity purposes Maxine angrily refused, explaining, 'I'm not going to make copy out of the most sacred thing in my life.'[43]

Donors like Noël and Maxine were just what Lady Northcliffe and her committee needed; each personal story behind the donations increased the public interest and kept the pearls pouring in. By the end of March, as the total number of pearls reached 300, no limit was placed on the numbers needed nor was a deadline set for receiving pearls. The *Daily Mail* simply told its readers, 'The sooner the string can be completed the sooner will the pearls be converted into the cars needed for the sick and wounded.'[44] Responding to this appeal, in bedrooms across Britain women raided their jewel boxes. A feature of the gifts was the fine quality of pearls contributed. According to the organisers, early in March one lady had taken her pearls to a jeweller to choose the finest in her rope, and had given that one. Even the practicalities about how to fill the gap left in a necklace when a pearl was donated were discussed in the newspapers. One proposal was that every donor should be given a memento as a memorial of their generous gift. A tiny bead of white enamel decorated with a red cross could take the place of the missing pearl in the necklaces of the charitable.[45]

However, the gossip columnists could not resist a little gentle mockery of the appeal. According to *Bystander*, no fashionable lady dared to turn down the call to donate a jewel. The columnist wrote, 'To wear a perfect pearl-chain puts you under suspicion of having, if not profiteered, then failed to contribute to the Red Cross Necklace. And the otherwise much be-jewelled lady is immediately suspect, these days, of laying up treasure.'[46] In another edition, it satirised the way vacuous society women vied with each other to appear self-sacrificing. With echoes of the self-indulgent Belinda in Alexander Pope's poem *The Rape of the Lock*, *Bystander* described the owner of a well-matched rope of pearls toying with her necklace, lost in reverie. When her friend asked sympathetically whether she was making up her mind which one to part with she replied, 'No, trying to decide whether to give the whole or only enough to spoil it for my own use.' She explained her logic:

> If I give it as it is to be sold for charity I shall scarcely miss it. It won't be in my jewel case that's all and when I want to wear a long chain, which isn't often, I can put on these white sapphires. They really suit me better. But if I break the rope and leave it too short for me to wear at all, I shall feel well,

you know how one feels about a thing of beauty spoiled. The odd pearls will be a small pang to me every time I see them or think of them. You see, I want to give away something that I want to keep.

Demonstrating her resolve, she fetched a silk bag and a pair of scissors and:

… cut the Gordian knot she had just manufactured for herself. As the lovely oyster's tears dropped one by one into the brocade sack, until there remained only nineteen orphans on the string, her colour rose and her eyes shimmered. 'There!' She said with happy regret, 'I do mind. Oh my beautiful pearl.'[47]

THREE

PEARLS FOR SOULS

One donor who represented the ambiguities of the Pearl Appeal was Violet, Duchess of Rutland. As always with Violet, it was difficult to disentangle her motives; was she simply driven by a desire to be at the centre of the most fashionable charity campaign of the moment, or was her intervention inspired by genuine sympathy for the suffering of others? Whatever her reasons, on 1 April, Violet wrote to *The Times* encouraging her friends to donate their finest jewels. Wearing her cream flannel kimono, sitting cross-legged in bed in Belvoir Castle, she took up her quill pen. Balancing a green morocco folding letter case, with blotting paper and a pot of ink on her knee, she wrote:

> In case those eagerly anxious to give pearls from their heirloom necklaces should be deterred by what they imagine an insurmountable difficulty, may I tell your readers that in view of the present Red Cross necessity permission has been given me by those concerned with the entail of this family to take from their necklace the pearl I have sent in their names? I know that the present wearer, and I hope that the future wearers, will see in their necklace an added lustre by reason of the pearl that has been given from it. It makes the necklace for ever more interesting.

To make certain that 'the wonderful reason' for its shortening should never be forgotten by future owners, the duchess had written a memorandum to be kept in the family as an interesting historical record. She added, 'Surely necklaces from which pearls have been taken, and given to such a cause, will possess a better glamour than ever they had before.'[1]

Pearls from the Duchess of Rutland inevitably oozed glamour. In her youth, as Lady Granby, Violet had been a prominent member of the 'Souls', an aristocratic social circle that favoured intellectual pursuits and avant-garde artistic tastes. The leading lights of the group were Ettie Grenfell (later known as Lady Desborough), Mary, Lady Elcho (later the Countess of Wemyss), and Violet. These intelligent women enjoyed stimulating conversations with the most promising young politicians of the era. The Conservative Prime Minister Arthur Balfour was the acknowledged philosopher king of the circle, but politicians from both sides of the political spectrum enjoyed the stimulating atmosphere around the Souls' dining tables. George Curzon, George Wyndham and Herbert Henry Asquith were equally welcome. Although they called themselves 'the Gang' rather than the Souls, they were given the title by Lord Charles Beresford because they were always so intently examining each other's souls.

Circulating between Mary's Jacobean Cotswold manor house, Stanway, Ettie's Thameside mansion, Taplow Court, and Violet's Belvoir Castle, the Souls turned flirtation into an art form. Each married woman had her admirers, who wooed her with a heady combination of philosophical discussions and courtly love.[2] These relationships were 'a little more than friendship, a little less than love'. More about romance than sex, the idea was that 'every woman shall have her man, but no man shall have his woman'.[3]

Although Mary had a brief affair with the womaniser and adventurer Wilfrid Scawen Blunt, who was the father of one of her daughters, the enduring love of her life was Arthur Balfour. Whether they were lovers in the conventional sense is uncertain, but their *amitié amoureuse* lasted for over thirty years and was the most important relationship in their lives.[4]

Reflecting the interwoven relationships that developed within the group, Ettie Grenfell bewitched countless admirers, including Mary's brother, George Wyndham, and her brother-in-law, Evan Charteris. The Duchess of Rutland also collected her own circle of adoring men. Disappointed in her philistine husband, after bearing him three children, Haddon, John and Marjorie, Violet felt free to take lovers. While the Duke of Rutland seduced actresses, his duchess had an affair first with Montagu Corry, Disraeli's former secretary, and then with the philanderer Harry Cust. It was rumoured that Corry fathered her daughter Letty and Cust her youngest child, Diana.[5]

Arguably the most beautiful Soul, the Duchess of Rutland's Pre-Raphaelite beauty had an ethereal quality.[6] Bohemian and unconventional, her auburn hair, pale complexion and slender figure were set off by her Aesthetic-style clothes in faded colours and soft drapings. Creating her own style, Violet rarely used her jewels for their true purpose. At balls and dinners, the family tiara was worn back to front to hold up her hair, the diamond 18in waist belt was divided into two pieces and formed her shoulder straps, while Nell Gwyn's pearl necklace, immortalised in a portrait by Sir Peter Lely, hung in festoons between two sensational diamond drop earrings.[7] Her spontaneous decision to give one of her historic pearls to the Red Cross Necklace was characteristic of her cavalier attitude to family heirlooms.

However, the duchess was a highly controversial figure to promote the appeal because, unlike most of her contemporaries, she had done everything within her power to prevent her son John from going to the Front. As the heir to the dukedom and the Rutlands' only surviving son, if he died the title and estate would pass to distant relatives. Violet believed that John's duty to his family outweighed his obligation to fight for 'king and country'.[8] Using her considerable persuasive powers, she did her best to keep her son out of danger. As her daughter Diana explained, Violet was obsessed with getting John a position on the General Staff at headquarters, where he would be out of the firing line.[9]

One of Violet's strategies involved pressuring Diana into seducing an American, George Moore, whom she thought might be able to influence Sir John French, the Commander-in-Chief of the Western Front during the first phase of the war. Moore showered gifts on Diana, giving her an ermine coat, a monkey called Armide and a huge sapphire said to have belonged to Catherine the Great. Twice weekly he sent a vast box of Madonna lilies to her home. Moore also held decadent dances in her honour, which were nicknamed the 'dances of death' because no one knew which men present would survive the war. No expense was spared as guests drank vodka or absinthe and ate terrapin, soft shell crabs and avocadoes then danced the night away to the seductive beat of Negro bands. The minute Diana left, the host turned down the lights and stopped the music. The only problem was that Diana found the squat, swarthy married man who was sixteen years her senior, repulsive, however, she had to accept his advances because her mother told her it was to save her brother.[10]

Despite the sacrifice of Diana, Violet's strategy did not go to plan. When John refused to take the safer post offered to him through Moore's intervention, his mother had to adopt different tactics. The family physician gave false evidence about John's health, claiming that he had recurring gastro-intestinal and heart problems so John was ruled unfit for active service by the army medical board.[11] Although at first John had resisted his mother's interference, he finally gave in to the relentless family pressure. Unlike many of his contemporaries, he had never glorified war. His sister Marjorie wrote to Ettie Desborough, 'He sees no glamour in the fight like Julian [Ettie's son] – for that I pity him poor boy – He sees it as sad work from beginning to end.'[12] By the summer of 1915, his plans of battling in the trenches with his regiment, the 4th Battalion Leicestershire, were over. While 249 men from the Belvoir estate were killed fighting on the front line in France, for the rest of the war John stayed safely at Field Marshall Lord French's side as his aide-de-camp.[13]

Although Violet's actions were considered outrageous by many in society, she was not the only aristocrat to pull strings. In March 1915, of the seventeen heirs to British dukedoms who were of military age, only ten were at the Front, the rest were assigned to staff positions or attached to home forces.[14] As well as the obvious motivation of dynastic self-preservation, there were deep psychological reasons for Violet's behaviour. It was rooted in her earlier experience of losing a child. In 1894, her 9-year-old eldest son, Haddon, died in a freak accident which involved an acrobatic trick at his brother John's birthday party. He suffered a twisted gut and, after six days of agony, died of starvation.

Violet was inconsolable, Haddon was her favourite child and she called him 'my beautiful big fair child of beauty'.[15] The only person she felt able to confide in was her friend and fellow Soul, Mary Elcho. She knew that Mary would understand, as she had lost her 3-year-old son, Colin, to scarlet fever shortly before. Mary had tried to hide her grief from her children by putting on a 'resolute almost jaunty brightness', but one day when her daughter Cynthia followed her out of the nursery she found her sitting on the stairs 'weeping as if her heart must break'.[16] Having been through it herself, Mary knew just what to say to comfort her distraught friend. She wrote to her of the bitterness, terrible longing and feelings of regret, and she added that nothing could ever fill the silent aching gap in her heart. However, she consoled her friend by reminding her that there was comfort in knowing that for Haddon all the pain was over.[17]

Violet was a talented artist so she expressed her all-consuming grief through her art. Withdrawing into a studio in London, she sculpted an effigy of her son. On the foot of the plinth was written:

> Hope of my Eyes
> Something is broken that we
> Cannot mend.[18]

The death of Haddon was the great tragedy of the Duchess of Rutland's life and she never got over it. Even at the end of her life, aged 80, she used to tell Lady Diana how the thought of this dead child could hurt her as agonisingly as ever, but that the thought grew ever rarer.[19]

After losing Haddon, Violet sent John away to her brother because his presence reminded her of Haddon's death. She also maintained a certain detachment from her daughters, Marjorie, Letty and Diana.[20] However, she was neurotic about their health and lived in constant fear that tragedy would strike again. For her, the thought of her son John going to the Front to face possible death was unendurable. She was well aware of the risk involved as she watched other mothers within her circle suffer.

The Souls remained a tightknit clan and many of their children fell in love. Violet's three daughters, who were known as 'the hot house' or 'the hotbed' for their daring attitudes and dazzling good looks, formed the focal point for the next generation. Most beautiful was Diana, known as a 'scalp collector' she attracted around her many of the Souls' children in a group which was known as 'the Corrupt Coterie'.[21] Enjoying fast cars, champagne, drugs and gambling, they were criticised by their elders for their bright flippancy but their wit concealed an underlying earnestness. They had a horror of cant and rebelled against the moral hypocrisy of their parents' generation.[22]

As Balfour had been the leading man of the Souls, Raymond Asquith, eldest son of Prime Minister Asquith, was the guiding light of the Coterie. He was known for his wit, which at times could seem callous. According to his friend, the writer John Buchan, he effortlessly destroyed homilies with a jest and scorned obvious emotion and accepted creeds.[23] Like so many of his group, both male and female, despite his brilliance he found it hard to find a role that fulfilled his potential. Educated at Balliol, and then becoming a barrister, he knew that with his brains, looks and contacts he had the world at his feet, but he lacked motivation. As he confessed to one friend, his great difficulty was not doing things but wanting to do them.[24] He questioned the value of his extensive education and felt that nothing of real importance ever happened to him.[25] Although by the beginning of the war he was married to the intelligent beauty Katharine Horner, he had a close relationship with Diana.

During the war years, Violet watched as, one by one, most of Diana's friends and suitors, including Raymond, were killed. It seemed as though a whole generation was being annihilated. All classes suffered heavy losses in the war, however, the upper classes' losses were proportionately greater than any other social group. Of the British and Irish peers and their sons who served during the war, one in five was killed. The comparable figure for all members of the fighting services was one in eight. These aristocrats were either professional soldiers or the first men to volunteer, and they were rapidly posted to the Front.

The idea of a 'lost generation' is not supported by the figures, as four out of five of all British peers and their sons who joined up came back. However, because the families were so interconnected and so many brilliant young men did not return it felt as though the myth was true.[26] Diana recalled that Violet was deeply sympathetic about the deaths of her friends, but for their mothers' sake more than her daughter's.[27]

Even though she tried everything within her power, the duchess could not isolate her family from the slaughter. The horror of the situation came closest to home when Violet's son-in-law Hugo (known as 'Ego') Charteris, Lord Elcho, was killed in the Egyptian campaign of 1916. Violet witnessed the shattering effects of this loss on both her daughter Letty and her old friend, Ego's mother, Mary Wemyss.

When, in 1910, Letty and Ego got engaged, both their families had been delighted. The Rutlands cried for joy and the Wemysses welcomed Letty with open arms. The young couple were shy and very serious when they came to see Mary in her sitting room at Stanway. With tears in her blue eyes, a pale Letty asked Mary if she would have her for a daughter.

Mary was overjoyed. The most inclusive of women, she collected an eclectic, often eccentric, circle around her including those nicknamed by her children as 'freaks and funnies'.[28] She already had six children who competed with her friends for her time, but there was room in her brood for more.[29] The engagement was the start of a bond between mother-in-law and daughter-in-law which was to deepen through the tragedies of the following years.

Letty and Ego were deeply in love. As the companion sketches of them done at this time by John Singer Sargent show, the young couple were perfectly matched. Her slightly fey, modern beauty complimented his dark, soulful good looks. However, Ego was typically self-deprecating about his handsome image, saying it was not his idea of himself. He felt he was 'a dreamy, comfortable, sheepish individual'.[30] Others always saw in Ego what he failed to see in himself. Diana described her brother-in-law as like a knight of chivalry but one who had the most wonderful sense of humour.[31] From his boyhood, he had an inherent integrity so that anyone contemplating a mean or dishonest action would feel ashamed if they looked into Ego's eyes.

Ego and Letty's wedding at St Margaret's, Westminster, in February 1911 was a joyous occasion, and afterwards Ego wrote to his mother from their honeymoon, 'You are not losing me and you have gained little Letty.'[32] There was never any jealousy between the two women for Ego's affections and they enjoyed each other's company. Mary had 'a dancing gaiety' which made her fun to be with.[33] Open-minded and tolerant, her large brown eyes lit up as she listened to the latest news from her son and his wife. She was delighted to see Ego so happy, and the once diffident young man grew in confidence as he basked in Letty's adoration.

When their sons, David, and then Martin, were born, Ego became a doting father who looked forward to giving them their first cricket lessons. The couple enjoyed spending time quietly with their children. Ego would read while Letty played the piano, then they would have a game of chess.

Although Letty adored her children, Ego always came first. There was great physicality in their love for each other. When they first fell in love, Letty wrote breathlessly to her 'beloved one' from her bed, 'Oh! I want you, my honey, yes I want you, want you, want you!!'[34] In the year before they married she dreamt of him every night. Several years into their marriage the intimacy between them was as great as ever. She wrote, 'It was perfectly heavenly, our afternoon yesterday wasn't it. I loved you better than ever.'[35] The couple hated being apart even for a short time. Seeing Ego off on the train for a short separation Letty lacked the courage to turn around on the platform as she did not want to make a fool of herself by bursting into tears. She minded him going away much more than she expected and could not bear the loneliness of life without him.[36]

In another letter to her 'darling love', she jokingly told him, 'I nearly killed myself with a hat pin when I failed to find your darling head on your uncrushed pillow!'[37] The empty bed made her feel for an awful moment that he was dead. She added, 'I would give everything I have in the world to know that you were undressing next door, and would soon come and snuggle!'[38] While they were separated she clung on to anything associated with him, from the envelope he had licked to his empty dressing room which smelt 'deliciously' of him. She described her excitement at being reunited with him as like being married over again, 'only better because I know how wonderful it is going to be – I don't merely make a shrewd guess'.[39]

War was to end the Wemyss family's enchanted life. The immutable quality of Stanway, with its time-tinted golden stone gatehouse, church and tithe barn nestling in the Cotswold countryside would remain the same, but the lives of those who lived there would change beyond recognition. First Ego and then his younger brother, Yvo, signed up to fight. Ego had always loved anything military. As a boy, every inch of the family's London town house was taken over by a war game invented by his mother's friend, the writer H.G. Wells, which involved playing with toy guns and tin soldiers.[40]

While Ego was training with his regiment, Letty rushed to wherever he was posted to spend the night with him. Sometimes their arrangements had to be changed at the last minute because Ego had to be on duty, leaving them disappointed. On other occasions, Ego found it hard to switch from his role as a soldier to a lover. After seeing each other during one of his leaves in September 1914, he apologised for making Letty cry. He told her, 'I would give anything to have those 48 hours over again and live them differently. I didn't behave in a very lover-like fashion to you I am afraid but I love you dreadfully all the same.'[41] However, although there were occasional misunderstandings, their brief encounters added intensity to their relationship. Ego told his wife, 'We have had wonderful times, much the best time together since we married.'[42]

In April 1915, Ego was posted to Egypt with his regiment, the Gloucester Hussars. After Turkey entered the war at the end of October 1914 on the side of Germany, the British Government declared Egypt a protectorate of the British Empire. Troops defended the Suez Canal which was a vital route for the British Empire. When Ego left Stanway for the final time, his mother remained strong during their last goodbye. She wrote that love and pride gave her strength, 'Ego had never failed me and I could not fail him then.'[43]

When Ego went to Egypt, Letty proved herself to be her mother's daughter by pulling every string possible to enable her to join him there, while her young sons were left in Mary's safe hands at Stanway. For Letty, it was a great adventure and those months in Egypt were among the happiest of her life, which she described as 'paradise'.[44] Although Ego was frustrated not to see active service, he resigned himself to enjoying a sybaritic lifestyle until he was called on to fight. Letty took a large, airy villa by the sea at Ramleh, near Alexandria, complete with a Berber cook and a houseman. When Ego was off duty, the couple spent time playing tennis or swimming and dozing on the beach. Letty described her husband as looking tanned and beautiful. He told his mother that in spite of 'this infernal' war they had real fun together.[45]

However, the war's sinister presence always lurked in the background. Letty did VAD work at the Deaconess Hospital, Alexandria, which was overflowing with the wounded from Gallipoli. During the mornings, she cared for two badly injured young men, one was paralysed and the other blind and dying from an infection in the brain. She found the work rewarding. On sunny days, she wheeled her patients along the white marble corridors onto the verandas where they could feel the sea breeze.

Letty was mortified when she caught scarlet fever and had to go into hospital herself. After returning to England for a few months, she could not wait to get back to Ego. In October 1915, just as she was about to sail, news came that Ego's little brother Yvo had been killed at Loos in France. Aged just 19, he looked so boyish that his men teased him that he was too young to be at the Front, but he was determined to fight. A few weeks after he arrived, Yvo was leading his men 'over the top' when he was hit by four bullets, he died instantly.

Young in spirit but old in understanding, Yvo had known that he might not return. Mary recalled the last time she had been with him at Stanway, they had gone for an evening stroll around the grounds. Yvo, with his hands in his pockets, had kept looking up and down, turning his face from side to side as though he was saying farewell to every twig on every tree of his beloved home. Just before he went out to France, Mary travelled on the overnight train with him to the family's Scottish estate, Gosford. As he lay stretched out asleep, Mary had a premonition:

> He looked so white and still, and though I said to myself, he is still safe, he is still alive and under my wing, yet all the time as I watched him sleeping so peacefully there lurked beneath the shallow safety of the moment a haunting, dreadful fear, and the vision of him lying stretched out cold and dead.[46]

Just weeks later, Mary's premonition came true. Her daughter Cynthia had to tell her the news. No words were necessary, Cynthia's face told her all. When her mother heard, Cynthia recalled, 'She was wonderful, quite calm after the first moment of horror. About five minutes afterwards she said something so sweet and natural, just what one feels when one is dazed, "What a bore!"'[47] Although, neither Letty nor Ego could be with Mary to comfort her, they both wrote letters. Letty told her mother-in-law that when she 'thought of his [Yvo's] love for you and all his family, and of Stanway and the birds, and I felt that he must have almost <u>enjoyed</u> fighting for his "loves" and that he knew it was all worth dying for'.[48]

Ego wrote his mother a profound letter which was to guide her in the years to come. He told her that his one consolation was that she could cope with the grief, 'Your soul is big enough, large enough for that purpose. The mere thought of your tackling it strengthens me. That sounds selfish and detached, but I have faith in you.' However, his assessment of the future was bleak, 'The only sound thing is to hope the best for one's country and to expect absolutely nothing for oneself in the future. To write down everyone one loves as dead – and then if any of us are left we shall be surprised.'[49] In the last lines of his letter, he added that Mary and his father should write off their sons and concentrate upon their grandchildren, 'which thank God exist'.[50] He signed off, 'Goodbye, Darling, I love you till all is blue.'[51]

In January, Ego's regiment moved to Salhia. Letty met him once a week to spend the night together at the camp. Then, in February Ego became ill with flu, and his recuperation allowed him to enjoy a holiday with Letty at Luxor. The weather was exceptionally hot and they napped in the afternoons before walking down to an orange grove for tea. They were given a sightseeing tour of the Tombs of the Kings by the archaeologist Howard Carter and then saw Karnak by moonlight. They both agreed that they had never been so happy before. Ego said they had 'a delicious time' and Letty described the five days as 'heavenly'.[52]

In a letter to mark their fifth wedding anniversary, Ego sent Letty his 'greatest love' and told her, 'You are a perfect wife – there is no question about that.'[53] He hoped they would see their diamond wedding anniversary together. However, it was not to be, after just one more brief leave, Letty saw Ego for the last time on 10 April, before his regiment was sent to Katia, about 40 miles east of the Suez Canal.

On the night of 22 April 1916, back home at Stanway, Mary had a strange dream. She wrote:

> The atmosphere of the room seemed to quiver with excitement – I felt the stress and strain and <u>saw</u>, as if thrown on a magic-lantern sheet, a confused mass of black smoke splashed with crimson flame. The flames and smoke were high up to the right of the picture and to the left I saw Ego standing, straight and tall. I saw him in profile, his dark eyebrows and moustache made his face look very pale. I got the impression that he was exercising all his forces with all his might and main. Round his chest was wrapped a golden banner, its colour very beautiful, it swathed his body in spiral folds and seemed to protect him as he stood there with his face set and stern.[54]

At a subconscious level, Mary felt that something had happened, but she did not know what. She did not feel anxious, just stunned. At about the time of her vision Ego had been killed. At Katia, on the night of 22–23 April, Easter Sunday, Ego's squadron was attacked by a large force of Turkish troops. The British were massively outnumbered and most of the men were killed or taken prisoner. Ego was wounded in the arm and leg but he insisted on going back to the firing line because he thought his presence might give courage to some of the younger men. After being wounded for the second time he picked himself up and put on a field dressing saying, 'Don't bother about me, go on fighting,' then shouted, 'No surrender boys, no surrender!'[55] According to witnesses, he was looking happy and cheering on his men with his arm bound up when he was instantly killed by a shell.

For months, his family did not know what had happened, they lived in a torturous no man's land where their emotions swung between hope and despair. Thousands of families faced similar uncertainty when their loved one was described as 'missing'. Throughout the war, members of the Red Cross and the Order of St John interviewed soldiers travelling to and from the battlefields hoping to find news of the missing. 'Watchers' were introduced in all hospitals, they were given a list of names of missing men and they asked new patients if they knew anything of them. They noted down their answers and forwarded them to headquarters. A year after the final sighting of the missing soldier, the Red Cross told his family that he was now on the list of 'presumed dead'.[56]

The Red Cross' work was much appreciated, and one mother wrote, 'We have heard nothing more from the War Office; only that he was wounded and missing, and but for your help and kindness we should still be waiting in suspense.'[57] Describing what that waiting was like, Mary wrote, 'Fate is playing with us (my heart) as a cat plays with a mouse.'[58] At first the news was that Ego had been wounded and taken prisoner by the Turks. When Mary heard the news she felt paralysed, she wrote to Letty with relief that he was not dead, tinged with anxiety about the extent of his wounds. She distracted herself by taking David and Martin to pick primroses and daffodils in Stanway's grounds. Letty was also suffering from mixed emotions, she hoped that if he was a prisoner he would be safe until the end of the war, but with Ego missing she felt cut off from her 'life and heart and soul'.[59]

At the end of May, Letty returned to England. When Mary met her among the crowds at Victoria Station her daughter-in-law's face looked totally white from the strain. Over the next few months there were contradictory reports. First there was news from the Red Cross that Ego was at Damascus, but there were no details. Almost insane with relief, Letty pictured Ego returning to Stanway with the church bells ringing and everyone crying for joy. At that moment, all she had suffered would be worthwhile as Ego's little boys would have a live hero to worship. But the news was too good to be true. In June, the message about Damascus was countermanded. One night at a dinner party, Mary heard Mrs Keppel say that an Arab servant had sworn that after the battle he had watched over Ego's body for hours. The Duchess of Rutland insisted that the bad news was kept from Letty but this deception was very difficult for Mary as it created an artificial atmosphere between them.

The uncertainty eventually ended on 1 July when an officer prisoner certified that Ego had been killed at Katia, and a few days later the news was confirmed in a telegram from the Red Crescent. When Letty's father-in-law, Lord Wemyss, came to break the news he found her alone with her two young sons, David and Martin, playing the piano. When Letty heard, she clung to him, and her sister-in-law Cynthia described the scene:

> It was just like somebody in a fearful, unimaginable, physical pain. The children were scared asking, 'What has happened to you Mummie? What is the matter with you? Will you be better in the morning?' Once the children were taken upstairs and Letty had been given some sal volatile she babbled away almost incoherently to her father-in-law, 'Oh papa, it can't be true! How could God be so cruel? There was no one else in the world in the least like him – no one – I have been so wonderfully happy […] Oh God! Oh God! It's no use calling to God – nothing is any use – nothing in all the world can help him. I'm only twenty-eight – I'm so strong – I shan't die!'[60]

Letty was then carried upstairs to her room and her two little boys were brought to her. As they were just 2 and 4 years old, one of her greatest fears was that her sons would not remember their father. She explained, 'David, I want you to understand Poppa's – you remember what he looked like – Poppa's never coming back to us.' David said at once, 'But I want him to.' However, he was too young to really understand and said, 'I must go now, or I shall be late for bed.'

The Rutlands were annoyed that Lord Wemyss rather than one of their family had told Letty the news. Later that night Violet arrived to comfort her daughter, but when Letty woke the next morning she was inconsolable. She began moaning in her sleep, 'Don't let me wake up to this ghastly day – I don't want to wake up.' She had dreamt that Ego was still alive but then the full realisation of his death came back to her and she cried:

> Oh God, make me mad – make me mad, if I can't die! Come back to me just for one minute my sweet Ego, just to tell me how to bear it, I can't bear

it without you to help. You must come back and see David just once. Oh God, the pain of it! I'm so frightened – I can't face the long years. What am I to do – I haven't got the brains to cope with it? I don't believe I've got any brains – only a heart, oh such a heart.[61]

Her younger sister, Diana, joined her to try to help her as the family feared her mind might crack under the crushing loss. Even Diana felt impotent, she said she would rather bear the despair herself than see Letty suffering. She believed that her sister was dreading that she would never know love again or have more children. Cynthia described her as 'pathetic beyond words' and like 'someone cut in two', she added, 'it makes one physically ill to see her'.[62]

Ego's mother, Mary, grieved in a very different way from Letty. She heard of her eldest son's death at her parents' home, Clouds. Mary's brother Guy brought a telegram from her husband to her bedroom. Echoing Ego's letter to Mary just months before, Lord Wemyss tried to comfort his wife by saying, 'We must see him again in those darling boys.'[63] When she returned to London, Mary's daughter, Cynthia, described her mother as looking physically better than she had expected and 'braced', but she said that she hoped no one would say that she was 'wonderful'. Diana kept phoning from Letty's house to know when Mary would be coming round. However, Cynthia did not think it was good for her mother to be with Letty, she wrote:

> For her, of course, it is a severe physical strain to be with Letty. She can help her but she cannot be helped by her. With Letty it takes the form more of a crisis, like an illness which in a sense can be ministered to. Mamma is so utterly different – no one can help – each person she sees is, I think, an effort and a strain. She is best left alone.[64]

However, instead of focusing on her own needs, Mary thought of her daughter-in-law, and in her grief Letty turned not to her own mother but to her mother-in-law. It was Mary who helped Letty to survive. As she admitted to one of Ego's friends, 'His mother has saved me with her infinite sweetness and wonder – I should have been a raving lunatic but for her.'[65]

In the days after hearing the news, the two women went down to Stanway. Behind the golden stone and mullioned windows, they retreated from the world to grieve together. Stanway was more than just a house, Mary felt that their home had a soul and that its mellow walls were steeped in the joys and sorrows of her family. She wrote that her children had been lucky to grow up in such a beautiful place and they all loved it with 'unreasoning ardour'.[66] When she was there she felt as if Yvo or Ego might walk in at any minute and sit by the fireside in her drawing room. At Stanway, in the hot July days sitting on the lawn under the tulip tree, Letty and Mary shared memories of Ego. Letty read old letters about her husband as a child and Mary's old diaries, fixing upon any mention of herself and Ego. When she felt overwhelmed with grief Mary tucked her up with a quilt and hot water bottle and left her to doze like a tired child.

The Duchess of Rutland had to accept that she now took second place to Mary in her daughter's affections. She wrote to Letty, saying that she was missing her but she knew 'in what tender loving – and beloved by you – hands you are in and how you are living his childhood over again with her'.[67] The duchess told her daughter, 'I never cease to think of your lovely crystal life – and its tragic smash.'[68] However, she admitted that she did not know what to say to comfort Letty.

In contrast, Mary said just the right things. As she was so childlike, the younger woman was very open to suggestion. Mary told Letty that sorrow was a very lonely thing but love and sympathy could lighten the burden. They did not compete for whose loss was greatest, instead they acknowledged that they had both loved Ego with 'body, heart and soul'. As Mary wrote, 'You and I Darling had such a perfect time basking in Ego's love we never were jealous of each other's happiness – therefore we never could quarrel over each other's woe!'[69]

Mary had emotional maturity and a strong Christian faith and she did everything she could to instil these values in her daughter-in-law. At first Letty was angry with God and found going to church difficult because she had prayed over and over again for Ego to come home safely and her prayers had not been answered. However, although her faith wavered, she believed that if she lived in a way which would make Ego proud she would see him again.

Both women knew that their duty now was to concentrate on bringing up Ego's sons as he would have wanted. Mary described David and Martin as our 'little bits of Ego'. At first, Letty felt that the children were no use to her because they were not her husband, but gradually she realised that they were all she had left of him. Mary asked Letty to let her help bring them up and she told her that Ego's home was her home. The two women tried to fill the massive void left by Ego's loss. Mary told Letty, 'The great thing in my life now is our love and confidence in each other.' She added, 'You and I are one – not only sentimentally but really for Ego is he not my son? – am I not your "Mama" for you and he were one and so I will be "darling Mum". And we will love him and one another "till all is blue".'[70]

The Duchess of Rutland was redundant as Mary had taken her place in Letty's life. When Ego's memorial service was organised for Sunday, 16 July at Stanway, at first the duchess was not invited. Mary just wanted the people 'who <u>knew</u> and <u>cared</u> and <u>understood</u>' to be there.[71] When Violet heard about it she wrote to Letty, saying she must be there, but only if it was no trouble. She said that she did not mind that she had not been asked, but she must have felt increasingly isolated from her daughter. Mary wrote to Violet reassuring her that both she and Letty would love her to be there. No doubt unintentionally increasing Violet's sense of exclusion, Mary added that Letty's 'love and trust and confidence in me and her sweetness are beyond all words'.[72]

On the day of the memorial service it poured with rain all day as Letty rushed from the house to the church taking Ego's sword and belt and arranging the flowers. The service was held at 6, it was an intimate occasion with only the people who loved Ego there. Letty was very brave but afterwards she looked ravaged and had to go to bed.

When the family went to Gosford in September the familiar estate made the new sorrow all the more acute. As the rain poured and the weather was unseasonably cold, Letty wrote, 'I have been <u>so</u> happy here in the old days – it seems so strange that the same things one enjoyed should now break one's heart.'[73] Mary described Gosford as like a tomb and admitted she felt sapped by seeing Letty so listless and sad, but then her daughter-in-law's mood would suddenly alter and she would smile and do something brave and sensible.

Letty still found it hard to believe that her husband was really dead. Like 528,104 other British and Empire dead, Ego had no grave as his body had never been found.[74] Until the end of September, Letty was tortured by the mystery surrounding Ego's death – there was still a lack of details, and her greatest fear was that it had not been instantaneous. She imagined that he might have crawled away wounded. She wanted to know exactly what had happened so that she could feel it with her senses.[75] Her mind was finally put at rest by a telegram from his sergeant major stating that a shell blew out his chest, which meant he would have died immediately. His sergeant major added that Ego had 'acted quite magnificently'.[76] These words became a talisman for both Letty and Mary and they were widely quoted to friends as evidence of Ego's heroism. Mary told her sister-in-law, 'I <u>love</u> those words coming from the quiet sergeant!'[77]

In October Letty joined her mother Violet in their Arlington Street home. Even when she was with her own family she missed her mother-in-law and wrote to her that she was feeling 'a dreadful coward about my new life – but I know I must face it […] It is wonderful for me to have you to help me to live it as you do – I dare not think what would become of me without you.'[78] For months she had not been able to conjure up Ego, even in dreams, but now for the first time since his death she dreamt of him. He was lying in state in Arlington Street in what she thought was a coffin but then she realised that he was in bed. He opened his large twinkling eyes and looked at her and smiled. He was very thin and suntanned and he held both her hands. She knew she was only dreaming but it was a comfort to see him looking well and happy.

The first Christmas was particularly difficult. The family got together at Stanway but the absence of Ego left an enormous void. Letty put on a brave face for the children but she could not help quietly weeping as she bent over their beds in the nursery to leave their stockings crammed with presents. It was the first time she had done it with her sister-in-law Cynthia instead of Ego beside her to share the intimate family moment.[79] Over the holiday period she had never felt so near to insanity and feared she would collapse under the strain. It was Ego's birthday on 28 December, and to mark it Letty wrote to her mother-in-law, addressing her in terms worthy of the Virgin Mary, saying, 'that day that made you blessed above all women'. She thanked Mary for shaping Ego and then for sharing him with her. She wrote, 'Few men are so much "their Mother's sons" as he was. Fewer men have had such a mother.'[80] Mary found that day particularly poignant. As she watched the sun rise above the black tracery of the old elms she wondered what was the point of life as the light of her life had gone out.

In a letter to one of Ego's oldest friends in January 1917, Letty explained her feelings. She wrote, 'For us who are left behind it is unspeakable. He was everything in heaven and earth to me, he was my religion, I cannot say more than that, and yet he was a million times <u>more</u> than all that.'[81] However, although she still found it inconceivable that she could exist without him, she had taken on board her mother-in-law's sound philosophy. She explained that Ego had trusted her to do the right thing and she could not fail that trust now. No matter how hard she found it she had to carry on for his sake and his honour. She added, 'I was his wife, his <u>adored</u> wife and therefore I am sanctified. I am the mother of his sons and they are a very sacred charge […] I am the proudest woman on this earth to have been thought worthy of his love and confidence.'[82]

Around the first anniversary of Ego's death Letty had a relapse. As Mary was going to bed at Stanway she heard a sound like a child crying. She found her daughter-in-law 'trembling like an aspen', shrieking and howling in an agony of passionate longing and grief. She was relieved to have Mary with her, saying, 'Oh! thank God you have come Mama, I think I should have gone mad if you had not come.' Gradually she calmed down as they talked of Ego's love and their happy memories. Letty then went to sleep, but the encounter had churned up Mary's emotions and it took her a long time to go to sleep.[83]

As the months became years, Letty and Mary's lives reverted more to their old routines. At times Mary still felt she was in a dream world, living in her memories, but then the voices of her grandsons charging around in their mackintoshes and sou'westers called her back to reality. Both women had a sense of pride that they had created something positive out of their tragedy. As Mary said, they had made the most of a bad job and by sharing their sorrow they had not become lonely or bitter. Instead, they had developed an unbreakable bond which sustained them both. They received peace, comfort and strength from each other but they also had real fun. Mary told Letty that '"Mum" would be quite a lame old dog without you!'[84] Both knew that it would have pleased Ego that they had become so close.

Although it took many years for Letty to come to terms with her grief, she did eventually marry again. In 1921 she married the artist Guy Benson and they had two more children. It was seen by the family as a good marriage, but it is clear that Ego still came first in her thoughts. When she remarried Letty told Mary that she was wonderfully happy as Ego would want her to be. Nor did she forget what her mother-in-law had done for her. She told Mary, 'You are my "Mama" aren't you? And my dear counsellor and beloved friend and helper and thank God you always will be. And I shall always be your "daughter" and shall always come to you as of old.' Using the phrase Ego used in his letters to Mary, she told her she loved her 'till all is blue'. [85]

Mary Wemyss was a very different woman from Letty's real mother, the Duchess of Rutland. Pragmatically, Violet had decided early in the war that she would rather save her son than see him suffer a similar fate to that of so many of his contemporaries. She did not feel she had done the wrong thing, she believed that she had to fight to protect him. Other mothers did nothing, and what did they get for their bravery? The worst. [86] Although, in one way, this was true and many modern mothers would do the same as the Duchess of Rutland, in her own era her behaviour was seen as unacceptable. There is no record of what Letty or Mary thought of Violet's actions, but a gulf divided them. Mary had a depth of integrity that Violet lacked and Letty recognised this. The Duchess of Rutland had saved her son, but she had lost her daughter to her oldest friend. Her gift of pearls to the Red Cross appeal symbolised the complex deal she had brokered with fate.

FOUR

MOTHER OF PEARLS

Although Mary Wemyss found solace sharing her sorrow with her daughter-in-law, in their relationship she always had to be the strong guiding hand, and so when she needed someone to comfort her she turned to her female friends. A camaraderie grew up among the mothers who had made the ultimate sacrifice. The Red Cross Pearl Necklace embodied this solidarity, their pearls strung together in the necklaces symbolised the close links that united mothers, irrespective of class. A letter from Edith Fielden of Twickenham, sent on 21 April with her pearl, eloquently expressed the feelings of all the bereaved mothers. She wrote:

> It is not a perfect pearl, but it is the only one I have. I send it in memory of a pearl beyond all price already given, my only son, and I feel that perhaps one pearl in that great historic necklace from me may hang side by side with those of greater beauty, even as the mothers of only sons stand side by side with those who, richer, could give more.[1]

Mrs Fielden's son, Granville John Henry, had joined the 2nd Battalion Seaforth Highlanders in August 1914 and was sent to France the following month. He was killed at St Julien in the Battle of Ypres on Sunday, 25 April 1915. He was just 19 years old.

The Red Cross Pearl Appeal became a dignified way for mothers to remember their sons and express their grief. In April, the first gift 'in memory' of a soldier who had sacrificed his life in the Great War was given. Soon, many pearls were sent in with simple messages, which in a few words spoke volumes about the feeling behind the gift. One from Mrs E.H.Villiers recorded, 'In memory of my Son-Heart's 21st birthday. July 21st 1918. Killed Feb. 4th, 1917.' There were hundreds 'in memory of my beloved son', or even more poignant, 'in memory of my only son'. The fact that many of the fallen were fresh-faced youths just out of school was emphasised in a gift from 'a mother and sister in memory of two boys'.

In the public consciousness, no woman represented war mothers more powerfully than Ettie Grenfell, Lady Desborough. When she became a patron of the Red Cross Pearl Appeal many other women followed; her example of uncompromising courage in the face of adversity was legendary. After she lost two sons, Julian and Billy Grenfell, within two months of each other in 1915 on the Western Front, a photograph of her sitting very upright and proud in her pearls and picture hat between her tall, athletic sons appeared in *Tatler*. Above the picture, a quotation from Rudyard Kipling said it all, 'If blood be the price of admiralty, Lord God, we ha' paid in full'.[2]

Ettie became the face of stoic war mothers across the country. This was the image she promoted, but behind this potent mythology of idealised motherhood lies a more complex story. With Ettie, things were not always what they seemed. She used her strong will to create an image for herself and her family which merged fantasy with reality. Ettie was shaped by her childhood and the brave face she showed to the world during the First World War was first constructed many years before.

Born Ethel Fane, she came from a wealthy aristocratic background – on her father's side, she was a Westmorland while her mother was the daughter of Earl Cowper. As a child she experienced more than her fair share of loss. Her parents had died by the time she was 2, her adored brother when she was 8 and then the grandmother upon whom she depended when she was 13. Instead of wallowing in grief, she learnt to hide her true feelings behind a carefully cultivated façade and appear happy. This mask was essential to her and an act of will because there was a strong strain of melancholy running through her family. Many of her relatives on the Cowper side suffered from depression and one cousin committed suicide. Throughout her life, Ettie battled against acute attacks of depression. To overcome these episodes, which she condemned as 'a kind of blasphemy against life', she was determined to enjoy every moment of her existence, however adverse the circumstances.[3] Her friends described her 'gospel of happiness' as 'Ettyism'.[4] It was partly based in her strong Christian faith, but it was also a reflection of her dominant personality that fought fate with sheer willpower.[5]

As a vivacious heiress, Ettie attracted many suitors. Friends described her as having 'a genius for life itself and for human relationships'.[6] Although she was not classically beautiful, she had the patrician air of a Gainsborough portrait as she was tall and elegant with heavily lidded blue eyes. It was more her compelling personality than her looks that drew people to her. Her immense vitality made every occasion exciting. She enjoyed intense discussions in which she would seamlessly switch from profound subjects to trivial gossip. She had a seductive way of lowering her eyelids when she was listening intently and then replying in her melodic drawling voice.[7] Her great gift was to make whoever she was with at that moment feel that they were the only person in the world. She was able to charm without seeming to flatter, to flirt without compromising her virtue and, once a man fell in love with her, the infatuation often lasted for life.

In 1887 she married the handsome, athletic Willie Grenfell. A year later, the couple had the first of their five children. Unlike many of the women of her era, Ettie was determined to be a hands-on mother. At seaside summer holidays at Swanage she gave up the whole of her time to her children, spending every moment doing things with them, either walking, butterfly-catching or yachting. Within the Souls, she became known as a model of motherhood, but this alone was not enough for her – she also had to be a femme fatale.

Although on holidays she devoted herself to her children, back home at Taplow, her turreted, mock-Gothic mansion between Windsor and Henley, her social life took up much of her time. She created an idyll for her friends; at her summer parties, beautiful women dressed in flimsy muslins and straw hats, and strolled in the balmy night air in gardens fragrant with the scent of ripe peaches, verbena and sweet geraniums.[8] As Ettie stood at the end of her long lawn surrounded by acolytes, it was often hard to get close to her. She needed to be adored by everyone and her children were always competing for her attention against her many admirers.

She demanded a great deal from those she loved. She wanted to be the centre of her children's world and she also expected them to always be the best. At times, these dual demands became too much for her sons. Just two years apart in age, Julian and Billy Grenfell were like twins; although they often fought, they were passionately attached to each other. First at Eton, then at Oxford, they were expected to succeed, not just academically but in sport and their social life. To their mother's delight, they grew up to look like tall, curly haired Greek gods. They were both exceptional sportsmen who enjoyed riding, rowing and boxing. However, friends noted there was something primitive, almost savage, in them which meant they were happiest in the elemental world of nature – hunting, shooting or fishing.[9]

By the time Julian was in his late teens, strains had developed with his mother. He became increasingly critical of her social life, which he considered superficial and hypocritical. They would have 'vehement discussions' which often ended with both of them in tears. Ettie wrote that they both held very strong opinions and could not bear the other not to agree absolutely. She admitted to feeling 'mildly depressed' about these arguments and thinking how dreadful it would be if anyone heard them, as there was 'very plain speaking on both sides'.[10] It was mortifying for her when Julian made their differences public in a series of essays he wrote attacking her world. He argued that the conventional values of the society he had been brought up in were based on fantasies, it crushed any individualism and hid reality. He believed that it was heading for disaster.[11]

His letters to her at this time reflect their complicated relationship and often it is hard to tell whether he was being ironic or deadly serious. In 1909 he wrote, 'Madam – On mature consideration I have come to the conclusion that our differences of view with regard to the moral sanction, Good and Evil, and social conventions are such as to make further intercourse impossible between us.'[12] However, the silence did not last long and he was soon back in touch, writing, 'I am longing to complete my newly established supremacy over you in argument. How are you? I am longing to see you, you are so much greater fun than anyone "besides being my mother".'[13] In another letter he wrote, in a tone worthy of one of her admirers:

You are wonderful; your wonder is inexhaustible, and keeps coming on me with a shock of newness every time, and your dark depths and your surface fun […] I want to see you again directly, because you are so far far better than anyone else, and I don't want to see you again ever, because everyone else is like flat soda-water afterwards.[14]

Hardly surprisingly, the oedipal dynamic between mother and son affected Julian's relationships with women. His brother, Billy, described him as 'a splendid creature, as beautiful as a panther, and no woman can resist him for ten seconds. I wish I did not feel such a centipede beside him.'[15] However, when Julian became interested in girls Ettie was jealous. He was particularly attracted to Marjorie Manners, the Duchess of Rutland's dark-eyed daughter and one of the three exhilarating Manners girls nicknamed 'the hot house'. Like Julian, Marjorie wanted to become independent from her dominating mother and be a singer. Ettie resented her rival and, for a time, refused to invite Marjorie to Taplow.

Similarly, Julian found it difficult to accept his mother's many flirtations. Particularly challenging was Ettie's intense emotional attachment to Archie Gordon, a friend of Billy's who was only three years older than Julian. When Archie was killed in a car crash in 1909, Julian could not cope with his complex emotions – already suffering from depression, he had a complete nervous breakdown. For a time he left university and spent hours just lying on the sofa in Ettie's sitting room fingering a loaded shotgun which rested beside him. During this difficult year, he wrote to his mother about his search for a purpose in life:

I utterly realise that what I am doing now is only secondary, and I'm longing for a real 'end' – I am truly, though you think I'm bolting, and barring, and banging. […] I agree that an ultimate end must satisfy all the needs of the soul; it must do more than that, it must be far far far above and beyond all those needs, a pure ideal, something wholly unattainable, you must have millions of miles of outlook. I think too that 'dedication and devotion and service' *are* very near to the roots of it […] Honestly I can't understand love at present, I can't think it, and I'm sure no ideal will come to me through love, though love may come through an ideal.[16]

Julian knew that to survive he had to separate from his mother. He described their arguments as his 'fight for life'.[17] After recovering from his breakdown he joined the army and went abroad to India and then South Africa.

Following in Julian's footsteps, Billy went to Oxford, but like his elder brother he became depressed when his academic achievements did not live up to his mother's exacting expectations. When he failed to get a first in his degree in 'Greats', he wrote to Ettie in August 1913:

> You must believe, my darling, that all your great love has not been wasted, though God knows you have got little enough tangible return for it; but it is there in the form of seed, and may flower some day, if you will continue to have faith in me and *will* me to be better.[18]

When war was declared, both Julian and Billy could not wait to fight. Like Raymond Asquith, until the war came they lacked motivation, but at last they seemed to have found their vocation. Julian now had a purpose in his life that had been lacking before. He wrote a letter full of excitement to his mother in August 1914 setting out his vision of what the war was all about. Steeped in ideas of honour, duty and self-sacrifice for his country, both at home and at Eton, he wrote:

> Don't you think it has been a wonderful and almost incredible rally to the Empire? […] It reinforces one's failing belief in the Old Flag and the Mother Country and the Heavy Brigade and the Thin Red line and all the Imperial Idea, which gets rather shadowy in peace time.[19]

It was not just the imperial ideal which appealed to Julian, he adored the whole adventure of being a soldier. When the Royal Dragoons arrived in France in early October, his letters home constantly repeated that he had never been so well or happy before. He wrote, 'Isn't it luck for me to have been born so as to be just the right age and just in the right place – not too high up to be worried – to enjoy it now.'[20] He described the excitement and independence of his life. He liked having no personal property to tie him down and even enjoyed sleeping on straw in the bottom of a trench rather than a bed. He was pleased that he did not have to be well-mannered and clean, recording his pleasure in getting really dirty and only taking his boots off once and washing twice in ten days. He enjoyed the camaraderie with his men, admiring their courage under fire, their filthy language and humour.

More controversial to modern listeners is his attitude to killing. He was not squeamish about shooting Germans. He wrote, 'The first time one shoots a man one has the feeling of "never point a loaded gun at anyone even in fun", but very soon it gets like shooting crocodile, only more exciting, because he shoots back at you.'[21] One night, he crept over to the German trenches and shot one of their soldiers who had been sniping at the British troops. He was awarded the DSO for his bravery. On another occasion, a German shell landed within 10 yards of him and knocked him off his horse, but he just got up and laughed – it had not even knocked the cigarette out of his mouth. He wrote of the war in his usual half ironic tone, 'It just suits my stolid health, and stolid nerves, and barbaric disposition. The fighting – excitement vitalizes everything, every sight and word and action. One loves one's fellow man so much more when one is bent on killing him.'[22]

For once, Ettie was able to give her son just what he needed. She kept him supplied with a Burberry mackintosh, lamp refills, pipe-lighters, whisky, copies of the *Daily Mail* and tins of café au lait. More importantly, she kept any fears she had for his safety to herself. Their relationship had never been better. He wrote to her, 'You are a really great War Mother. All emotion is fatal now.'[23] At last he knew that he had become the hero she had always wanted.

In May 1915 Julian's regiment was involved in a major action near the Ypres–Menin road. At 4 a.m. on 13 May the Germans started a heavy bombardment of the trenches. Julian went up what he called 'the little hill of death' to try to take some observations. He was knocked over by a shell but it only cut his coat and bruised his shoulder. He took his findings back to his colonel, who was pleased with him and got him a whisky and soda. Julian then volunteered to take a message through to the Somerset Yeomanry. He walked very coolly through heavy fire to deliver his message. When he returned, he went up 'the little hill' again with General Campbell.

At about 12.30, Julian was hit in the head by a splinter of shell. At first his feet felt cold and he said to the general, 'Go down, Sir, don't bother about me, I'm done.' However, the general helped to carry him down and while doing so was slightly wounded himself. Julian put on a cheerful front, but he said to a brother officer, 'Do you know, I think I shall die.' When his comrade said, 'Nonsense!', Julian replied, 'Well, you see if

I don't.'[24] Julian was one among many of his regiment seriously injured or killed in the encounter; out of his fifteen brother officers only three survived.[25]

The following Sunday morning, a bloodstained letter arrived at Taplow from Julian, explaining what had happened in his usual light-hearted way, 'I stopped a Jack Johnson with my head, and my skull is slightly cracked. But I'm getting on splendidly. They said I did well. Today I go down to Wimereux, to hospital, shall you be there? All all love, JULIAN OF THE HARD HEAD.'[26]

Pulling strings with friends in the Admiralty, his parents travelled to France overnight on an ammunition boat and were able to be with him in hospital. Julian had an extensive fracture of the inner skull and severe laceration of the brain; a splinter had penetrated 1½in into the brain and an immediate operation was necessary. Julian was in good spirits when he saw Ettie and Willie, but he told his mother that the journey down from the Front had been terrible to endure.

Billy had just been sent to France and, on 20 May, he came to visit his brother. He was overcome by seeing him looking so ill. However, Julian was delighted to see him and said afterwards, 'I am glad there was no gap.' It was thought he meant that just as he had to give up serving his country his brother stepped in to take his place.[26]

In the following days, Ettie and Willie stayed by Julian's bedside willing him to get better. As Ettie fed him brioches with Devonshire clotted cream he said to her, very slowly in a weak voice, 'The right way to eat is to swallow enormous mouthfuls of food, washed down by huge gulps of liquid.' When she did not disagree, he was quite disappointed and, referring to their old battles, said, 'Why don't you <u>argue</u>, Mummie? I would not give up one of our ructions.'[28]

Julian, like his mother, had a strong Christian faith and during this time he prayed that he would be able to bear the pain. On Whit Sunday morning, 23 May, he had Communion with his family. When the doctors saw him at 9.30 a.m. they found further inflammation of the brain and said that a second operation might give him a narrow chance of recovery. He was operated on at 11 a.m.

Afterwards, he was in terrible pain and his left arm was paralysed. His parents stayed with him night and day. The next day he seemed better and asked if his doctors had thought he was dying. 'Did they think I was going off the rocker?' he asked Ettie, adding, 'I thought I was; but now I've never been so well, and I've never been so happy.'[29]

In those final days, while his father rubbed his paralysed hand, Ettie read aloud poetry, psalms and hymns he had known since he was a child. On the Monday he clasped his mother's hand tightly, she said, 'That is what you do when you are asleep, and think that I am going away.' He replied, 'No, it is only affection.' At times he groaned, but he reassured them that it was 'only contentment'. Ettie wrote, 'The thought that he was dying seemed to go and come, but he was always radiantly happy and he never saw any of the people he loved look sad. Never once through all those days did he say one word of complaint or depression.'[30]

On Tuesday, 25 May, he deteriorated. He talked a little, and then said to Ettie, 'Hold my hand until I go.' A shaft of sunlight came in through the darkened window and fell across his feet. He smiled at his mother and said 'Phoebus Apollo', referring to the god of the sun whose irradiating powers have not yet separated from destructiveness.[31] At 2.30 p.m. he said his father's name and snapped his fingers for a cigarette but could not smoke it. He never spoke again, and died the following afternoon. Although he could not talk, he knew his parents to the very end and, just before he died, he moved his mother's hands to his lips. Ettie wrote, 'At the moment that he died he opened his eyes a little, with the most radiant smile that they had ever seen on his face.'[32]

On 28 May Julian was buried in the soldiers' cemetery on the hill above Boulogne, looking over the battlefields. His grave was filled with green oak leaves and wild flowers. As she stood in the wind on the hillside, Ettie refused to wear mourning, it was a symbol of her defiant stand against grief. The following day she was staying nearby in the Forest of Hardelot, trying to write to Billy, when she suddenly looked up to see him there beside her. Ettie wrote, 'It was almost like seeing a vision [...] Julian and he had been like one person, but he did not seem to have a thought that was not of faith and triumph.'[33] Billy stayed with them for three hours but then had to go back to the Front. Ettie wrote that it was 'almost impossible to let him go'.[34] She never saw him again.

After Julian's death, Billy wrote a letter to their friend Norah Lindsay which perfectly captured his brother's complex character and helps to explain his attitude to war and death:

You know all the mysticism and idealism and that strange streak of melancholy which underlay Julian's war-whooping, sun-bathing, fearless exterior. I love to think that he has attained that perfection and fullness of life for which he sought so untiringly. I seem to hear him cheering me on in moments of stress here with even more vivid power. There is no one whose victory over the grave can be more complete.[35]

Billy was inspired by Julian and wanted to live up to his example; like him, he was ready to die for his country. His fellow soldiers noted his fearlessness during attacks. He spoke of death as 'a gateway, not a barrier, and a path I am sure to joy and freedom'.[36] He wrote to the mother of a friend who had been killed, 'Death is such a frail barrier out here, men cross it so smilingly and gallantly every day, one cannot feel it as a severing in any way. Pray that I may bear myself bravely when the burning moment breaks.'[37]

Two months after Julian's death, and only a mile away from where his brother was wounded, that moment came. Billy was killed leading his platoon in a charge near Hooge on Friday, 30 July. As he led his men into the tremendous fire from machine guns he knew he faced almost certain death. He was killed instantaneously.

Ettie responded to the death of her sons in the same way she had reacted to other tragedies in her life. She turned to her Christian faith and stuck to her positive creed of 'Ettyism'. Her courage and refusal to wallow in self-pity made her a role model for other bereaved mothers. Her friend Mary Wemyss wrote to her imagining these women as an army led by Ettie. She explained that there was 'the double column', the sons who fought and the mothers 'who have to give their all and sacrifice their dearest hopes and aspirations – with open hand and hearts – without looking back – without regret'. She told her friend, 'Darling you are leading a Brave Battalion and if I am called – I pray I may not "fall out" from the ranks – but whatever way things go this I know, we are Comrades – once and for all, comrades now and for ever.'[38]

The relationship between Mary and Ettie shows the importance of this camaraderie between mothers. Although they responded to the loss of their sons in different ways, they always supported each other and offered sympathy and love. Mary wrote to Ettie when Julian was wounded, 'Of course you will know what I feel for you – as you would for me, <u>elemental</u>

mothers – like you and me and life-long friends like you and me – don't need <u>much</u> to explain!'[39]

Once Mary heard that Julian had died, she immediately wrote to Ettie. Perhaps because of her earlier experience of losing her 3-year-old son, Colin, she could identify with her friend. She wrote, 'Alas there is absolutely <u>no sorrow or pain</u> like it and the mother's wound is one that never really heals and with you the intimacy the love the close interdependence was so wonderful.'[40] Mary's letter expressed more pain than her bereaved friend's reply. Ettie wrote to her in almost euphoric terms, 'Darling, what curious words of Terror we weave about life and death, then they vanish away when reality draws very near.' She described Julian and his comrades as like a heavenly army, 'One could never feel fear of death again after seeing Julian die: after seeing them all out there marching so gaily across the river, with the trumpets sounding, to take up their "quick promotion" on the other side, and carry on what work may be required'.[41]

Recognising her friend's need to remain the dominant partner in their relationship, Mary replied:

It seems as if <u>you</u> in your wonderful courage and faith were giving consolation to <u>me</u>! I feel I could not be so splendid – but if the supreme trial of parting with one's own Beloveds come upon me –then I pray God I shall not falter or fail and if I stand firm – it will be <u>you</u> who have helped and led my footsteps.[42]

The strange dynamic between them continued once Ettie returned home. Mary offered to visit her at any time, day or night, but knowing Ettie's need to appear strong, she claimed that she came to receive comfort rather than give it. Ettie replied that she wanted to tell her friend about 'all the happiness and beauty' of her last days with Julian and share 'all the revelation of happiness and help now, his arms tight about one for evermore'.[43] After seeing her, Mary described Ettie as 'quite wonderfully calm, and upheld by a sense of Julian's continued presence and love'.[44] She seemed to show a remarkable immunity to grief, she still wore coloured clothes instead of mourning, refused to break down and would scarcely admit that she should be pitied at all. Mary's daughter Cynthia Asquith wrote in her diary:

Can it last? One feels there must be a reaction to flatness and just the daily longing. The only thing is, she has got such marvellous powers of bluffing herself that she may succeed, and then, of course, her abnormal sense of the importance of things will help. One would feel 'What does it matter, to others, if I do break down and just give up?' She will always feel it is of vital significance to keep her flag flying.[45]

At the end of July, Cynthia went to see Ettie for herself. She found her lying on a sofa in her sitting room looking 'curiously unwound for her', but later when they went for a walk together she seemed quite normal. She talked about Julian and also gossiped about other subjects, showing her humour and zest for life. Having spent time with her, Cynthia revised her earlier analysis, writing, 'I loved her. She inspires one with tremendous admiration. There seems nothing strained and artificial about her marvellous courage, just a sort of alchemy which has translated tragedy to the exclusion of all gloom.'[46]

When Billy died, Ettie's friends were anxious about how she would survive this second tragedy. Cynthia wondered how she could 'face such utter desolation, such extinction of joy, glamour and hope'.[47] At first, her life seemed to be ebbing away from her as all she did was cry, but then she decided to make a supreme effort to survive for her other children.[48] In public, Ettie continued to put an unrelentingly positive slant on her loss. She wrote to Mary's sister-in-law, Evelyn de Vesci, that 'in the brave moments – which are the true moments – I feel happier now that Billy is gone too, even than when it was only Julian. Knowing that neither of them can ever be sad or lonely now.' Her unshakeable belief in the afterlife sustained her and she liked to imagine her boys laughing together as they always did when they were alive.[49]

Her reaction sounds unbelievable to modern listeners but, as her biographer explains, to understand her reaction involves acknowledging the depth of her Christian faith. She was steeped in the Christian creed and firmly believed that Jesus had died and risen again, that he was her Saviour and would save her soul and bring eternal life. After her sons' deaths, she told one friend that she had believed in the Resurrection all her life but now she knew it was true. She relied on daily prayer for her strength and even when she faced the most devastating tragedy she believed that it was her Christian duty to continue praising God.[50] However, maintaining her equilibrium was not easy and it involved an extraordinary degree of self-control. Shortly after Billy's death, she wrote to a friend, 'What a knife edge among the mountains we walk on now – destruction on every side – eyes must never leave the hairbreadth of space just ahead.'[51]

Watching what was happening to her closest friend was a painful experience for Mary. Julian and Billy had grown up with her sons and she had loved them. It also constantly reminded her of what she might soon have to face. When, just months after Julian and Billy's deaths, Mary lost her youngest son Yvo in October 1915, her eldest son Ego wrote:

> I suppose the misery of people like Ettie breaks the shock. A woman with sympathy loses many sons before her own. If anything could dwarf one's own tragedy, it is the agony of millions of others. But it doesn't – it's the other way about – one's sluggish imagination is stimulated, and one merely realises for the first time other people's miseries as well as one's own.[52]

Helping each other provided a purpose for mothers who were left at home anxiously waiting for news. As soon as Ettie heard of Yvo's death, she wanted to be with Mary at Stanway. She knew just what to say to ease the pain of her oldest friend. They cried together, Mary described 'tears of love' coursing down the cheeks of Ettie's 'grief-stricken and beautiful face and you deep in the waters of woe holding out both hands to help and save me: We save others, ourselves we cannot save – but others; the love of others saves us: and the God of Love saves us all.'[53]

The letters between the two women show that, although they were close friends and from a similar background, their response to their sacrifice was very different. While Ettie remained steadfast in her mantra of glory, Mary wavered between accepting the party line and questioning the assumptions of a glorious death. Shortly after Yvo's death while trying to rush a German trench, she wrote to Ettie:

> I don't suppose it helped the military situation one scrap getting this trench – it may have been ordered for countless other reasons or for none, and they still seem to think it necessary to pit infantry against machine guns! But one must not make these sort of remarks – and they do not really affect us – you are so wonderful as regards the attitude and the aspect, the only one, we mothers must take![54]

Ettie's attitude was based in the assumption that God and England and honour were all facets of the same thing.[55] Her belief in the sacredness of patriotism, the glory of battle and sacrifice was typical of many of her class and generation. The hundreds of letters of condolence written to her echoed many of her sentiments. However, as the slaughter continued, particularly after the Battle of the Somme in 1916, the idea of the futility and pity of war seemed to reflect the reality more closely.

Many of the younger generation in the Coterie ridiculed Ettie's ethos. Raymond Asquith believed that the formulae of consolation were futile. When his closest friend lost his mother, he told him that between men of intelligence there was no room for the platitudes of Christianity nor the paradoxes of stoicism. The only advice he could give was that time took the edge off grief.[56] During the war, members of the Coterie argued against the concept of a glorious death, claiming that it did not make any difference to your feelings whether your son was killed by a bullet or a bus. Even Cynthia Asquith, who admired Ettie's 'stubborn gospel of joy' more than the Coterie's cynicism, began to question the patriotic line.[57] After her younger brother Yvo's death she wrote:

> Somehow with the others who have been killed, I have acutely felt the loss of them but have so swallowed the rather high-falluting platitude that it was all right for them – that they were not to be pitied, but were safe, unassailed, young, and glamorous for ever. With Yvo – I can't bear it for him. The sheer pity and horror of it is overwhelming, and I am haunted by the feeling that he is disappointed.[58]

Unlike many of the British people who 'hated the Huns', Cynthia and Mary had a more sophisticated understanding of the conflict. Before the war they had often visited Germany and they had many German friends. They knew that the average German had gone to war with Britain through no choice of their own. They were able to distinguish between ordinary German soldiers and the criminals among the enemy who committed atrocities. Cynthia's friend, the novelist D.H. Lawrence, captured this magnanimity in his portrayal of 'Lady Beveridge', who was modelled on Mary, in his novella *The Ladybird*. Despite what happened in the war, Lady Beveridge continued to love humanity and she refused to join the general hate. He wrote that she was not to be pitied for her sorrows because her life was now in her sorrows and in helping others cope with their grief.[59]

When Ego was killed in 1916, Ettie was one of the intimate circle Mary wanted at his memorial service. Afterwards, she wrote about her pleasure at seeing 'dearest brave Ettie with the two <u>swords</u> in her heart', as she was one of the few people 'who <u>knew</u> and <u>cared</u> and <u>understood</u>'.[60] Echoing her friend's language, Ettie wrote about her feelings on that occasion, 'The thought of Mary is like a sword, I would have given the soul out of my body to save her from this – one knows it too well, the long long pain, the <u>crushing</u> of the second blow.' However, she added, 'But I think her spirit is indestructible – and what held up Ego and Yvo, Julian and Billy, will hold her too.'[61]

Although Mary tried to remain strong for the younger generation, in her letters to her contemporaries she was candid. Unlike Ettie she explored her feelings of loss. She described 'the shivering misery' of waking up the first morning after receiving the news of her son's death and having to drag herself back into a world that was forever changed. It was hard to continue with daily tasks 'when the earth has opened and swallowed one up and avalanches have poured over one's head, and one's soul is wandering in a great and lonely void'.[62] She admitted to feeling 'battered and bewildered' and often not knowing what she wanted to do.[63]

Although she felt able to tell Ettie some of her true feelings, she was more open with other friends. It was as if she censored herself to protect her friend, in case the truth would shatter the carefully constructed shell Ettie had created to survive. Mary wrote to her sister-in-law, Evelyn de Vesci, 'One's mind is startled and paralysed and one's soul faints so at the sense of mountains of piled up corpses/bodies – the young, the bright, the beautiful laid low.'[64] Her grief affected how she saw herself. She feared that she created an oppressive atmosphere around her and was surprised anyone could bear to sit in a room with her. She wrote, 'They would have to fly away from me – with shut eyes and closed nostrils – as from a charnel house if they felt about me – what often I feel.'[65]

As the loss of her boys undermined every aspect of her life, for a time Mary questioned conventional Christianity and, like many of the bereaved, she briefly dabbled in spiritualism. Many of her friends and family, including her mother and sister, Pamela, were evangelical about spiritualism and they firmly believed that communication with the dead was possible under certain conditions. However, Mary's daughter Cynthia was very critical of mediums, who she believed exploited the grief of the vulnerable. In August 1916, a friend of Cynthia's wrote to say that when they had been table turning at Knebworth, the name Yvo Charteris was spelt out. When a message was asked for, the sentence 'I question duty night and day' was given. They asked who it was for and the answer was 'Mother' and when asked where she was, the response came, 'Ireland', which was where Mary was staying. They asked if there was anything more, and 'Kiss her' was spelt out. Cynthia was not convinced, she wrote, 'I don't know why, but the whole thing is <u>distasteful</u> to me. It gives, I think, a sad idea of survival. To be hanging around unable, though longing, to communicate and having to use a middle-man in the form of some revolting medium – No! No! No!'[66]

Missing both her sons, Mary was perhaps more susceptible than her daughter. In November 1916, she told Cynthia that although she was agnostic about spiritualism she thought that perhaps she ought to just give it a chance. She said she was doing it more for Yvo than Ego because she had a feeling that he might want to speak to her. It was only at this point that Cynthia told her about the Knebworth table turning.[67] Later that month, Mary went to a séance with a medium in Tavistock Square.[68] In December she asked Cynthia to attend another session with her. It confirmed Cynthia's cynicism, the medium got on the wrong track and thought Cynthia's husband had been killed in the war. When she realised her mistake, she claimed the younger woman's scepticism was acting as a mental screen to communication. Cynthia concluded, 'It wasn't even a good exhibition of telepathy, and I thought the whole business unpleasant.'[69] This unsatisfactory experience left Mary more bereft and confused than ever. She wrote:

> I felt a very deep feeling of disappointment and sadness though I know one must expect all that I'm afraid the <u>rush</u> of people seeking help that way is a great incentive to cheating and will stimulate a veritable growth of quacks and charlatans – I feel very <u>mixed</u> about it all, as if patience and faith were the only <u>attitude</u> and the subtle one.[70]

As she struggled through the many stages of grief, Mary felt angry about what had happened to her sons. She most coherently expressed her resentment in her letters to her old lover, Arthur Balfour. Perhaps this was partly because he had some influence over the situation, as in May 1915 he had succeeded Churchill as First Lord of the Admiralty in the coalition government. Her letters to him have a different tone from her ones to Ettie – they are more direct with less purple prose. Finally she was able to say what would have been heresy to Ettie; that the war seemed to be a 'shambles' and, rather than being a glorious sacrifice, the deaths were 'a sickening waste'.[71] In one particularly frank letter, she wrote:

> What I mind is that <u>others</u> should not have their time – supremely fitted for life and love – and sorely needed in this world to set it right, to save and help many – cut off in golden youth. No one can maintain that that is not tragedy – pure and unadulterated, that it is draped in all the glamour of romance and admired by onlookers does not mean the price is less to pay to those who pay […] If you hold your breath you hear the sound of widows weeping, sisters sobbing and the ceaseless falling falling of the mothers' tears, the whole air is stifled, surcharged with sadness, which eats into the soul – (at times!) I will not believe that sadness is not sadness – or say it is God's will and all is for the best.[72]

In contrast, Ettie rarely revealed any anger or vulnerability, perhaps fearing that if she ever let go she would succumb to the Cowper melancholy. In a letter to a friend she admitted, 'My heart feels almost bled to death about Julian and Billy,' but she rapidly added, 'the thought of <u>them</u> and of all that shining company is always joy.'[73] However, in 1917, after the death of one of the last of her sons' circle, and around the second anniversary of Julian's death, her self-discipline finally gave way. She wrote, 'Two years after is rather a bad time – one ought to have found out the new roads, and new ways of treading them, and yet reconstruction is such a slow and difficult work.'[74] Now it was Mary's turn to help Ettie. Sending her words of consolation she had found helpful from the Bible she wrote:

> Your little pencil letter today had such an anguished cry it pierced my heart […] I only want to tell you that you have all my love and devotion and I'd cut

myself into hundreds of tiny bits if I could only help you to know how I love you and that you are a prop and stay to me and my prop seems to be reeling with misery and right now all seems tragedy and failure and darling you have helped so many and now there seems no one to help you.[75]

Characteristically, Ettie was determined not to be downcast for long. Although at times she felt like a dead woman who was just going through the motions of being alive, she explained that for the sake of her other children she 'could not bear to grow numb and unresponsive to this world […] "we must live among the living" – not let all that counts go on ahead, and leave only a sleeping and walking, eating and laughing self here, an automaton'. She finished with a characteristic quote:

I'll lay me down and bleed awhile;
And then I'll rise and fight again.[76]

Her determination to go on fighting was admired by many, but her old friend, the professor and poet Sir Walter Raleigh, complained to Cynthia Asquith that Ettie was never restful to be with because she was constantly 'battling' against life and swimming against the current. He added that her 'deliberate activity made her mechanical and prohibited any real friendship or the finest companionship'.[77]

Although Ettie was indispensable to many of her friends and the person they turned to in a crisis, she was not an easy person to be intimate with; her unwillingness to show her vulnerability put her at a distance from most people. As Raymond Asquith wrote to her, she seemed 'removed into a tragic world beyond our small horizon and far beyond the range of mortal vision and mortal voices. One does not offer consolation to the heroine of a Greek tragedy – It seems hardly less impertinent to offer it to you.'[78]

Like her sons, Ettie was determined to be heroic and set an example. She was an inspiration to others, but perhaps Mary was a more attainable model of maternal grief for many women. She comes across as more human and representative of the way attitudes to war changed as the conflict continued. As Mary wrote at the end of December 1917, 'Our darling boys are killed by her country's bullets – When shall we learn that there is some <u>better way</u> than War? But even sin and Death and War <u>do not</u> prevail over love.'[79]

For both women, there was a need to make sure that their sons were never forgotten, and to do this they wrote books immortalising them. In her *Pages from a Family Journal*, privately published in 1916, Ettie recorded every detail of Julian and Billy's childhood and war experiences. She gathered tributes to her dead sons from among their friends and then published seventy pages of them at the end of the book. Circulated only among her friends, it had a profound effect on its readers, reminding them of happier days and what they had lost. Diana Manners could not stop sobbing as she read it. For Ettie, it was her last chance to control her sons' lives and shape their lasting image for posterity. Her book helped to establish the narrative of the lost generation of golden youth cut off in their prime. However, some members of that generation, like Raymond Asquith, who was still fighting and was to lose his life later that year, were critical of Ettie's glossing of reality.[80] In one of his final letters to his wife, Raymond complained that Ettie had doctored his contribution to her book. She had cut out his comment that Billy was 'insolent'. She had also changed the facts about where Billy, Julian and Raymond had fun together, inserting the grandest houses owned by their friends, partly through snobbery, but also to make every moment of her sons' lives seem as perfect as possible.[81]

Although modelled on Ettie's example, Mary's *A Family Record* has a more truthful, nuanced tone. It took her years to write and only appeared in 1932. She told Balfour that writing it nearly killed her with misery as it reminded her how all her hopes and aspirations had been cut off by the 'holocaust' of the war.[82] At the end of her book, she listed the young men of her circle who had died – fourteen were members of the Coterie and another eleven were sons of her friends – she had known them all since they were little boys. Except for Ego and Raymond, they had all been under 30.[83]

It was only long after the conflict that Mary finally felt free to say to Ettie what she really thought. When Yvo died, Ettie had written to Mary that it was the only end worthy of his beginning. In 1931 Mary, albeit very tentatively, challenged her friend. She wrote:

During the passage of years does not one slightly change not one's point of view – but perhaps the manner of expressing it? […] I only feel that […]

(altho' we know that it was wholly glorious right and noble that they <u>did</u>) we do not quite think that any other way (their lives, lived out here) would have been <u>unworthy of their beginning</u>? Perhaps you'll think me mad [...] but they <u>might</u>, as thank God, many did – they might have fought and lived?[84]

FIVE

PATRIOTIC PEARLS

In some ways, the Pearl Appeal could express better than words the wide range of emotions unleashed by the war. Like the subtly different shades of the pearls, each woman who donated had a slightly different experience and reaction to the conflict. Whereas words often seemed inadequate to capture the ebb and flow of complex feelings, and sometimes pinpointed differences even among the closest friends, the enigmatic element of the Pearl Appeal, which symbolised rather than stated the emotions of the giver, united the donors in a common cause.

During the crucial months of the spring and early summer of 1918, as the threat of defeat hung over the British, donating a pearl became a way for women to reaffirm their patriotism and show they would not acquiesce. After the overwhelming German attack in March, the Allies fought back, appointing the French General Ferdinand Foch to co-ordinate the Allied armies. He immediately sent reinforcements to stop the German advance. As the Allies recovered their strength, the Germans found themselves overstretched; they lacked the reserves and supply structures to consolidate their gains and they had advanced well beyond the support of their artillery.[1]

The Allies' line was holding and, crucially, they managed to prevent the Germans reaching Amiens. When Ludendorff realised his troops had failed to make this breakthrough, he called off the offensive and turned his attentions further north, launching a second offensive aimed at driving the British from Flanders and capturing the Channel ports.[2] On 9 April the German Army attacked again in the valley of the River Lys, with a secondary assault towards Ypres, using the methods of 21 March. At this time, there was a real fear that Britain might lose the war. On 11 April, General Haig issued his famous Order of the Day, calling on the army to fight to the last man:

> With our backs to the wall and believing in the justice of our cause each one of us must fight on to the end. The safety of our homes and the Freedom of mankind alike depend upon the conduct of each one of us at this critical moment.[3]

At home in Britain people wanted to demonstrate their support for the men at the Front. Reflecting this desire, there was a surge in donations. By the end of the first week in April nearly 700 pearls had been given and before the month was out the first thousand was passed. By the end of May the total number of gems received had reached over 2,000. They came in from all over the country and were given by women from different walks of life. The pearls ranged in value from one worth a few shillings sent from a country vicarage to a pearl of great price from a stately home. As 'K.R.' from Eastbourne wrote, 'As a drop in the ocean, this small pearl seeks to swell the ocean of England's gratitude to her heroes.'[4]

No donation more poignantly reflected General Haig's call to fight to the last man than Lilian Kekewich's gift. Her family had given their all for love of their country – three of her sons and her brother-in-law died in the war. She gave pearls to the appeal on several occasions because it symbolised the self-sacrificing concept of duty that her family believed in. Before the conflict, the Kekewichs had lived a privileged life. The daughter of a wealthy brewer, Samson Hanbury, Lilian had grown up in a large Italianate former bishop's palace in Torquay. In 1884 she married Lewis Kekewich, the son of a well-known Devon family, who owned Peamore House, an elegant Regency mansion at Exminster, near Exeter. The Kekewichs were deeply rooted in the local community and took a paternalistic interest in their tenants and neighbours. They believed in public service, and members of the family had served in the local army regiments, as Justices of the Peace and as high sheriffs of the county for generations.

As Lewis was a younger son, he left Devon to pursue a business career in London. The couple moved to Sussex, buying an estate, Kidbrooke

Park, where they could enjoy country pursuits. Lewis loved shooting and a round of golf, while Lilian was a keen horsewoman and a member of the hunt. They had seven children, but sadly two of their three daughters died in childhood.[5] Their four sons, Hanbury, George, John and Sydney, were brought up on exciting stories of military glory. Their father's brother, Major General Robert George Kekewich, was a hero of the Boer War, who had been commander-in-chief of the garrison during the siege of Kimberley. Uncle Robert provided a role model for his nephews.

When the boys went to Eton their family's ethos of public service and militarism was reinforced. Like Julian and Billy Grenfell, they were encouraged to be keen sportsmen. John excelled at football and cricket and, in 1909, he played in the Eton Cricket XI at Lords. The Kekewich boys were brought up in a public-school culture that taught them to conceive of war in the language of the playing field. The right qualities needed for war had been firmly instilled in them, and they were taught to value sportsmanship, leadership, loyalty, honour, Christianity and patriotism.[6] Eton had prepared them well for their future. As the *Eton Chronicle* wrote of its many former pupils who were now serving their country, 'It was there that they learnt the lessons which are to enable them to withstand the ordeal which must now be undergone.'[7] For the four young Kekewichs, it was to be only a brief interlude before they had to put the values they had learnt on the playing fields of Eton into practice.

On leaving school, Hanbury and George joined their father in business. In his spare time, George became a Master Scout, founding a Boy Scout troop in Sussex. Following in his uncle's footsteps, John went to Sandhurst, but instead of taking up his commission he went to Alberta where he ran a ranch. He then returned to England for a short time before going to Penang in 1913 to become a planter. When war was declared, John gave up his new life abroad and returned to England to fight.

His brothers also soon signed up, with their background it seemed the natural thing for them to do. Every man in the Kekewich family was expected to do his duty. At the outbreak of war in 1914, although he was now 60 years old, Major General Robert Kekewich commanded the 13th (Western) Division, which was stationed at Salisbury Plain. Robert's health was not good; he suffered from gout, insomnia and heart problems. He began to worry that his illness would prevent him from serving his country as he wished. On 5 October the camp doctor sent him home on sick leave because he was having a nervous breakdown. For several weeks, he was cared for in the Home Hospital in Exeter where his treatment included massage and rest. At the end of the month he was considered to have improved enough to return to his home, Whimple Rectory, near Exeter. However, his doctor noted that he still experienced waves of depression when he worried that he was not serving his country and his anxiety was exacerbated by the frequent reports of the deaths of his friends and fellow officers.

A few days after his return home, his sister Julia spent the afternoon with him. She noticed that he seemed very depressed about the war but she did not think he was suicidal. After having dinner together, he seemed more cheerful, although he went to bed early at 9.15 p.m. Early the next morning, Julia was awakened by the sound of a gunshot coming from Robert's bedroom, followed by a heavy thud. She knocked and entered to find her brother lying in a pool of blood on the floor with his head on a gun case and a shotgun by his right side. He had shot himself in the head and died immediately. After finding him, Julia ran into the cook's room and instructed her to send the groom into the village for a doctor.

The inquest into his death recorded a verdict of 'suicide whilst temporarily insane'.[8] Even for a man of his military experience, the reality of the First World War was destabilising. In fact, his reaction to the war was not insane, the conflict was enough to test anyone's sanity. If he had remained in command of the 13th Division, within a year he would have led his men into the bloodbath of Gallipoli.

The major general's death shook the whole community. In the close-knit local villages where Robert had grown up and was known by everyone as 'the General', his neighbours tried to make sense of his suicide. He had always seemed rock-like, the man villagers went to if they were in trouble, knowing that he would always be there with sound advice or a helping hand. In Whimple Parish Church on the Sunday after his death, his friend the Reverend Sanders recalled the 'kindly neighbour' who was 'all that an English gentleman should be'. In his sermon, the vicar asked his parishioners:

> Who will hesitate to say that our brother who is gone has died for duty? Full well he knew that he was not the man he had been – not the man he had been in the Kimberley days and the far off Egyptian days. Full well again, did he know what the task before him - the training of a new Army – was like.

What of that? He recognised it as the call of duty. Cost what it might, in the hour of his country's need he would do his best. Only as he goes down under it, as it costs him his life, in charity let us say that he is entitled to a place on the roll of honour as clearly as if he had died on the battlefield.[9]

Major General Kekewich was given full military honours and his funeral was one of the largest military funerals Devon had seen. The coffin was brought from Whimple Rectory to the crossroads near Countess Weir, where it was placed on a gun carriage. A long procession formed behind the coffin as 400 officers and men of the 3rd Battalion Devon Regiment and 400 officers and men from nearby Topsham Barracks gathered to pay their respects. Many of the villagers lined the route to say their final farewell to the General, the old soldiers among them stood to salute. As the cortege wound its way slowly towards St Martin's, the ancient, red sandstone church at Exminster, the band of the 3rd Devon Regiment played Chopin's 'Funeral March'. After a brief service, the buglers sounded the last post before Robert was laid to rest beside his ancestors overlooking the River Exe.[10]

Three of Robert's nephews, Hanbury, George and John, were among the mourners at the funeral that day. They were also soon to lose their lives doing their duty. Less than a year after his uncle's death, on 26 September 1915, John was killed near Loos. A captain in the Buffs, he was involved in heavy fighting and was hit in the thigh and disabled, but he refused to let his brother officers try to get him back to the British lines because he believed it would needlessly jeopardise their lives. Later, a sergeant found him, but he again refused help and sent the man on, only asking that a stretcher might be sent out for him at night when the heavy firing had decreased. The night-time rescue proved impossible and he was declared missing but presumed dead.[11]

The next to die was George. In September 1914, he joined the City of London Yeomanry. A brave soldier, who was mentioned in Despatches, he was serving in Palestine when he died on 20 October 1917, from wounds received the previous day on the Gaza Front. Just a few weeks later, the Kekewichs' eldest son, Captain Hanbury Lewis, who had served seven years in the Sussex Yeomanry and was also in Palestine, was killed in action near Sheria on 6 November 1917.

Of Lilian's four sons, only the youngest, Sydney, survived the war. He had been badly wounded in a frontier fight in India in September 1915. It seems that the authorities recognised that the Kekewichs had sacrificed enough as, for the rest of the war, Sydney continued to serve the army but in a desk job at the War Office headquarters.

After seeing so many of the next generation killed in the war, owning such a large house as Kidbrooke Park seemed meaningless to Lilian and Lewis. Leaving behind their memories of happier times, they moved into a house in Hove and sold Kidbrooke. Unlike Mary Wemyss and Ettie Desborough, there is no written record of Lilian's reaction to her losses but an insight into the family's attitude is provided in a speech given by her brother-in-law, the head of the family, Trehawke Kekewich, in 1915. He recognised that Britain was fighting in 'the most horrible, the most terrible, and most atrocious war' that had ever been waged, but his tone was defiant. For his family, like the Grenfells, it was a matter of honour. He said:

> Many wars had been fought and many brave men had fallen sometimes in a cause which was not exactly holy. This was a holy cause. They were fighting for the civilisation of the world; they were fighting to make treaties respected; they were fighting to teach the German that it was not in his power to say: 'I am super-man. I stand over the laws of the universe, I stand above everything.'[12]

Mr Kekewich's attitude was shared by the vast majority of the British people at the start of the war. Fighting the Germans was about more than opposing the violation of Belgian neutrality; they believed that the choice was between going to war and allowing the German domination of Europe, which they thought would be a disaster.[13] For many patriotic people, including some who had previously been pacifists, the war was about enforcing acceptable behaviour in the international sphere and maintaining the belief in lawful behaviour among nations. Germany was seen as a bully that ignored values of peace and negotiation.[14]

Mr Kekewich was proud of his family's military record. In 1915 he was involved in a recruiting tour which went around the Devon villages encouraging local men to sign up. He told a rally in Exminster that he had thirty-two nephews and first cousins serving, and sixteen were fighting on the front line. He added that he would be ashamed of himself if he had a single relative who was eligible but not serving his king.

After conscription was introduced in 1916, Trehawke Kekewich sat on tribunals that were held to make judgements on who should be exempt from military service. Clergymen, teachers, doctors, coal miners, those working in the iron and steel industries or in specialist manufacturing were among those not required to join up. Their jobs were described as 'Scheduled (or Reserved) Occupations'. Other men who felt they should not have to fight due to poor health, potential damage to their business, family hardship or conscientious objection had to plead their case in front of a tribunal, which then made the decision whether they should be exempted.

About 1,800 local tribunals were set up across the country and it is estimated that between 20,000 and 40,000 citizens served on them.[15] Tribunals were usually made up of a member of the military, eight or nine local dignitaries, such as Justices of the Peace, councillors and mayors, and ideally a representative of labour, usually a trade union official, also served on the board. They were supposed to be impartial. However, their judgements were often inconsistent, varying from one locality to another.

In 1916, tribunals were inundated with work as many people decided to appeal. Although the majority of cases had a serious foundation, there were some bizarre attempts to avoid conscription. One man appealed in Leeds for a three-month delay in order to complete a course of hair restoration – understandably, his plea was rejected. Across the country, success rates varied but ranged between 20 and 50 per cent, usually for a temporary exemption.[16] Those who won their case were provided with papers and badges to prove that they were involved in war work, they needed this official recognition to avoid the social stigma attached to not fighting.

At the tribunals, Mr Kekewich always took a draconian line with any man he considered to be shirking his duty to king and country. In November 1916 he was particularly scathing about a Bratton Clovelly farming family where seven brothers had not gone to the war because they argued they were needed on the farm. Mr Kekewich felt that to have so many able-bodied men at home was wrong. He told the boys' father, 'It is a scandalous case – seven sons.' The chairman of the tribunal said that it was hoped that the family would not go through the war without a single member fighting for their country. The farmer should go home and think over what the opinion of his neighbours would be after the war if none of his sons went.[17]

However, Mr Kekewich and his colleague's attitudes were soon outpaced by events. In fact, the government did not want too many farm labourers going off to fight. During the second half of the war food imports were squeezed. In spring 1917 there was a wheat crisis due to U-boat attacks and the bad American and British harvests of 1916. In response, ministers tried to stimulate agriculture. From 1917 a Food Production Department was created in the Board of Agriculture with a mission to boost arable farming, as this was seen as the most efficient means of feeding the population. From this time, most agricultural workers were protected from conscription.[18]

While sitting on the Devon tribunal, Trehawke Kekewich was never afraid to show his prejudices, particularly when conscientious objectors came before him. During the war there were between 16,000 and 20,000 conscientious objectors on the grounds of political, humanitarian or religious beliefs.[19] However, whether or not a man's plea was accepted often depended on who was sitting in judgement. In April 1916, Charles Baker of Highweek appealed to the Devon tribunal on conscientious grounds to be exempted from military service. The 30-year-old animal skin curer and sorter was the Newton Abbot chairman of the No-Conscription Fellowship, district secretary of the Trades & Labour Council and treasurer of the local Independent Labour Party. He told the panel that he was an International Socialist who saw the war as the greatest hindrance to human progress.

Charles Baker's beliefs were anathema to Trehawke Kekewich. While Mr Kekewich and his friends were trying to encourage new recruits, Mr Baker and his colleagues in the No-Conscription Fellowship were distributing leaflets and holding meetings claiming that they intended to 'deny the right of any government to make the slaughter of our fellows a bounden duty'. No doubt, Mr Kekewich agreed with the *Daily Express*, which claimed that these 'anti-conscriptionists' were fighting against their country 'as much as if at this moment they were trying to poison gas the British Army in the trenches'.[20]

Like many of his class, Mr Kekewich also harboured a deep distrust of the Labour Party and the working class which Charles Baker so vocally represented. Although the Labour Party and the Trades Union Congress had declared an 'industrial truce' and supported an all-party recruitment campaign at the beginning of the war, the Independent Labour Party maintained an anti-war position.[21] For the first two years of the war there was minimal industrial unrest, but there were exceptions with strikes in the South Wales coalfields, which provided essential coal to the Royal Navy, and in the shipbuilding industries on the Clyde. Any strikes inflamed middle and upper-class fears.

David Lloyd George believed that industrial unrest was a more serious menace to Britain's chance of ultimate victory than even the military strength of Germany because the contentment and co-operation of the workforce was essential if Britain was to win the war.[22] He was careful to keep the powerful unions happy, although his own suspicions of some of the most militant strikers' motivation were aroused when he addressed a mass meeting of shop stewards in Glasgow in December 1915. The meeting got completely out of hand and there were fears for his safety as he was shouted down by the angry audience. Lloyd George told his mistress, Frances Stevenson, that he believed that there was German money behind the unrest and the men had been misled into believing that the war had been engineered by capitalists to keep the working class in their place. For them, the war was not against Germany but against capitalism.[23]

It seems Charles Baker held similar sentiments to some of the Scottish shop stewards. As a trade unionist, an International Socialist and an anti-war campaigner, he threatened everything Church, king and country Conservatives like Mr Kekewich stood for. This clash of cultures was played out in the tribunal. When the young man admitted that he did not come to the tribunal on religious grounds as he was an agnostic, but rather his conscientious objection was to war, Mr Kekewich scathingly asked him, 'How can an Agnostic have a conscience?' Refusing to be intimidated by the question, Baker showed that he was no coward by saying that he was willing to spend the remainder of his life in prison or face a firing squad rather than take part in the war. His speech was not hyperbole, members of the No-Conscription Fellowship, who refused to do war work only narrowly escaped execution by the military authorities. At least 1,540 conscientious objectors were condemned to two years' forced labour and seventy-one died as a result of their ill treatment by the military or prison authorities.[24]

The tribunal was not impressed with Charles Baker's arguments; it decided it was not satisfied that he had sincere conscientious objections so they put him into a combatant force and gave him 'the privilege of defending' his country. Using his closing comment to make a political point, Baker replied, 'I have no country. The country does not belong to me or to any of my class.'[25] Although his principles were the opposite of the Kekewichs and Grenfells, he too was willing to make a personal sacrifice for his beliefs. A week later, Private Baker was court-martialled and imprisoned for six months for refusing to obey army orders or to undergo a medical examination.[26] He joined the 6,000 so-called 'absolutists' among the conscientious objectors who refused to accept conscription and were jailed, often repeatedly, for their convictions.[27]

To see the battle of ideas between Charles Baker and Trehawke Kekewich purely in terms of class, however, is to oversimplify the situation. No doubt Baker did see the conflict in terms of class war, but that was because he was part of a politicised minority which was not typical of the working class as a whole. As the war progressed some of the early idealism about sacrifice for the country was replaced by class antagonism on the home front, but the majority of workers did remain patriotic.[28] In 1917 and 1918 there were more strikes, but to put this in perspective, the number of days lost in the entire war was fewer than had been lost in 1912.[29] Reflecting the underlying loyalty of the workforce, strikes drastically decreased when Britain was most under threat in April 1918 and only increased again in the second half of the year as a British victory became likely. A recent historian claims that, although a few of the strikes had an ideological element, they were less an indication of revolutionary defeatism than a protest by the working class about their living standards. To calm the situation the government usually responded to these disputes by making concessions to the unions.[30]

It is clear that on both the home front and the battlefields no one class had a monopoly on patriotism. Although the middle class was keener to fight, in their different ways men and women from all sections of society showed their sense of duty and willingness to do their best for their country.[31] For many, 'love of country' was a nebulous concept, nor did they see themselves as fighting for the king. However, they wanted to protect their families and prevent Germany invading Britain.[32] Other young men treated the war as an adventure and a change from the humdrum existence of their daily lives. However, after the slaughter of the Somme, the war ceased to be seen as an adventure and, increasingly, new recruits were not enthusiastic about the prospect of serving 'king and country'.[33] They continued to fight, but few had any illusions, and by 1918 their attitude was 'we're here because we're here because we're here'.[34]

Not every war hero or heroine came from a family wealthy enough to donate a pearl, but the public showed a determination that their sacrifice should also be recognised in the Red Cross necklaces. Wealthy women who had not suffered personal losses but wished to show solidarity with those who had been bereaved gave on their behalf. One of these generous women was Ada Bey. In May she donated her jewel for 'the fallen men of Otley'. Her first husband was William Henry Dawson, the well-known printing machine manufacturer whose firm was one of the biggest employers in the West Yorkshire industrial town. The daughter of a butler, Ada was a local girl from Wharfedale whose life changed dramatically when she married one of the wealthiest men in the area. She enjoyed the privileges of her new role, collecting an extensive jewellery collection which included a diamond tiara, a brooch with a spray of diamonds representing a waterfall and, of course, a pearl necklace. However, as well as her glamour she was also known for her generosity and warm sympathy for the poor people in Otley.

After her husband's death in 1905, Ada was left a wealthy widow and 'sole governing director' of the family firm. Two years later, she caused a minor scandal by marrying Henry Bey, an attaché at the Turkish Embassy who was six years her junior. Although Ada kept her mansion, Maple Grange in Otley, the couple spent much of their time in her London flat or travelling on the Continent. After 1914 their marriage became even more controversial since Britain was at war with Turkey. Perhaps giving a pearl was Ada's way of demonstrating her patriotism and showing she had not forgotten her roots. Ada's donation was in memory of the 187 men listed on Otley's war memorial – a large number of the fallen had worked at William Dawson & Sons.

As soon as war was declared, many of the workforce rushed to volunteer.[35] Ada and other local employers rewarded their patriotism by paying a war bonus of between 3–5s a week to the soldiers' wives.[36] Many of the Otley men joined the 4th West Riding Howitzer Brigade, which was made up of the 10th (Otley) and 11th (Ilkley) Batteries, the Burley Ammunition Column and No. 4 Section of the Divisional Ammunition Column and Brigade Headquarters. On 14 August 1914, crowds lined the streets to see the brigade leave Otley to begin their training at Doncaster.

The first casualty occurred on 20 January 1915 during manoeuvres. A wagon limber carrying four men hit a hidden tree stump. The wagon overturned, trapping Gunner George Lawson underneath, he died almost immediately. Fortunately, his two brothers, who were also serving with the 10th Battery, did not see what happened.[37]

In April 1915, the Otley men sailed from Southampton to Le Havre on the *Anglo-Canadian*. Once across the Channel they were soon moved to the front line. The officers and men worked very well together because they came from such a close community where people both worked and socialised together. Their commander, Major Kenneth Duncan, wrote to his father in December 1916, 'The men are keeping wonderfully well and marvellously cheery. They really are a top-hole lot and Wharfedale has need to be proud of her sons.'[38] However, as the unit was so interconnected any losses were particularly painful. The most devastating disaster occurred on 3 November 1917 during the attack on Passchendaele. A German shell exploded an ammunition dump near to the right flank of the battery position killing ten non-commissioned officers and men and severely wounding seven.

With many of Otley's men away fighting, the women played an important part on the home front. At William Dawson's almost half the men employed at the firm in August 1914 had gone to war by January 1915. At first Britain had been slower than France and Germany to employ women and there had been reluctance from some employers and the trade unions to engage female workers. However, after the 'shell scandal' in the spring of 1915, it was clear that female labour was needed.

From April, Ada's firm was one of the local businesses that took women into the workforce to fill the gaps. Instead of peacetime production, Dawson's was converted into a war-work factory where women worked night and day to produce the small lathes needed for turning shells and shell cases. By 1918, women made up nearly a third of the work force at William Dawson's.[39]

The contribution that women munitions workers were making to the war was recognised by Winston Churchill, who, as munitions minister, told the House of Commons in 1918 that the 750,000 women working for the munitions ministry produced more than nine-tenths of its shells. He described their contribution as beyond praise and added that without their labour the war effort could not carry on. However, the women at Dawson's received a lower wage of, on average, 10–15*s* less each week than the men. This was largely due to an agreement negotiated between employers, the unions and the government in March 1915, which stated that women undertaking skilled men's work would receive equal piece rate payments, although not the same time rates if men were still required to do the setting up.[40] The combination of a decreased wage bill and the award of lucrative government contracts meant that Ada could certainly afford to give a pearl to the Red Cross appeal. Her firm's profit increased from £3,340 in 1913 to £6,054 in 1916.[41] Knowing that many of the war widows in Otley would never own a pearl themselves, she made the donation on their behalf.

The idea of a well-known local woman donating a jewel to represent her community's role in the war became an essential element of the Pearl Appeal's success. In Hampshire, Alice Shrubb sent her pearl for the men of Boldre and Pilley. The Shrubbs were important figures in the area. They lived in Boldre Grange, an impressive Victorian house designed by the architect Norman Shaw and, like the Kekewichs, they took an active part in public life. Mr Shrubb served first as a county councillor, then as mayor of the nearby town of Lymington.

Before the war the villages of Boldre and Pilley were reminiscent of the static, hierarchical societies in a Jane Austen novel – the same families had taken the same roles in the community for generations. In Pilley, the squire, Justice of the Peace and vicar lived in ivy and creeper-clad mansions while the other villagers lived in cottages tucked behind thorn hedges and shrubbery. On the boundary of Pilley was the hamlet of East Boldre, which had grown up when landless labourers had set up 'squatter' settlements on the forest common land. The surrounding countryside was noted for its peaceful, picturesque beauty. Dotted across the landscape were smallholdings where cattle and ponies grazed.

However, the sleepy serenity of the area was disturbed in 1915 when East Boldre was chosen as a base for a flying school by the Royal Flying Corps. The first airfield in the area had been built five years earlier by William McArdle and John Armstrong Drexel, who established the New Forest Flying School on the site. It was one of the first flying schools in Britain. Although it only lasted until 1912, the training centre became an exciting addition to village life. In May 1910, the headmaster of East Boldre School sketched a plane in the school logbook, many of his pupils had never even seen a train, but they could now boast of being among the first to watch aeroplanes flying overhead.[42]

During the war, the site became home to No. 16 Training Squadron. Hangars were built and grass runways were marked out, and then the first men arrived for training. In 1917 the site was extended to become a large complex. Added to the existing hangars were new Bessonneau canvas ones; there were also accommodation huts, mess halls and workshops. Three new squadrons were trained at the airfield.

In April 1918, the naval and military wings of the RFC were merged to establish the Royal Air Force and the base at East Boldre became RAF Station Beaulieu. The trainee pilots came from all over the world to the base – there were men from Canada, the United States, South Africa, Australia and Belgium. In their late teens or early twenties, they were full of bravado.

Women were also stationed at the airfield; some drove lorries or acted as officers' chauffeurs, while others were employed as waitresses in the Officers' Mess or as shorthand typists. Women worked in the sewing room, in the workshops stitching material onto the wings of planes, or in the doping room, where the material was dipped in a foul-smelling stiffener.

The life expectancy of pilots was short so they seized every moment and made sure they had plenty of fun. When they were off duty they would cycle over to the local pubs at Boldre and Pilley, making the most of the old-world charm. Dances were held regularly in the Sergeants' Mess. A lorryload of girls would come up from the villages to dance to music played on the piano and fiddle. At midnight, flirtations were forgotten and their dancing partners were unceremoniously helped back into the lorries and sent home. On Sundays, when the camp was less busy, there was time for roller-skating on the hangar floor. Occasionally there would be a camp concert with plenty of beer and comic choruses.[43]

The airmen were risk-takers, who enjoyed showing off. Against the rules, one pilot took up a single-seater plane with a fellow airman sitting astride the fuselage and waving to a gasping audience beneath. There were about a dozen pilot instructors who were allocated three student pilots each. One of the most popular instructors was Tone Hippolyte Paul Bayetto. He had joined the RFC in 1915 and seen extensive service in France. During a mission in September 1917 his plane was shot down. In the subsequent crash landing, he fractured his skull and he was sent home to recover. In March 1918 he was posted to East Boldre. His daring flying stunts, which included flying between the hangars, gained him the nickname 'Mad Jack'. A few months after his arrival he was involved in an accident – while flying in formation he turned back to look for his pupil pilot, 21-year old Sergeant Patrick Hogan, but their planes collided killing both men. Bayetto's plane crashed into the trees on a nearby hill and his dead body was found spread-eagled on the ground below.[44]

As aviation was in its infancy, crashes were common. Planes landed on top of the hangars or upside down on the landing strip. One pilot clipped the chimneys of Norfolk House, in the village, before crashing into a neighbouring garden. On 24 October 1917, a plane crash-landed on the roof of the village post office, above the bedroom of the postmaster's daughter. She was just getting dressed when the ceiling came down around her head. Thankfully no one was injured and the pilot was provided with a ladder to climb down to safety.

Villagers became used to seeing planes flying in formation overhead, and many attended air shows at the base, where they were entertained by displays of stunt flying. However, the high level of risk involved could never be forgotten. On 28 April 1918, a large crowd was watching as one of the most senior officers, 28-year-old Major John Lawson Kinnear, did rolls, loops and spins. The atmosphere of excitement changed in a second to horror as one set of the wings of his Sopwith Scout plane became detached. As he spun to the ground, he switched off his engine just before impact; he was killed immediately.[45]

From March 1918, not a month was to pass without at least one fatality at East Boldre. During the war years, twenty-three trainee pilots were killed at the base. Their dynamism and courage would never be forgotten by the villagers, and a lasting reminder remains in the village churchyard where nineteen of the airmen were buried.[46] They had become as much a part of the community's wartime story as the local men whose names were engraved on the village's war memorial. Alice Shrubb's gift of a pearl commemorated all their brief lives.

The courage of pilots like the men trained at East Boldre was essential to the British fightback against the Germans in 1918. On 12 April, the newly-created RAF dropped more bombs than on any other day of the war. Its pilots were told that 'very low flying is essential. All risks to be taken.'[47] With the Allied forces working effectively together, the German advance was halted and General Ludendorff had to change his plans again, turning the attack on the French.

East Boldre pilots had proven themselves prepared to make the ultimate sacrifice to prevent the Allies' defeat and Alice Shrubb made sure their contribution was remembered. Mrs Shrubb was just the type of woman that

Lady Northcliffe had been looking for when she launched the Red Cross appeal. It was thanks to dedicated provincial women that the fundraising spread to cover the whole country. Local committees had been formed in forty-three counties. In twenty counties the collections were organised by the wives of the high sheriffs, and in most of the other areas mayoresses like Mrs Shrubb took the lead.

Lady Northcliffe and her committee encouraged competition between the different areas to keep the pearls coming in. Donors were kept informed of which areas were doing best, and a few months into the appeal it was made known that the southern counties had been more generous than the northern ones. Areas that were falling behind were chastised.

The wide geographical range of the donations, and the fact that they were given in memory of men from all classes, showed that, like the men in the trenches, the women at home believed that they were all in it together. The necklace became a symbol of the determination that even when their 'backs were against the wall' they would not surrender.

SIX

PEARLS FOR HEROIC NURSES

Pearls were not only given for soldiers who died in action, they were also donated for nurses who made the ultimate sacrifice. In the first week of June 1918, a pearl was added to the collection 'in memory of the heroism of our nurses on May 19'.[1] The tragedy that prompted this gift marked a new low point in the conduct of the war. During May, German airships bombed hospitals clearly marked with the Red Cross sign. It was never proved that the Germans had adopted a deliberate policy of bombing hospitals; they claimed not to have seen the Red Cross symbol and argued that the hospitals were placed near railways, army camps and depots which were legitimate military targets.[2] However, their actions were seen by many as a war crime that went against all moral and international law. On Whit Sunday, 19 May, the No. 1 Canadian General Hospital at Étaples was struck, killing three nursing sisters and many patients.

One of the nurses who died was 25-year-old Katherine Maud MacDonald. Katherine had everything to live for. Attractive and full of *joie de vivre*, her strong conscience made nursing her vocation. Born in 1893, before the war she had lived in Brantford, Ontario, in Canada, with her mother and sister, Florence, who was chief operator of the Bell Telephone Company in the town. When Katherine graduated from Victoria Hospital, London, Ontario, in 1915 it was a proud moment for the whole family. She was photographed at her graduation in her immaculate uniform surrounded by bouquets of flowers. She then nursed privately in her home town before enlisting in the Canadian Expeditionary Force and the Canadian Army Medical Corps. Unlike nursing units in other Allied forces, the Canadian nurses were fully integrated within the military structure and assigned a rank. They were nicknamed 'Bluebirds' by soldiers because of their blue dresses, white aprons and sheer white veils.

At Easter 1917 Katherine left home for England, full of excitement and travelling with two other local nurses. A pipe band played and a crowd of friends cheered Katherine off as the train pulled out of the station. Looking forward to the adventure, on the journey she wrote home, 'Oh what a lovely time I have. I just adore being on the train. This suits me fine.'[3] She proudly explained that she had been chosen to be in charge of all nineteen nurses in her unit, although some were as old as her mother. Leadership came naturally to her and she enjoyed booking their hotel rooms, arranging meals, organising their tickets, documents and luggage, and taking them to matron if they became ill. Evidently her easy charm made her popular, the porters could not do enough for her, calling her group of nurses first for meals and thus annoying the other nursing unit from Toronto, who had arrived before them. When they set sail to cross the Atlantic on HMHS *Essequibo*, life on board ship had plenty to keep them entertained, and Katherine particularly enjoyed a grand concert put on by the stewards' minstrel troop.

Once in England, Katherine was posted to military hospitals in Eastbourne and then Brighton. Her life on the south coast is captured in the red leather scrapbook she kept. As well as the serious side of life, there are snapshots that recall the fun she had with her fellow nurses and army officers. She was loved by both her patients and colleagues. In one photograph, Katherine is the only nurse sitting in the middle of a group of wounded soldiers; some have bandaged heads, others have crutches, but several are fit enough to be larking about in the background. One grateful patient wrote Katherine a poem:

My work is on Ward Number Seven
The day sisters there, they simply remind one of heaven.
The patients all say
That it was lucky that they were admitted to Ward Number Seven.[4]

The hospital at Eastbourne was a large Gothic building set in well-manicured gardens. When she was off duty, Katherine went for walks on the seafront or the nearby clifftops, followed by a picnic on the beach with other nurses and officers.

Katherine had many admirers, including Dr Fleck Graham, an earnest young doctor who had grown up just a couple of streets away from her in Brantford. When the war began, Dr Graham had just graduated in medicine from Toronto University and was taking a postgraduate course in New York. He immediately enlisted in the 86th Machine Gun Battalion but just before his unit was sent overseas he was badly injured in a railway crash. The damage to his back was so severe that he could have been invalided out of military service. However, he was determined to do his duty. Wearing a plaster of Paris cast for his back injury, he went to England and worked with Katherine in the military hospital in Eastbourne. At dances, while Katherine energetically joined in with equally exuberant young soldiers, Fleck was restricted by his back problem and, instead of joining her on the dance floor, was left playing bridge with the 'serious'.[5]

During this time, Katherine met and fell in love with a Canadian captain in the 12th Canadian Reserve Battalion called John Ballantyne. Spending time together at Eastbourne when he was on leave, the relationship developed quickly and they got engaged. John captured some of their precious moments together with his camera. One particularly relaxed photograph shows Katherine standing on a windswept clifftop; she is holding on to her hat while laughing flirtatiously at the photographer. However, although she was so happy during her time in England, she was always looking for the next challenge. Her fiancé counselled her against going to France but she was determined, as Captain Ballantyne later wrote to her mother, for Katherine 'duty was ever foremost and prevailed'.[6]

Her opportunity came after she impressed doctors by helping in a difficult operation. When she was first asked to scrub up and help 'a big man' who had come down from London in the operating theatre she was nervous. She wrote to her mother, 'I was a fussed girl when they told me.' However, she was delighted afterwards when 'they all said it was fine and our Colonel was tickled to death, praised me sky high'.[7] When she heard that some nurses would soon be selected to go to France, Katherine asked the colonel if she could be one of them and, recalling her competence in the recent operation, he agreed, saying 'we want some good nurses'. She warned her mother and sister that she might be gone before they got her letter and added enthusiastically, 'hope so'.[8]

In March 1918, she set off for France. Her arrival coincided with one of the most intense phases of the fighting. Vera Brittain, who was nursing at a hospital near to Katherine's, described the experience as like being in Dante's *Inferno*. There was constant and deafening noise, crashes and thuds from the battlefield mixed with the roar of ammunition lorries and ambulances travelling along the broken roads day and night. The flashes of fire on the horizon were a reminder of how close they were to the fighting as the Germans advanced.[9]

Canadian Nursing Sisters served in military hospitals and casualty clearing stations in France, Belgium, Greece, Malta and the Eastern Mediterranean. The casualty clearing stations received the wounded first. Ambulances rolled up in a steady stream and then stretcher bearers would move the wounded to the wards. Often the men were gassed and choking for breath or bleeding copiously from their wounds. The nurses would care for them immediately, feeding them and clothing them in clean outfits.

The base hospitals in France were part of the casualty evacuation chain. Further back from the front line than the casualty clearing stations, they needed to be close to a railway line for casualties to arrive. Most of them were located not far from the coast because they also had to be near a port so that men could be evacuated for longer-term treatment in Britain. There were two types of base hospitals, known as stationary and general hospitals. Often, they were established in large buildings which had been seaside hotels or châteaux before the war.

The Canadian Red Cross made sure that the hospitals were kept well equipped and both nurses and patients were supplied with what they needed. The organisation was responsible for building some special wards for chest and fractured femur cases, and in all the larger Canadian hospitals there was a special Red Cross storeroom where supplies were kept and were looked after by a Red Cross orderly. As well as necessities, members of the Red Cross also provided a personal touch, handing out cigarettes, chewing gum and maple sugar to cheer up wounded men.

In December, 38,235 Christmas stockings stuck with bright seals and tied with multi-coloured ribbon were sent from Canada to soldiers in hospital in France. It was a reminder to each man that people at home were with him in spirit at Christmas. Mary Macleod Moore, a contemporary chronicler of the Canadian Red Cross, explained that it allowed 'a soldier who has fought for years, and known all the horrors and privations of a long campaign' to be a child again.[10] Mrs Macleod Moore saw many of the Red Cross' activities in maternal terms, writing that the Information Bureau of the Canadian Red Cross might be called 'the Mothering Bureau', because it made sure that each Canadian soldier when he was admitted to hospital had a visitor to comfort and befriend him and make sure he was given what he craved. They also kept in touch with the man's family in Canada.[11] Mrs Macleod Moore wrote, 'It was a deputy for all the mothers and wives longing to make the time of suffering easier. In a word, it represented a human and personal side to that awful thing called War.'[12]

Katherine was based at No. 1 Canadian General Hospital at Étaples. Many of the wards were devoted to patients with leg injuries and by May 1918 they were nursing more than 300 patients with fractured femurs.[13] Wounds to the femur carried high mortality rates, but at Katherine's hospital they were using a new method of treatment which was improving outcomes. Major Meurice Sinclair, a Regular Army Medical Officer, had transformed the management of gunshot fractures of the femur by introducing a system of traction on the Thomas splint, in suspension. It was very successful and in his own hospital, where the treatment was first used, the death rate in open fractures of the femur was reduced from 80 to 7.3 per cent.

The work at the hospital was demanding and after a hectic day Katherine was often too tired to write letters. During this final phase of the war, hospitals were working at high pressure. As the Germans advanced, casualty clearing stations had been bombed and field ambulances wiped out so patients were sent directly to the hospital from the battlefield. Wounded in the morning, soldiers would often be at the hospital by the afternoon.

Convoy after convoy of men arrived, often unattended, in any vehicle that would carry them, from ambulances to cattle trucks. Lying on stretchers, often moaning or crying out with pain, the wounded lay in their blood-soaked khaki uniforms torn open to expose their wounds. Many went to England just a few hours later, after just a wash and change of dressing. Others never made it home, instead they were sent to the cemetery after a hurried laying out that was too rushed to be reverent. The operating theatres were fully stretched day and night, with nurses and doctors often working fourteen-hour days. There was no time to tidy the wards or finish off one job before another convoy arrived demanding immediate attention.[14]

In a letter home, Katherine described the relentless flow of men at her hospital:

> Poor fellows, they have some awful wounds. We have one very sick man. Amputation of both legs above the knees. He lost so much blood that I am afraid for him. We had to send him to the Operating Room again tonight and when he came back he would not rest unless he had my hand and there I sat and thought every minute my back would break. He is a dear but I am so afraid he will go out.[15]

In Katherine's scrapbook there is a handwritten poem called 'The Nursing Sister', by Captain Ronald Gordon Cumming, who she had met in the Eastbourne hospital. As it is undated, we do not know when he wrote it or gave it to her, but the verse recreates the tender care she gave her patients. In the 'long, long nights of suffering' the nursing sister battled hard with death trying 'to ease a sinking sufferer' by smoothing his forehead and just watching over him during 'the last grim tussle' before he died. However, the last lines of the poem were an uncannily accurate forecast of Katherine's fate:

> For throughout a life of mercy
> That has much to teach and learn
> She must always face the prospect
> That in time will come her turn.
> May some spirit haunt her pathway
> To help her down that road.
> With willing hands to lead her
> And to help her bear her load.[16]

At times, Katherine's load seemed very heavy and her duties in France tested her to her limits. After two months at this unrelenting pace she had asked for a transfer back to England to the Canadian Hospital in Brighton, which she considered to be her home. She was hoping to leave the hospital soon and was looking forward to returning to her old friends, but she knew that while they were so busy in France they would not want to let her go.

By May there was a shortage of trained nurses in France and it was estimated that another 342 nurses were needed.[17] The Germans had gone quiet for a few weeks, but it was clear they were still planning something.[18] In her last letter home, written the night before she died, she wrote reassuringly to her mother and sister, 'I suppose we will have another big push again. Hope they make one grand one and finish but don't worry we are far from harm.'[19] However, the final paragraph of her letter suggests that like everyone else, male or female, at the Front, death was never far from her mind. The night before, she had visited the war cemetery where there were 'millions' buried. She looked for Canadians but did not find any she knew. Showing a surprising interest in the details of the burials, she noted that the officers had graves to themselves but the privates were two to a grave although 'each have a wooden cross at the head and all are fixed up nicely'.[20]

Those were the last words she wrote to her family, just a few days later one of those simple wooden crosses would bear her name. On 19 May, after a long day on the wards, Katherine had attended the Whit Sunday Communion service. When it finished at 9.30 p.m. she went with her friend, Margaret Lowe, to drop into the room of another sister. Together they talked of the sermon and service and then they set off for their own rooms. As they did so, bombs began to drop on the men's quarters. There was no time to think of getting to the bombproof shelters.

Katherine was with several other nurses when the fatal shell fell directly on the building where they were. None were killed outright, but Katherine was wounded by a piece of shrapnel which severed the femoral artery causing extensive bleeding and shock. She told her friends that she felt faint. Another sister suggested that the others tried to move her but Katherine then said, 'I am fainting,' and wilted in front of them. She died a few minutes later.[21]

The matron of the hospital, Edith Campbell, wrote, 'Poor little soul, she did not suffer long, death came very soon.'[22] Drawing on her Christian faith, the matron added, 'It was a terrible night. It's only God's mercy that any of the Sisters were saved. They simply hammered at us for hours it seemed.'[23]

The matron and sisters had shown great courage during the raid. All night the sisters remained at their posts and, despite the heavy bombing, many of those who were off duty went up to the hospital to help. Their bravery was widely recognised. Queen Alexandra sent a telegram to Miss McCarthy, matron-in-chief, expressing her deep shock at the terrible casualties 'to our dear nurses'. She wrote:

> Please tell all those at Étaples how truly I sympathise with them in the terrible ordeal they had to undergo. It is too dreadful to think that our brave nurses whose lives are devoted to looking after the sick and wounded should have been exposed to such wicked and uncalled for trials.[24]

Two Sisters were awarded the Military Medal for distinguished service in the field for their bravery that night. Nursing Sister Helen Elizabeth Hansen 'worked devotedly in the operating room throughout the period of the severe bombardment, which lasted for 2 hours'. Her citation stated that she 'was ready for any duty, and exhibited qualities of coolness and courage'. Nursing Sister Beatrice McNair also 'carried on her duties throughout the night without interruption'. During the period of severe bombardment, she 'showed great solicitude for the patients in her wards, and was wholly unmindful of her personal safety'.[25] The bombing destroyed the quarters where Katherine and her friends had been and the adjacent building of HRH Princess Victoria's Rest Club for Nurses was also in ruins. The only thing left intact in the building was Her Royal Highness' picture, which was on a small table on the ground floor – neither the table nor the picture had been touched.[26]

Rather than shattering morale, the German atrocities made the doctors and nurses all the more determined to continue with their vital work. 'Carry on' became the motto of the Canadian Nursing Sisters in all the hospitals after the bombing. The colonel of one hospital decided to send his nurses off to a distant hospital on the coast where they would be safe, but the women refused to go and the colonel allowed them to continue. Each night the sisters on duty were provided with shrapnel-proof shields to wear under their uniforms.

Emergency operations continued to be carried out, although the surgical hut rocked with the force of explosions from bombs that dropped a few yards off. In other huts, when the raid siren was blown, the nurses went through the wards and gently lifted helpless patients to the floor where, protected by the sandbag barrier that lined the hut, they were comparatively safe from flying shrapnel. Only after they had completed all these tasks would the nurses go to the bombproof shelters. If a ward was hit by a bomb, nursing sisters would rush to the rescue, ready to calm the men who were in their care.[27] When the sisters' quarters were no longer considered safe after dark the nurses spent their nights in trenches in the woods.[28]

In the days after the raid Katherine's fiancé, Captain Ballantyne, wrote to her mother about his darling 'Christy'. He wrote that she was 'a brave girl and so devoted to her duty in the cause of justice and relief to the suffering that she has made the supreme sacrifice. Her heart and soul were in her work and nothing was too extreme for her powers.'[29] Comforting Mrs MacDonald, he assured her that she was 'always her chief thought' and that Katherine adored her. He credited her mother with instilling strong Christian values in Katherine and making her 'a sterling character'.[30] He then turned to his own feelings, explaining:

> My personal relations with her were most intimate, as you no doubt know, and to me she was ideal in every respect and our love meant much to us. Now that bond is severed, but her memory will always be one to inspire me to higher ideals and may I be able to avenge her loss.[31]

Still in shock, he added, 'I can scarcely realise that all this has come to pass and that I am not to enjoy her companionship again. She was everything to me and our hopes were for the future.'[32] In his overwhelming grief he tried to cling on to what little he had left of her. Spending time looking at the photos of them together during the more carefree days at Eastbourne, he attempted to recreate that time by asking Katherine's sister, Florence, what she had told them about him. He wrote, 'Could you give me some idea of Christy's esteem for me from things she had written home. It seems strange to ask such a question but it would be so self-satisfying.'[33]

Mrs MacDonald also needed a tangible link with Katherine to help her grieve; she requested that her daughter's body should be brought home to Brantford. Although Captain Ballantyne wrote many letters on her behalf and even offered to go over to France to arrange it, the authorities would not allow it so Katherine was buried in France. At 9.30 a.m. on 21 May, 110 Canadian sisters, with seven generals and many British and American officers from the area, attended her funeral. Her fellow sisters showed their high esteem for her by lining her grave with white and purple lilacs and pink peonies. Flowers were also sent from all the hospitals in the area. At the service, the Canadian Army chaplain read from Corinthians and

Revelations. Describing the great multitude standing before the throne of God to a congregation who were still in shock from recent traumatic events, he read, 'These are those who have come out of the great tribulation; they have washed their robes and made them white in the blood of the lamb. Therefore [...] He will lead them to springs of living water. And God will wipe away every tear from their eyes.'[34]

The two other sisters who were seriously wounded did not survive. Thirty-five-year-old Nursing Sister Gladys Maude Mary Wake died from a compound fracture of the femur two days after the attack. Nursing Sister Margaret Lowe, aged 32, suffered a fractured skull and wounds to the chest in the air raid. She was operated on three days later, when a portion of her rib was removed and fluid was drained from her chest. Her head wound was also examined and some of the bone was removed.[35] She was nursed in a hut as her condition was too serious to allow her to be moved to the Sick Sisters' Hospital at the Villa Tino. A few days after the attack, she was just conscious but very ill, and she died on 28 May.

All of the staff and patients in the hospital were deeply affected by the three deaths. The chaplain wrote, 'Those of us who are alive, live very much in our thoughts with those who have gone.'[36] The strength of feeling among their fellow nurses was evident at Margaret's funeral as a long line of nurses in uniform followed her coffin. Three small white crosses mark the graves of the heroic Canadian sisters in the Military Cemetery at Étaples.

Five other nurses had also been wounded during the raid. Their injuries included wounds to the back, wrists and eyes. Three of them were sent to the Sick Sisters' Hospital to recuperate, but Sisters Wishart and Gallagher, whose injuries were only slight, asked to remain on duty after a brief period of rest. However, when another heavy barrage happened it was too much for Sister Wishart, she 'became unnerved' and had to be taken to the Villa Tino.[37]

She was not the only one to suffer from shattered nerves. Vera Brittain admitted that her teeth chattered with terror when she heard the deafening noise of the German planes overhead. One nurse who, like Sister Wishart, had previously been shelled completely lost her nerve and ran screaming through the mess until two sisters grabbed her, forcibly put her to bed and held her down until the raid was over to prevent panic spreading.[38]

The strain on nurses was at times unbearable and all matrons were instructed to send off duty any nurses who were overtired. Since 1 April

1918, the Red Cross had opened a rest home for nurses in Boulogne. Previously run as a hotel, it was made to feel like a real home with the prettiest chintzes, freshest curtains and good china. Nurses could relax in the terraced garden, which provided freshly grown vegetables for their meals. However, even at the rest home they could not escape the German threat. During the air raids all the guests and staff went down to the large concrete cellar where, by the light of electric torches, they told stories and played games until it was safe to emerge.[39]

Back in Canada, as Mrs MacDonald tried to come to terms with her loss the letters of condolence continued to arrive. There were the official ones from King George V, the Secretary of State for War and the Governor General of Canada, but the ones that moved her to tears were from Katherine's friends. On opening one letter a few pressed flowers fell out, a Canadian sister had sent flowers from Katherine's grave to her mother, writing, 'I hope you will keep strength Mrs MacDonald. It is hard I know that you should not see Katherine again. She was a dear girl – you know loved by all – Dear Girl. She is "often, often with you when you think her far away".'[40]

However, perhaps the most poignant letter was from Katherine's admirer, Dr Graham. When he wrote to Mrs MacDonald he was serving in No. 3 Canadian Stationary Hospital at Doullens. Recalling their time in England, he wrote, 'You don't know how difficult it is for me to write to you. So many little things come to mind. I can close my eyes and look back over the joyous times spent together. The climax seems so strange.'[41] He added that it was difficult to realise how 'wonderfully brave' the nurses were under the bombing until you saw it at first hand, but their calm conduct made a huge difference to the wounded soldiers. Knowing how close Katherine was to her mother and sister, he tried to comfort them by reassuring them that it was beyond doubt that:

> ... were Maudie [his name for Katherine] to do it all over again she would most assuredly tell you that to have been such a service as Canadian Nursing Sisters are to the wounded in pain racked body and the heroic spirit of our Tommies – to be of service is worth the price.[42]

Dr Graham was also to pay the ultimate price. He died only a few months later on 20 September 1918. When No. 3 Canadian Stationary Hospital was bombed at the end of May he carried on his crucial work in the resuscitation and chest wounds ward, even when he heard the German planes overhead. Remaining calm and cheerful, he reassured his critically ill patients with his usual kind words.[43] As German bombs descended on the hospital, a huge triangle in the Citadel was destroyed and in the rest of the building the roof fell in leaving only walls. He survived, but three nursing sisters and two medical officers died. The whole of the operating theatre and X-ray appliances had been wiped out and the medical staff who had been working in the theatre were unrecognisable. Those who were not killed were badly wounded.[44] Revealing much about his own ethos, at the funeral of his colleagues Dr Graham was most forcibly struck by the words of the bishop who, in speaking of the nurses, said it was 'such a glorious ending to such a glorious life of service'.[45]

Dr Graham only narrowly escaped death again in August 1918 when a German bombing raid killed his roommate and destroyed all Fleck's possessions. A week after that incident, more people were killed at the hospital and the unit moved to Rouen. In a letter home, Dr Graham expressed the belief that if he met the almost inevitable death in France he felt that he had been of just as much use to humanity as if he had returned and lived to be an old man in Brantford.[46] Although he remained cheerful, the constant physical and mental strain was debilitating. He had never fully recovered from his earlier back injury and was in constant pain from severe sciatica. The night before he died he was quite positive and was talking about returning to work, so it came as a shock to his colleagues when he was found dead in his bedroom early the next morning. He had died from cardiac failure and exhaustion – he was only 34.

The self-sacrificing valour of the Canadian nurses and doctors was captured in a painting by Gerald Moira, entitled 'No. 3. Canadian Stationary Hospital at Doullens'. Disappointed that Canadian achievements had not been recorded visually, Lord Beaverbrook had commissioned British artists to document the Canadian war effort. The Canadian War Memorial Fund eventually employed more than 100 artists, including Gerald Moira. Born in 1867, Moira studied at the School of the Royal Academy of Arts and later taught at the Royal College of Art in South Kensington. Inspired by the Pre-Raphaelites and Symbolists, many of his works of art were allegorical.

In 1917, he wrote that he would like the opportunity to go to France and do decorative paintings for the nation because it was essential that the country should have memorials of the war.[47] Moira visited the hospital in early 1918, before the raids, and made sketches for his picture. The hospital had been set up inside the chapel of a fifteenth-century château in Doullens. Reflecting the religious environment, Moira set the tender care of these nurses in a Christian context. Designed like a triptych which could go above an altar, the left panel depicts convalescence and healing, the central panel illustrates the chapel turned into a receiving room where the wounded had their field dressings removed, while the right panel shows the wounded being evacuated to a base hospital. Moira portrayed the nurses tending wounded soldiers like angels of mercy. Emphasising the importance of nurses in the war, they are placed in the foreground and centre of the painting. They are shown tending wounds and bandaging injured soldiers lying on stretchers. Linking their care to Christian ideology, in the central panel a nurse carrying bandages is placed below a statue of the Virgin Mary cradling Christ's wounded body. The connection between the sisters and Mary is further highlighted by the nurses' clothing, reminiscent of the Virgin they wear white veils and a blue dress.

Like the Red Cross Pearl Necklace Appeal, Moira's painting showed that amidst death and destruction there was a need to remember the humanitarian values that were under threat. Moira's work of art reflected the importance of Christianity for Canadians during the First World War. Many Canadians saw it as a Christian battle fought under the banner of Christ.

The Canadians were not the only ones to view the war in religious terms. Many people in Britain, France and Germany believed God was on their side. Despite the fact that Catholics, Protestants and Jews – people of all different faiths – were fighting on both sides and that there was an almost complete lack of any clear denominational differences between the Allies and their enemies, these people saw the conflict as a kind of war of religion. The idea that they were engaged in a holy war was exploited by some of the clergy in the different countries to spur their congregations on to ever greater sacrifice.[48]

In trying to make some spiritual sense out of the carnage of the battlefield, the devout identified the suffering with Christ's crucifixion. One army chaplain, the rector of St Giles in Dorset who was serving at No. 42 Stationary Hospital during Holy Week 1918, wrote to a friend explaining that he believed that the Passion of Christ was reproduced in the life of nearly every soldier. On a physical level, he compared the pack each soldier carried to Christ's cross, claiming that it weighed the same, and each man's tin hat to the crown of thorns. However, it was the spiritual suffering, the agony and the loneliness of the helpless, wounded soldier waiting to be picked up on the battlefield that most reminded him of the Via Dolorosa.[49]

The idea of giving a pearl to the Red Cross often appealed to people who were seeking a spiritual dimension amidst the horror of war. In medieval times, pearls were associated with the purity of the Virgin Mary, Christ and the Kingdom of Heaven, and this sacred symbolism made the Pearl Appeal a particularly apt way to commemorate the nurses killed in May 1918. It tapped in to the same vision of the saintly sisters that Moira promoted in his painting. Pearls were also an appropriate jewel to remember Katherine and her colleagues by because the gems had a long history of being thought to have healing powers. During the Renaissance, scholars promoted the medicinal and magical properties of pearls. Some were pulverised and taken in a drink, while others were worn as amulets that were believed to cure illnesses of the mind and protect patients.[50]

Nurses were not only remembered through the pearls, they also gave to the appeal themselves. One of the most generous contributions was a fine necklace of eighty-nine pearls from 'Blue Bird' – perhaps she was one of the Canadian nurses who had already given so much.

Katherine was the first of forty-six Canadian nurses to lose their lives during the war.[51] It was right that a pearl in memory of her sacrifice should take its place in the pearl necklaces alongside other jewels in memory of soldiers who died in action. In Katherine's local paper, her photo appeared next to all the soldiers who had died in London's Honour Roll. As the Brantford newspaper explained:

> She has fallen on the field of battle, on behalf of the cause of human liberty, just as surely as those who have given their lives on the firing line, and her name will rank with other heroines who have demonstrated their loyalty and self-sacrifice in the time of stress.[52]

SEVEN

PEARLS FOR TRANSFORMATION

Not all the pearls given to the appeal had a sacred significance or were donated to remember loss. Since Queen Elizabeth I in the Armada portrait had worn pearls in abundance to signify her purity, chastity and wealth, another layer of symbolism wrapped itself around these jewels. During the Elizabethan age, pearls became associated with female empowerment. In the 1588 painting celebrating the defeat of the Spanish fleet, the queen, resplendent in a jewel-encrusted gown and festooned in ropes of pearls, stands beside her pearl and jewel-set crown, her hand resting on a globe to suggest that she controls even time and space.

During the Great War, many women found they also had more power and control over their own destinies. Society had to change to adapt to the demands of war and, with thousands of men away, women took on many of their roles on the home front. During the war, 100,000 women were nurses or worked in hospitals, another 100,000 served in the auxiliary forces and 800,000 women worked on making munitions and in engineering. Another quarter of a million had worked on the land.

Women took on many of the jobs previously done by men, even driving trains and buses.[1] In Lord Northcliffe's *War Book* in aid of the Red Cross, the press baron wrote about the effect this work had on women. Describing it as one of the great surprises of the war, he suggested that the new jobs open to women released their 'tremendous pent up energy'. He wrote that before the war thousands of 'nice girls' living in 'dreary, manless suburbs' did not work because their families thought it was beneath their dignity. They preferred the barren existence of 'keeping up appearances on small dress allowances to an active participation in daily life'. During the war, women had been able to prove themselves and they had taken on their tasks with 'joyousness'.[2]

His wife's Pearl Appeal allowed some of these women to express this joy in their new experiences by giving jewels. As one donor of a very beautiful pearl wrote, 'If "every pearl is a tear", may this one represent only a tear of laughter.'[3] Although they were often working harder than they had ever worked before, the combination of camaraderie and a sense of purpose meant that some women actually had fun in the war.

Many of the patrons of the appeal not only donated their gems, they also gave their time to the Red Cross. Working for the first time, they found a fulfilment and freedom they had never known before. One woman who experienced this transformation was Constance Edwina, Duchess of Westminster. Known to her friends as Shelagh, her metamorphosis from society butterfly to a woman with a mission is recorded in photographs.

Posing provocatively, playfully stretching her long string of pearls across her cleavage to accentuate her waspish waist, Shelagh stares knowingly at the camera. Her hair is coiffed into a hundred curls and a tassled brooch is pinned strategically just below her low neckline to draw attention to her pert bust. This photograph, taken in 1906 at the fashionable Lafayette Studio in New Bond Street, could not be more different from the one taken eight years later. In her 1914 photograph, the seductive diva has vanished to be replaced by a demure nun-like woman in a high-necked nurse's uniform and apron. Every bit of hair, except her fringe, is concealed in a nurse's white hat while, reflecting the practical requirements of her new role, all her jewellery has been removed. The sexually knowing look has gone and, in its place, her eyes express a deeper, sadder knowledge.

Before the war Shelagh had led a hedonistic life. Married to one of the richest men in England, Hugh Grosvenor, 2nd Duke of Westminster, known as Bendor (after his grandfather's chestnut Derby winner), she had been one of the most envied women in society. It was estimated that the duke's income was the equivalent today of almost £47,000 per day. However, her wealth did not bring Shelagh happiness. Her mother,

Patsy Cornwallis-West, was a manipulative matchmaker who taught both her daughters that they had to marry for money and position rather than love. Patsy's eldest daughter, Daisy, married the German Prince of Pless. Upon the death of her husband's father in 1907, Daisy became the chatelaine of Furstenstein, a palace in Silesia with more than 600 rooms, and the Castle of Pless, which had an estate larger than an English county. A trendsetter, Daisy was responsible for changing the fashion in pearls. In 1900 the height of sophistication was the *bayadére*, composed of several strands of seed pearls plaited together and often decorated with a pendant or tassel. From around 1910, its place was taken by long *sautoirs*, modelled on the Princess of Pless' string of pearls, which was more than 7m long.

After Daisy's marriage, Patsy's next mission was to snare an equally eligible husband for her second daughter. Bendor and Shelagh had been childhood sweethearts. As children, they took part in a mock wedding ceremony with Daisy officiating as the vicar. For years afterwards they called each other 'my darling wife' and 'dearest husband'.[4] Once Bendor came of age, Patsy was keen to turn the play acting into a reality.

At a house party at Blenheim Palace, Patsy persuaded the Prince of Wales (the future Edward VII) to speak to Bendor and suggest that, having been discovered alone in the garden with Shelagh, the only course of action for a gentleman was to marry her. Bendor later claimed that Patsy had orchestrated it all by sending the two of them into the garden for a walk, with the intention of accusing him of compromising her daughter's reputation. Whatever the truth, her machinations worked and in February 1901 Shelagh was married to Bendor. Although the ceremony was scaled back because the country was in mourning for Queen Victoria, it was still one of the grandest society weddings of the season. Shelagh was swathed in Brussels lace, while the pages wore satin 'Blue Boy' costumes copied from Gainsborough's portrait. The reception was held in Park Lane where the centrepiece was a huge wedding cake topped with replicas of the bride and groom's ancestral homes. On the wedding day, Princess Daisy noted that her new brother-in-law showered presents 'not unworthy of an Empress' on his bride'.[5]

At first, the couple seemed compatible as they shared a love of hunting, polo playing, yachting and motor racing. They also enjoyed entertaining on a lavish scale at Grosvenor House in London and Eaton Hall in Cheshire. The young couple were at the heart of Edwardian society. Bendor's widowed mother, Lady Sibell Grosvenor, had married George Wyndham, Mary Wemyss' brother, so they were leading members of the Souls. However, Bendor and his bride were also close to the less intellectual Marlborough House set. At their house parties at Eaton Hall, the two groups mingled. Edward VII and Queen Alexandra, Alice Keppel and Lady Sarah Wilson visited, as did the Duchess of Rutland and her daughters.

Redesigned in the Victorian era by Alfred Waterhouse, the architect of the Natural History Museum, Eaton Hall was a Gothic palace which unkind observers compared to St Pancras Station.[6] With unlimited money to spend, Bendor developed his estate to his own taste, creating a boy's paradise with a steeplechase course, nine-hole golf course, hunting, shooting, cricket, tennis and croquet. The highlight of the year was the annual polo tournament when ten teams and ninety-two polo ponies descended on Eaton Hall for a week.[7]

The Westminsters entertained with equal extravagance in London. In 1902, the duke and duchess gave a ball at Grosvenor House for the coronation. It was the height of Edwardian glamour as royalty and aristocracy, glittering in evening dress and jewels, filled the ballroom. The supper hall was decorated with blue hydrangeas and white lilies and the finest silver. It was the culmination of Patsy Cornwallis-West's social ambitions, as her two daughters and their extremely rich husbands took centre stage, but then an unfortunate incident ruined Patsy's evening. Somehow, she managed to break her string of pearls and, as the orchestra stopped playing and guests crawled around the floor to collect her jewels, someone whispered that the pearls were not real. Soon the gossip had spread throughout the party and Patsy's moment of glory was ruined.[8]

The duke and duchess' marriage was also not what it outwardly seemed. In the first years the young couple had a daughter, Ursula, followed by a son, Edward, but increasingly Shelagh was away from home, living a fast life in every sense of the word. In 1907, a month after she was featured looking flirtatious in a large picture hat on the front cover of *The Car* magazine, she appeared in court on a charge of dangerous driving. She admitted to having driven her car at up to 11 miles per hour and was fined £5.[9]

Still under the influence of her sister and mother, she was often away from home visiting Daisy at her palaces in Pless and Furstenstein. As their marriage deteriorated, husband and wife were unfaithful to each other. Bendor had an affair with Gertie Millar, the daughter of a Bradford millworker who had become one of the most popular musical comedy stars of the era. Their relationship continued until she found out that Bendor was being unfaithful to her with the ballerina, Anna Pavlova.[10] Retaliating, Shelagh surrounded herself with handsome, unmarried men and it was soon rumoured that she was having an affair with the urbane Duke of Alba. Already a regular guest at house parties held by the Desboroughs at Taplow, Jimmy Alba was soon top of Shelagh's guest list for Eaton Hall. In 1908 Shelagh and Daisy went to visit him at his luxurious home in Spain. While the duchess enjoyed her holiday, she left her young children with their grandparents for three months.

Shelagh immersed herself in a decadent lifestyle, but it did not satisfy her. She was looking for something more meaningful to give purpose to her life. Strong-willed and with a complex personality, the shallow existence of a society hostess did not stretch her. Although she always appeared outwardly cool and poised, she often seethed within when her spoilt husband flew into a rage if he did not get his own way. Clashes between the couple were inevitable as Shelagh could also be difficult to handle.[11]

The final blow to the Westminsters' marriage came in February 1909 when their 4-year-old son, the heir to the dukedom, died from septicaemia following an appendix operation. Shelagh was too distraught to attend her son's funeral. She wrote to her sister of the 'big blank he has left in my life; I feel as if the world had grown suddenly dark, and I am groping to see and touch a little light'.[12] Later that year she wrote again, saying how she missed Edward's little footsteps and thought she heard them all the time.[13] Bendor was equally bereft, the sorrow of not having a son to succeed him was to pervade the rest of his life. However, rather than turning to his wife in his grief, he blamed her for the tragedy, claiming that she had neglected their son.[14]

For a time the duke and duchess kept up appearances, attending and hosting events together. During this period, Shelagh seemed to be living her life in fancy dress and going to endless parties. Typical of this time, there is a photo of her in 1910 at Lord Winterton and Lady Birkenhead's ball at Claridge's. Shelagh is dressed as a Gypsy, with a rose pinned in her hair and her ubiquitous pearls around her neck.

To repair their marriage, the Westminsters tried for another child. However, when in June 1910 a girl, Mary, was born instead of a male heir, the marriage was over. At first Bendor did not even bother to visit the new baby. For the following three years, although living in the same house, the duke would rarely see or speak to his wife. In 1913, the duke requested a separation and offered Shelagh an allowance of £13,000 each year and the use of his yacht. She rejected the offer as derisory and wrote to her husband appealing for 'restitution of conjugal rights'. Bendor refused and informed her that Eaton Hall and Grosvenor House would no longer be available to her. On 30 June, a legal separation was finally agreed upon, which was very similar to Bendor's original offer. Their two daughters, Lady Ursula and Lady Mary, were made wards of court.[15]

For both Shelagh and Bendor the war provided an escape from their unhappy private life. While the duke joined his regiment and introduced the first armoured cars into battle, the duchess sailed to France with a group of friends, her faithful wolfhound and a copy of Longfellow's poetry to start a new and very different life. Within weeks she had founded a military hospital at Le Touquet which became known as the Duchess of Westminster's Hospital. Run under the auspices of the British Red Cross, the organisation insisted that a fully trained nursing staff should be appointed.

A highly qualified team of surgeons and nurses who had been trained at St Bartholomew's Hospital agreed to join the Duchess of Westminster's Hospital. Under the military Commandant-in-Chief Major Douglas, there was the senior surgeon, Major Charles Gordon Watson, and five medical officers. A trained matron and assistant matron were appointed to oversee the nursing department.[16]

Before the war was declared, the duchess had been invited to be a guest aboard the entrepreneur Sir Thomas Lipton's yacht *Erin* to watch the America's Cup races. Using her considerable charm, Shelagh persuaded her host to convert his luxury yacht into a hospital ship instead and bring her entire field hospital, including doctors, nurses, orderlies and medical equipment, to France.[17] Once across the Channel, the unit was temporarily housed in the Hotel de France at Choiseul, in Paris, while it awaited the allocation of a hospital. However, Paris was very different from the fun-loving capital Shelagh had known before – in fear of what the war had in store for them, many of the Parisians were now dressing in black.[18]

Shelagh did not just lend her name to the hospital, she took a hands-on role. On 24 October 1914 the duchess and her team received a telegram from British Headquarters ordering them to start for Boulogne in twenty-four hours. The duchess, the matron and one of the medical officers went ahead, but were disappointed to find that there was no building available for the hospital in Boulogne itself and so Shelagh travelled to Le Touquet and used her contacts to find a suitable site. Fitting the duchess' previous incarnation as a playgirl, she chose the local casino to become her hospital. It was a picturesque building, with its turrets and colonnades giving it a fairy-tale appearance. The gossip was that Shelagh had been in competition with Lady Dudley who wanted the casino for *her* hospital, but the duchess had won against her rival.[19]

The next morning, the whole unit gathered at the Gare S. Chapelle. It was like a military manoeuvre to get to Le Touquet, with the hospital equipment alone filling a dozen railway trucks on the train.[20] There was a festive atmosphere as the team gathered. The sixty orderlies, from a Bristol unit of the St John Ambulance Association, arrived garlanded with flowers which had been presented to them on their march to the station. The men and women of Paris had greeted them with gratitude, kissing them, calling them '*les braves Anglais*' and even singing 'God Save the King'.[21]

At 1.40 p.m. on 28 October, the duchess' team set off on the train. The journey took almost nine hours as the Chantilly route had been disrupted by the blowing up of the bridges along the Oise. Looking out of the train windows, they saw houses burnt by the Germans. After arriving at Étaples, the team travelled by tramway to the casino at Le Touquet and then moved into the Hotel des Anglais nearby. Le Touquet had the feel of a seaside holiday resort off season, there were the famous sand dunes, the woods and the smart golf club where the flags were still flying and the groundsman was rolling the grass.[22] However, the holiday atmosphere did not last long as there was urgent work to do.

Within days the casino was transformed into a military hospital. Shelagh gave £1,000 to start the hospital and then guaranteed £400 a month to keep it running. Her husband sent her a £500 donation 'for old times' sake', but when she wrote him a thank-you letter hinting at the possibility of a reconciliation he did not reply.[23]

However, the duchess did not have time to dwell on personal disappointments. The next three days were spent unpacking instruments, dressings, tables, linen and crockery that had been brought over from England. In the gaming rooms, beneath the ornate ceilings and crystal chandeliers swathed in linen covers, rows of beds were lined up awaiting the first casualties. The *salles privées* were transformed into an operating theatre, and a pathological laboratory and an X-ray room were set up on the ground floor.

Now all the hospital needed was patients. Boulogne was crowded with British wounded, and injured soldiers were lying at the station waiting to be taken to England. But at Le Touquet the medical team waited for patients in vain for several days. On 4 November, the commandant, Major Douglas, went to Boulogne and returned with the promise that a hospital train would arrive later that day.

At about 7.45 p.m. in the evening the first cases arrived by ambulance car from Étaples Station. Then the cars kept coming, returning to collect more men, until by 1 a.m. there were about 200 patients. Many of the injured had been travelling all day, they looked exhausted and their wounds badly needed redressing. From now on there would be little respite for the duchess and her medical staff. The next morning they were up at 8 a.m. to care for their patients.[24]

The duchess became a familiar figure on the wards accompanied by her Irish wolfhound. One patient wrote to his fiancée about being visited by the duchess who 'promised to bring a big dog she is awfully proud of' the next time she visited.[25] One of the hospital's nurses, Lynette Powell, described the duchess at this time as looking beautiful in her uniform, which always included a very dainty cap. A professional nurse herself, Lynette found Shelagh and her friends were useful because they could do the jobs the trained nurses did not have time for; they read to the men, wrote letters for them and kept them entertained. They also did the administration and clerical work and saw to the medical supplies, linen and food.

Shelagh and her friends also provided glamour. The duchess thought that one of the best things that they could do was to raise the morale of the soldiers. When the convoys of casualties came in, the nurses all rushed to attend to their medical needs while the duchess and her team took down their details on slips of paper. They always dressed themselves up to greet their patients. 'It's the least we can do to cheer up the men,' the duchess used to say. Whenever they got word that a convoy was coming in, even if it was early in the morning, they changed into full evening dress with diamond tiaras. Dressed for a ball, they would stand at the entrance to the hospital and take the names of the men. Adding to the party atmosphere, they played uplifting music on the gramophone. The contrast between the elegant ladies and the muddy men lying on stretchers was a surreal sight, but it did what the duchess had intended and cheered up the men. Lynette recalled one soldier saying, 'We thought we were going to Hell and now it seems we are in Heaven!'[26]

Beneath the superficial frivolity the duchess took her role seriously and was deeply affected by the patients she saw. Finding the cases of tetanus were the worst to watch, she gave the patients a little chloroform each time an attack came on to ease their pain. She particularly admired the cheery and amusing young boys who came in. She told her mother about two Irish lads who both had their rights arms off and 'did nothing but chaff each other and ask for the loan of each other's arms'.[27]

Shelagh went back to England for Christmas, but she found it a difficult experience. Her two daughters, Ursula and Mary, stayed with their father at Eaton Hall so Shelagh spent the holiday with her parents. During the war years, Shelagh rarely saw her daughters. They stayed with their grandparents and were raised by governesses because for both the duke and duchess their war work came first. They let the day pass without celebration, and separated from her children the duchess wanted to be very quiet.[28] It was a relief to return to her work at the beginning of January.

However, even in France Shelagh could not totally escape her mother's unhelpful interference. Patsy used to send her six rashers of bacon for her breakfast, and on the outside of the package she had written, 'If anyone opens this and won't let my poor little girl have it, I hope it will make them very, very sick.'[29]

Many of the women who were involved in the Red Cross Pearl Appeal ran hospitals. Like the Duchess of Westminster, Lady Sarah Wilson set up a hospital in France in 1914. By October, the chief surgeon and thirty-three nurses were on their way to join her at Étaples. Wanting her patients to have the best of everything, Lady Sarah had arranged for Harrods not only to equip the hospital but also to do the catering. Lady Sarah's friend, Alice Keppel, who was also a leading member of the Red Cross Pearl Appeal, joined her and helped with secretarial work. One of Lady Sarah's patients told a journalist that it was 'the jolliest place to be ill in'. Favourite ragtimes were played on the gramophone and Lady Sarah herself was 'a veritable tonic' as she was always so bright and cheery.[30]

From 1915, some of the smartest addresses in London and grandest stately homes in the country were turned into convalescent hospitals. As many of the Duchess of Rutland's friends were setting up hospitals in France she decided that she would like to do the same, but at the last minute the Red Cross refused to sanction the unit. Disappointed, she decided to turn her Arlington Street home into an officers' hospital. At first the duke resisted as he feared his house would be knocked about, so the duchess turned to his ex-mistress, Maxine Elliott, and asked her to persuade him. A compromise was reached in which only half the house was converted into a hospital; the duke's part would be reserved for his use only. Violet reassured her husband that this was not a purely philanthropic move, it was to prevent their daughter, Diana, from becoming a nurse in France.[31]

Diana had been scheming to become a nurse since the start of the war and had written to the Duchess of Sutherland, Lady Dudley and the Duchess of Westminster in the hope of joining them. She had also contacted Maxine about helping on her barge in Belgium. However, using similar emotional blackmail to the pressure she exerted on her son, John, the Duchess of Rutland had prevented Diana from going to the Front. When bursting into tears and saying the anxiety would kill her did not work, Violet persuaded her friend Lady Dudley to give Diana a lecture on how wounded soldiers might rape the nurses who looked after them.

Diana thought this argument was ridiculous, but she was unable to go against her mother's wishes and instead trained as a nurse at Guy's Hospital in London. Violet resented even this compromise because it threatened her authority over her daughter. Although the work at Guy's was gruelling, for the first time in her life Diana felt free, until then she had never been allowed out on her own on foot and her every move had been known by her mother. Diana's newfound liberty did not please Violet, so she plotted to curtail it. By establishing her own hospital, her daughter would once more be under her domination.[32]

At Arlington Street, the golden drawing room became a ward for ten patients, while the ballroom held another ten men. The walls were hung with glazed linen, the floors covered with linoleum and the duchess' bedroom was equipped as an operating theatre. After Diana's training in the more professional, spartan environment of Guy's Hospital, she felt that her mother's hospital 'seemed soft and demoralising'.[33] When the hospital opened there was no discipline for the nurses. Instead of the unflattering, utilitarian uniform she had worn at Guy's, Diana was now dressed in a flattering red uniform with a big organdie Red Cross headpiece. Chestnut-cream cakes from a top patisserie and sherry were provided for elevenses and there were plenty of boltholes with telephones from which Diana could keep in hourly contact with her friends.

The Duchess of Rutland was not the only one to put her own personal stamp on her hospital. Using the skills they had honed as society hostesses, the women running hospitals tried to make their patients as comfortable as possible. From 1915, Lady Northcliffe ran a twenty-bed hospital for officers at 14 Grosvenor Crescent, Belgravia. A journalist from the *Pall Mall Gazette*, who visited the hospital, wrote, 'The wards have been decorated with unerring good taste under Lady Northcliffe's personal direction, the furniture having been obtained from one of Lord Northcliffe's country houses.' A large bowl of flowers was placed beside each bed and a comfortable day room was created for the officers. The journalist described Lady Northcliffe, 'In the most becoming of white nursing outfits [she] moves about like the presiding angel of the house with a smile on her lips and a cheerful word for all'.[34] She was as much at home in the little white marble operating theatre as in the cosy, fire-lit apartment where the nurses rested.

Patients appreciated Lady Northcliffe's efforts. Major Wingrove, who had been wounded in the leg at Neuve-Église in April 1918 and had lost part of his right calf to gangrene, was sent to her hospital. He wrote, 'I am now recovering rapidly in one of the best hospitals in London. Everything possible is done for us and no expense spared. Lady Northcliffe is a charming hostess and comes round to see us almost every day.'[35]

The rush to offer their houses for use as hospitals, charity headquarters and convalescent homes was so overwhelming in the early months of 1915 that in May the War Office was forced to announce that no further offers of private houses were needed. The numbers of women volunteering to become nurses in the VAD was also overwhelming. From 9,000 members in August 1914, the organisation had grown to 23,000 nurses and 18,000 hospital orderlies by 1918, with many VADs serving in France, Gallipoli and Mesopotamia.[36]

Like Lady Diana Manners, many of the young women who helped in the hospitals found the experience liberating. There was a reality to the work which was often lacking in their pampered pre-war existence. Cynthia Asquith wrote in her diary about her time in a hospital:

> I have <u>loved</u> it, to an extent that puzzles me. I quite understand one's liking for the human interest side of it and the absorbing, feverish desire to satisfy the Sister and please the men, but I rather wonder why one enjoys the sink tray, Lysol, bustle side of it quite so much. [37]

Analysing her emotions further, Cynthia wrote, 'I think one reason that makes me like it is my entire lack of shyness with the men. It is the <u>only</u> human relationship in which I haven't been bothered by self-consciousness.' [38] Away from the stilted conventions of society, where strict etiquette and chaperones kept the sexes apart, young women like Cynthia at last felt able to be themselves. They related naturally to men as fellow human beings rather than potential suitors. For the first time, these girls had a genuine purpose which went beyond their previous restricted roles as lovers, wives or mothers.

The press picked up on the idea that these women gained at least as much from their work as the men they cared for. Journalists satirised society ladies who were falling over themselves to nurse the wounded. A cartoon in *The Sketch* portrayed a Tommy bandaged like an Egyptian mummy complaining to an orderly as a smiling lady prepared to treat him, 'Lummy 'er Ladyship again? Look 'ere George! Be a sport. Go tell 'er I'm too bloomin' ill to be nussed today.' [39]

There was some scepticism about whether untrained aristocrats were the right people to run hospitals. The politician Lord Crawford thought women like Millicent, Duchess of Sutherland, and the Duchess of Westminster were particularly troublesome. According to him, they overspent and then expected the Red Cross to extricate them. They shamelessly exploited their contacts and they were so eager to keep their hospitals filled that they became known as 'body snatchers' for carrying off invalids 'willy-nilly'. Apparently, one of the ladies employed an 'admirable' ambulance driver who would wait at a railway siding and then whip a wounded man out of the train while the orderlies were not looking. Lord Crawford hoped that the Red Cross would veto any more expeditions by these 'adventuresses'. [40]

However, despite the mockery, most of these women did a good job, they conscientiously cared for the sick and provided the funds that kept the hospitals going. They were not just 'lady bountifuls' playing at nursing. As one officer told a journalist, the Duchess of Westminster was 'a little brick a dead hard worker a sport very unassuming always there when you want her – the best of the bunch'.[41] Her hospital gained the reputation for being one of the best in France. *The Sketch* described it as 'quite the perfection of a ward'. They added, 'The surgeons say that it is astonishing how quickly wounds heal and bones set in the quietude and the splendid atmosphere of the forest by the sea.'[42]

Although they were dealing with dreadful mental and physical wounds, the duchess and her nurses made a great effort to raise their patients' spirits. According to *The Sketch*, 'All the ladies are expert masseuses.'[43] Often the sound of a piano could be heard, accompanied by a cheerful singing voice. One of the best-loved nurses was 33-year-old Martha Frost from Yorkshire. Always kind and optimistic, she would sing at the top of her voice while encouraging the patients to join her in a singalong. One solider wrote, 'Here's to jolly Martha, who is all cheerfulness and brightness itself, with such splendid care, how can any patient help but be affected by her charming personality?'

There was humour and laughter as well as sorrow on the wards. In a 'ditty' a patient wrote, 'Martha we love you, dear old thing. If you can't do much else, you surely can sing.' Recreating the teasing banter between nurses and patients, another soldier penned a poem, 'A cheeky old thing by name, Martha, when dealing with wounds was a "strafer", she'd just pull, tear and rip; at the pads round my hip; but by Jove a good sort she's not half a […] Potter!' Showing how the men courageously made light of their life-changing wounds, in Martha's autograph book one of her patients signed himself, 'Deepest love and best gratitude from the one-legged rabbit'.[44]

Lasting friendships were made on the wards of the Duchess of Westminster's Hospital. Social class became irrelevant as professional nurses like Martha, who had nursed in Yorkshire before the war, worked side by side with girls from the aristocracy and landed gentry. Martha became great friends with Lady Alba Painter and after the war she used to visit her at her stately home. Whenever Lady Painter's children were ill, Martha was asked to nurse them. Although Martha never married or had children of her own, her niece was named Alba to mark the special relationship.[45]

While some of the medical staff changed over the years, the Duchess of Westminster was a constant reassuring presence. Proving she was no longer the restless socialite of the pre-war years, she showed lasting commitment to her hospital and worked there throughout the war. In the spring and early summer of 1918 the pressure on all the hospitals in France was reaching a peak. At the Duchess of Westminster's Hospital the number of beds had increased from 160 at the start of the war to 250. Red Cross reports show that for the four weeks ending 18 May 1918, the hospital had treated 634 patients, 201 operations had taken place and 125 X-ray examinations had been done.[46]

The unrelenting workload continued following the Battle on the Aisne on 27 May. As thousands of German guns shelled the French from north-east of Paris, the earth shook and an inferno raged. Within a few days the Germans had advanced about 40 miles to reach the Marne. However, the Germans faced stiff resistance from the French who were reinforced by American troops.[47] Giving the Allies hope for the future, the Americans acquitted themselves well in their first major action of the war at Château Thierry and Belleau Wood.[48]

Amidst the growing pressure on her hospital, the duchess remained calm and collected; her grace under strain was widely admired. Later that year, Shelagh was made a Commander of the Order of the British Empire for her service in the war. Through her work, the duchess found the fulfilment which had been lacking in her previous life.

While developing her new identity she also found new love. One of her patients was a dark-haired, slightly built, 25-year-old airman called Captain James Fitzpatrick Lewis. A keen sportsman, before the war he had lived at Woking and worked at Lloyds Underwriters. When the war broke out he gained a commission in the Royal Flying Corps.

Early in the war the RFC had set up an aerodrome at Le Touquet near the duchess' hospital. As the fatalities at East Boldre training school highlighted, military flight was very dangerous. Once trained and in France it became even more perilous and, as Captain Lewis 'conceded nothing in daring', inevitably he was injured.[49] After his accident he was sent to the duchess' hospital.

Although James was twelve years Shelagh's junior, when they saw each other it was love at first sight. A newspaper reported, 'From their earliest acquaintance an attachment sprang up between them.'[50] As the duchess was still married, they tried to keep their romance secret but there was gossip. However, the couple were undeterred by what other people thought. When Shelagh was spotted at a performance of *Seraglio* at Drury Lane in summer 1918 she was looking radiant. The columnist noted, 'The Duchess of Westminster always seems to be resplendent in diamonds these days whenever I see her. She was a vision of jewels and lace.'[51] When James was demobilised, the duchess appointed him as her private secretary so that he could be constantly with her.

After the war ended, in 1919 the duchess divorced the duke on grounds of his adultery and desertion. The decree was made absolute on 19 December and just a few weeks later on 14 January 1920 Shelagh secretly married James. Unlike her first wedding, the couple had an unostentatious register office ceremony at Lyndhurst in Hampshire with just Shelagh's maid as a witness. After the wedding, Wing Commander and Mrs Lewis left to start a new life in the South of France.

For the former duchess, giving away one of her pearls to the Red Cross had been a symbol of her liberation from a life which had offered her everything money could buy, except happiness.

Lady Northcliffe as a young society hostess. (© LaFayette/Victoria and Albert Museum, London)

DAME GRAND CROSS OF THE ORDER OF THE BRITISH EMPIRE: VISCOUNTESS NORTHCLIFFE.

Left: Lady Northcliffe ready to launch her pearl campaign, 1918. Photograph after she received her OBE. (© Illustrated First World War online/Mary Evans Picture Library)

Above: Princess Victoria, president of the Pearl Appeal, wearing a long string of pearls in 1914. (Royal Collection Trust/© Her Majesty Queen Elizabeth II 2018 RCIN 2913342)

Left: The Countess of Cromer, as she appeared on the cover of *The Queen* newspaper when promoting the Pearl Appeal, March 1918. (© The British Library Board. News 12539, p.1)

Noël, Countess of Rothes, wearing her pearls shortly after surviving the sinking of the *Titanic*. (© Mary Evans Picture Library)

Anthony Wilding in uniform, photographed in France. (© Mary Evans Picture Library)

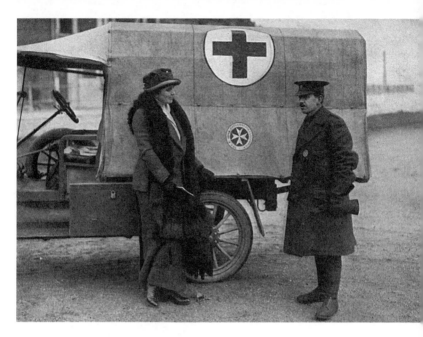

Maxine Elliott with a Red Cross ambulance. (© Mary Evans Picture Library)

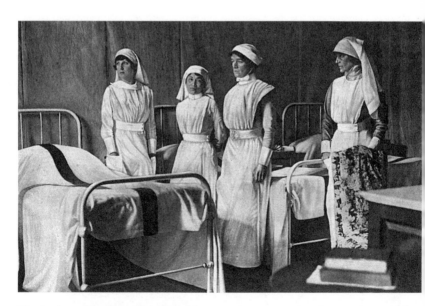

The Duchess of Rutland with her daughter Diana wearing nurses' uniforms in the Rutland Hospital. (© Mary Evans Picture Library)

Violet, Duchess of Rutland, photographed in profile wearing her pearls. (© Mary Evans Picture Library)

Mary Wemyss with her son Ego when he was a child. (© Lord Wemyss, Stanway)

ONE OF THE BEAUTIFUL MANNERS GIRLS — AND CHILDREN.

1. WITH HER SONS: LADY ELCHO, WIFE OF THE ELDEST SON OF THE EARL OF WEMYSS, WHO IS GOING TO EGYPT TO VISIT HER HUSBAND (OF THE GLOUCESTERSHIRE YEOMANRY).

2. PLAYING AT SOLDIERS—WITH RED INDIANS! THE HON. FRANCIS DAVID CHARTERIS AND THE HON. MARTIN MICHAEL CHARLES CHARTERIS, CHILDREN OF LORD AND LADY ELCHO.

Lady Elcho, who is going to Egypt to visit her husband, was, before her marriage to the eldest son of the Earl of Wemyss, Lady Violet Manners, and she is the second of the three beautiful daughters of the Duke and Duchess of Rutland. Her wedding took place in 1911, and her two little sons are the Hon. Francis David Charteris, born in 1912; and the Hon. Martin Michael Charles Charteris, born in the following year. Lord Elcho is a Lieutenant in the Gloucestershire Yeomanry, and a barrister of the Inner Temple.

Photographs by Speaight.

Letty Elcho and her boys. (© Mary Evans Picture Library)

Ettie Desborough with her two sons Julian and Billy when they were boys. (© The Rt Hon. N. Viscount Gage/ The British Library, 10864, p.27)

ie Desborough with her two
s during the war. (© Mary
ans Picture Library)

"If blood be the price of admiralty,
Lord God, we ha' paid in full."—*Kipling.*

LADY DESBOROUGH WITH HER SONS—THE LATE HON. GERALD GRENFELL (ON LEFT) AND HER SURVIVING SON, THE HON. IVO GEORGE GRENFELL (THE LATE CAPTAIN JULIAN GRENFELL, INSET)

The deep sympathy of all of us goes out to Lord and Lady Desborough in their recent loss of their second son, the Hon. Gerald Grenfell, who is seen above with his mother and surviving brother. Few parents have been privileged to suffer more greatly for their country and in the cause of humanity, as their eldest son, the Hon. Julian Henry Grenfell, D.S.O., a portrait of whom is inset, who was a captain in the Royal Dragoons, died of wounds in May last. Their surviving son is still at Eton. Lord Desborough is famous as a great sportsman, and both he and his wife are very popular, particularly in the neighbourhood of Taplow, their charming riverside home

Katherine MacDonald wearing her nursing sister uniform. (© George Metcalf Archival Collection, Canadian War Museum: CWM 19950037–011)

Funeral of the three Canadian nursing sisters and a Canadian doctor. (© George Metcalf Archival Collection, Canadian War Museum: CWM 19930012–179)

Painting by Gerald
Moira of the No. 3
Canadian Stationary
Hospital at Doullens.
(©Beaverbrook
Collection of War Art,
Canadian War Museum:
CWM 19710261-0427)

Constance Edwina
(Shelagh), Duchess of
Westminster, looking
flirtatious. (© LaFayette/
Victoria and Albert
Museum, London)

The Duchess of Westminster dressed as a nurse, with her dog. (© Mary Evans Picture Library)

A ward in the Duchess of Westminster's Hospital. (© Mary Evans Picture Library)

THE SKETCH.

THE WEDDING OF THE EARL OF ST. GERMANS AND LADY BLANCHE SOMERSET: BRIDE; GROOM; AND MAIDS.

The St Germans' wedding.
(© Illustrated First World War
online/ Mary Evans Picture
Library)

Blanche St Germans after
the death of her husband,
looking desperately sad
in a large hat and pearls.
(© National Portrait Gallery
Picture Library)

Violet Astor looking poignant in her pearls, 1917. (© Mary Evans Picture Library)

Violet Astor looking happy again after her second marriage, in a large hat and pearls. (© Philip Astor)

The Grafton Galleries poster for the Red Cross Pearls Exhibition. (Imperial War Museum/ © British Red Cross Society)

Queen Alexandra attending the Red Cross Pearls Exhibition on 22 June 1918. (Royal Collection Trust/© Her Majesty Queen Elizabeth II, 2018, RCIN 2303822 b)

Queen Mary looking at pearls at the exhibition on 22 June 1918. (Royal Collection Trust/© Her Majesty Queen Elizabeth II, 2018, RCIN 2303822 a)

Lord Lansdowne and his grandson, both in soldiers' uniforms. (© Trustees of the Bowood Collection)

Lord Kitchener and Julian Grenfell. (© The Rt Hon. N.Viscount Gage/British Library, 10864, p.27)

Cartoon of Christie's Red Cross Auction by Max Beerbohm. (© Christie's, 2018)

Cartoon 'Objects of Desire, For the Wounded'.
(© Christie's, 2018)

The pearl necklaces, photographed
in the Red Cross Auction Catalogue.
(© British Red Cross Society)

In the autumn of 2018, after reading about the story in a magazine, a family got in touch saying that they have a Red Cross pearl necklace. The lustrous natural pearls, each unique in slightly different shades, have been treasured by the family down the generations and are still worn today. They come in an original blue velvet box with a white lining, on which is shown a red cross. (Private collection)

EIGHT

PEARLS FOR MARRIAGE

The complex combination of motives that inspired each donation to the Red Cross Pearl Appeal were as varied as the multi-layered mythology that surrounds pearls. For thousands of years pearls have symbolised love and marriage. However, the superstitions associated with the jewels were often contradictory; these desirable gems were variously thought to symbolise seductiveness or to embody purity, to bring good luck in marriage, or be unlucky to wear on your wedding day as they represented tears and misfortune.[1] For some of the women who gave pearls to Lady Northcliffe's appeal, these superstitions were echoed in their lives. During the war, the accelerated cycles of love and loss resulted in them experiencing the extremes of emotion within a few years which were enough to fill a lifetime.

In a June edition of *The Queen*, opposite an article announcing that the Red Cross Pearls were to be displayed at an exhibition at the Grafton Galleries later that month, the 'Fashionable Marriages' page celebrated the wedding of 'Mousie', Earl of St Germans, to Lady Blanche Somerset. It was to mark this joyous event that Mousie's mother, Emily St Germans, had donated her pearl from Empress Josephine's necklace. Emily had already known tragedy, when before the war her eldest son had shot himself at the St Germans' Cornish estate, Port Eliot. In 1916, she had nearly lost her only remaining son, Mousie, when he was severely wounded at the Front. In recognition of his bravery he received the Military Cross.

Emily's gift of a pearl was given in hope of a new beginning. She was delighted to welcome Blanche (known as Linnie) Somerset into the family.

The daughter of the Duke of Beaufort, Blanche had grown up on the family's Badminton estate. Fortunately, she was an unpretentious girl who preferred the outdoor life to society balls, because she was one of the war debutantes who missed a proper season as no courts were held during the conflict. In 1915, *The Sketch* explained, 'It is not a propitious year for debutantes if to be one spells a passion for dances and ices. But Lady Blanche Somerset has no use for those stuffy pleasures.'[2]

Her engagement photograph showed Blanche's determination to be a thoroughly modern woman; her hair is cut short and she is wearing a fashionable headband and long tasselled seed pearl necklace. Her openness to new ideas is further emphasised by the statue of an Oriental deity that was prominently placed on the table next to her. Blanche was happiest on the hunting field and she had followed the hounds as soon as she was able to ride. Responding to her future daughter-in-law's passion, as one of her wedding gifts Emily gave her a fine riding crop. Mousie shared his bride's love of horses but he also had the touch of the showman about him. It was said that if he had not been an aristocrat, his talent for acting and mimicry might have made him a fortune on the music-hall stage.[3]

The St Germans' wedding, which was held at 2.30 p.m. on Tuesday, 11 June 1918 at St Margaret's Westminster, had the appearance of the pre-war Cup Day at Ascot. Crowds of well-dressed young men and women jostled to get a better view of the young bride. The church was decorated with palms, variegated maples and white flowers. Recognising the groom's distinguished war service, troops from his regiment, the Scots Greys, formed a guard of honour inside the church. The congregation stopped gossiping and fell silent as the bride, dressed in a gown of silver tissue over charmeuse, with a train of old Brussels lace given by her mother, walked through their ranks with her father, the Duke of Beaufort, to the chancel where Mousie awaited her. According to the gossip columnist from *The Sketch*, 'the bridegroom looked far more nervous than he used to do in those very far away days when he was such a popular figure at the rag time dances that used to follow expensive suppers at Ciro's'.[4] Fortunately he had his best man, a brother officer, the Earl of Leven and Melville by his side to steady his nerves.

For the packed congregation, the soldiers in uniform were a physical reminder of the war that had transformed their lives. Across the Channel, a few days earlier the German General Ludendorff had launched his latest offensive against the Allies. Unleashing an overwhelming bombardment, the Germans managed to force the French back and were able to cross the Matz River. However, on 11 June, the day of the wedding, the French counter-attacked with a well-organised operation which combined troops, tanks and low-flying aircraft. After much bitter fighting, the Germans were forced to call off their offensive.[5]

At such a tense moment, thoughts about what was happening in the war were inevitable. Like so many wartime weddings, this was an occasion for reflection. Watching as their friends said their vows, 'till death do us part', Lady Diana Manners and her sister Letty, Lady Elcho, must have been reminded of the admirers and husband they had lost. Although the ceremony revived poignant memories, the wedding was an opportunity to give thanks. The *Sketch* columnist wrote, 'There are some things still so entirely joyful in their character that they almost waft us back to the peaceful atmosphere of pre-war days.'[6] As the couple signed the register, the anthem 'Rejoice in the Lord' was sung.

It seemed that the St Germans had every reason to look optimistically to the future. Within a year their first child was born. The new countess gave birth to a daughter, Rosemary, at Lowther Gardens, London, in February 1919, and two years later the couple had a second daughter, Cathleen.

The St Germans were not the only ones to have something to celebrate. Pearls were also given to mark second marriages. The bittersweet legacy of the Red Cross Pearl Appeal is illustrated in the story of Lady Violet Astor.

In 1909, at the age of 19, Lady Violet Elliot, daughter of the Earl of Minto, married Lord Charles Fitzmaurice, youngest son of the Marquess of Lansdowne. The wedding was held in Calcutta because the couple had met in India, where Lord Minto was the viceroy and Charles had been his aide-de-camp. Although Charles was fifteen years Violet's senior, it was a love match. Violet was known for her sharp wit and beauty while Charles' kindness and sense of humour endeared him to everyone he met.

Within the first years of their marriage they had two children, Margaret and George. Lord Charles' career was also flourishing and from 1909 until the beginning of the war he was equerry to the Prince of Wales, later King

George V. When not needed at court, Charles and Violet enjoyed escaping to their estate of Meikleour, in Perth. When he inherited the Scottish estate Charles took the name Mercer Nairne. The family became part of a close community and their tenants took a personal interest in Lord and Lady Mercer Nairne and their children.

At the outbreak of the war in August 1914 Charles requested that he might go on active service with his regiment. A major in the 1st King's Royal Dragoon Guards, he arrived in France on 8 October 1914 as part of the British Expeditionary Force. Shortly afterwards, he wrote to his father, saying, 'Tell Mother not to fuss about me, it is no good and I am only one of thousands.'[7] Just weeks later, he was killed at Ypres on 30 October 1914.[8]

Friends wondered how Violet would cope. Only a few days after Charles' death, Lord Lansdowne wrote to his colleague Andrew Bonar Law that Lady Lansdowne and 'Charles' poor little wife are very brave, but it is not easy'.[9] Like Letty Elcho, Violet was left a widow with two young children. Margaret was just 4 and George not yet 2 years old, so they were too young to really understand what had happened. In the days immediately after the news, Violet's sister-in-law, Evie, Duchess of Devonshire, helped with the children. Evie wrote to her mother:

> Margaret explained to me that her father had gone to Heaven and that God would no longer have to look down to find him, she illustrated this by standing up and staring at the carpet. She thinks it must be very difficult for God to see everybody at once.

George was too young to remember his father properly. However, his aunt said that when he saw a 'soldier boy' at his grandparents' house, Bowood, he was fascinated, blowing the soldier's whistle and crying bitterly once he had to go up to bed.[10] Evie wondered whether he had mixed this military figure up with his father, but she was reassured when he made it clear that he knew it was just a boy.[11]

Violet's desperate loneliness was plain for all to see. As the months went by she tried to turn her sorrow into something more positive by doing charity fundraising for other victims of the war. Charitable work was a prerequisite for society ladies during the war. Inheriting a tradition of philanthropy from their Victorian grandmothers, it was now seen as part of their patriotic duty to use their connections and time to raise money for war charities. However, not everyone felt that this was the best use of these women's time and there seems to have been a pecking order of what was considered the worthiest war work. Margot Asquith argued that if young women only served in this way it was not as 'humanising' as facing the horror and squalor of more hands-on duties like nursing. She believed that the 'committee girls' were missing a wonderful opportunity which could have been the making of them.[12] She wrote to her step-daughter in 1915 describing committee work as unimaginative as it added nothing to a girl's experience of life.[13]

While making her sweeping statement, Margot seemed completely oblivious to the fact that she was criticised for not serving on enough charity committees or doing any obvious war work herself. Admittedly, she did make private visits to London hospitals to talk to troops and she regularly drove to Folkestone or Dover on Sunday mornings to meet refugees, but she believed her main war work was to keep Asquith and their family happy. She was honest about her limitations and when Queen Mary organised a group of society women to sew for soldiers, Margot said she believed that it would be wrong to compete with shops that were already struggling to survive. Instead, she suggested that they should supply surgical shirts which were not sold in shops and immediately ordered a large number from her sewing woman.[14]

Although Margot was not the most appropriate person to criticise others, there was an element of truth in her wariness of committees. There was a danger that the fundraisers' enthusiasm for organising charity events could be counter-productive because so many bazaars, sales and auctions were held that people lost interest in them and potentially valuable items sold for low prices. At one sale, a waistcoat once worn by Edward VII only fetched 6s, while a glove belonging to Queen Victoria received no bids at all.[15] Appearing charitable could become a competitive chore, as Cynthia Asquith complained in her diary. As crowds of women swarmed around her stall at the great Caledonian Market Fair, Cynthia 'hated' trying to sell 'filthy bits of jet trimming, *alleged* to be off Queen Alexandra's dress'. Apparently the jet did not appeal to anyone and Cynthia felt thoroughly humiliated because she was faint with fatigue after manning the stall for an hour while 'that Bovril Duchess of Rutland' was still full of energy after 'selling assiduously' for two days.[16]

In November 1915, Violet Mercer Nairne was a stallholder at a grand bazaar and variety festival held at Claridge's Hotel in aid of War Emergency

Entertainments, which provided hospital concerts to wounded soldiers. Valuable gifts donated included oil paintings by John Singer Sargent and William Orpen and a court train of Duchesse lace worth 200 guineas. If these eclectic items failed to attract visitors, it was hoped that unusual entertainments including palmistry, thought reading and lessons in conjuring would encourage them to pay the 2s 6d entrance fee. Joining Violet as stallholders were the Princess of Monaco, the ever-energetic Duchess of Rutland and Lady Diana Manners.

These women would be reunited to support the Pearl Appeal, three years later. Unlike so many of the other charity appeals, Lady Northcliffe's well thought out campaign was focused, and captured the public imagination. It became so fashionable that even Margot Asquith abandoned her wariness of committees and served on the one set up to promote the pearls.

Although Violet tried to distract herself with good works, nothing seemed to lessen the emptiness left in her life by Charles' death. She was one among an army of widows. It is estimated that 160,000 women lost husbands and double that number of children were left fatherless by the war.[17] So many young women were widowed that society's customs and attitudes had to change. From the Renaissance, widows had worn black clothes and no jewellery except pearls as a sign of humility. During the Victorian era, the rules became more complicated; one etiquette advisor stated that no ornaments except jet could be worn by a widow in the first year of mourning, while a rival advised that diamond ornaments or pearls set in black enamel were acceptable.[18]

However, during the war, strict rules about mourning were modified. It was partly a matter of morale because it was soul destroying for troops on leave from the trenches to see the streets full of thousands of women of all ages shrouded in black crepe. With so many women needed for war work it was also impossible for bereaved wives to retire into the periods of seclusion demanded by the old etiquette of mourning. It was felt that alternative forms of mourning dress were needed to reflect the fact that soldiers had not died in the normal way, but for their country.[19]

Violet's mother-in-law, the Marchioness of Lansdowne, and her sister-in-law, the Duchess of Devonshire, campaigned for the abolition of wearing black in public. They suggested that, instead, a white armband should be worn to symbolise their pride in the dead. In a letter to newspapers in August 1914, before Charles had been killed, the marchioness and the duchess wrote that they had close relations serving in France and they 'did not know what their fate has been, or yet may be, but if it is their fortune to die for their country we shall not show our sorrow as for those who come to a less glorious end'.[20] Many women followed their lead. In June 1915, *The Sketch* commented that there was 'still extraordinarily little mourning to be seen in London'. Setting the standard, Lady Desborough refused to wear black because she was 'determined to fly no flag of distress over the glorious death' of her sons. She believed that to do so would 'be casting shadows' over their triumph.[21]

An even greater change was in the attitude to remarriage. Instead of frowning upon widows remarrying soon after their first husband's death, it was positively encouraged. With so many young widows it was no longer realistic to expect them to behave as though their emotional and sexual lives were over for ever, which was the underlying message of the ritual of mourning.[22] There was also the pragmatic reason that, with so many men being killed during the war, there was a need to replace them by those who remained having more children. Cynthia Asquith noted in her diaries a conversation with Lord Curzon who was 'rather amusing about the war-born necessity of some sort of polygamy, and we agreed that widows must have babies, even if their husbands have been dead for more than 9 months'.[23] Equally keen to boost the population, and with the hint of a eugenic agenda, Cynthia's step-mother-in-law, Margot Asquith, wrote in her diary that she thought that for the sake of the race 'splendid boys' like the unmarried Grenfell brothers should all have children before they were sent to fight.[24]

Two years after her first husband's death, Violet Mercer Nairne remarried. Her second husband was Captain John Jacob Astor. Part of the American Astor dynasty, John was the second son of William Waldorf, who was one of the richest men in America. In 1890 Waldorf moved to England and became a newspaper proprietor, owning the *Pall Mall Gazette* and *The Observer*. There was much rivalry between the Astors and the Northcliffes, as Waldorf disapproved of Lord Northcliffe using *The Times* to promote his own views.

John Astor was known for his charm and courage. At the outbreak of the war, he volunteered for the British Expeditionary Force and went to France as a Household Cavalry signalling officer. In October 1914, he was wounded at Messines and invalided home.[25] John had first met Violet in India when her father was viceroy, and while he was convalescing they renewed their friendship. Soon he fell deeply in love with the stylish young widow and wanted to marry her, but it took time for Violet to agree. Her grief for Charles was still raw and the thought of loving, and then possibly losing, a second husband who would be returning to fight in France made her feel vulnerable. In 1916 she finally accepted his proposal. Friends understood the ambivalence she had experienced. One wrote, 'I send you all my love and my sympathy for I think one needs as much sympathy in one's joys as one's sorrows. I know what you have been going through these last weeks and what an agony of decision you have been through.'[26]

In an environment where death was ubiquitous, no one saw Violet's remarriage as hasty. Her friends and contemporaries were all too aware that life could be short and so it had to be lived to the full. Many wrote letters of congratulations to Violet, expressing their relief that her loneliness was over. Ettie Desborough, who understood the pain of bereavement more than most, was particularly effusive, she sent her 'one line of _great_ love and every happy wish that I can think of in the whole world'. Typical of Ettie, with her penchant for younger men, she could not resist adding, 'I have always been deeply in love with John […] I do think you are both very blessed and lucky people.'[27]

Violet's late husband's family were also supportive. According to the Duchess of Rutland, Violet's mother-in-law, Lady Lansdowne, had helped to persuade her that it was the right thing to do. She told her, 'He is a man who has loved you always – you must think of him!'[28] When the tenants on Meikleour, Charles and Violet's estate, were informed, they looked forward to welcoming Captain Astor to Scotland. The estate manager, John Renton, told Violet, 'They all expressed their pleasure and asked me to convey their congratulations to you.'[29]

Both of Violet's sisters, Ruby and Eileen, also encouraged her; they were pleased that love and joy had come back into her life. John's family were equally delighted. Knowing how much his son loved her, John's father wrote to Violet, 'For some years it has been a fervent wish with me that he should marry in accordance with his inclinations, and this I know he is doing.'[30]

Her friends and family understood that the isolation of widowhood, particularly for very young women, could be stultifying and detrimental. One friend wrote that she was so young to have known such great sorrow, another claimed, 'No lady under 50 is able to take care of herself.' It was seen as the right move, not only for Violet but for her children. A new husband could provide love and support and become a father figure to George and Margaret. Blanche St Germans' mother, the Duchess of Beaufort, who had been left a widow with two small children in 1893, but had married the Marquis of Worcester two years later and went on to have three more children, including Blanche, wrote, 'Dear I can't wish you better than you may be as happy in your second marriage as I have been in mine and that you and dearest Charlie's beloved children may have found as kind and dear a friend as my boys found in Worcester.'[31]

The news also gave others hope for the future. With typical tactlessness, the Duchess of Rutland held Violet's remarriage up as an example to Letty Elcho when she was at the height of her grief for her husband, Ego. She wrote, 'Little Vi adored her husband – She is managing again – if he lives!'[32]

Marrying John, Violet did not try to replicate her first marriage. On 28 August 1916 the wedding was solemnised very quietly at Christ Church, Lancaster Gate. The bride's dress reflected the changing fashions of a world which bore little resemblance to the formal pre-war Edwardian years. Violet wore a short dress of cream georgette, trimmed with tiny pleats of taffeta and finished at the wrist with a band of cream ribbon. Her picture hat of cream brocaded velvet was lined with pink and trimmed with a single pink rose. Her only jewellery was her string of pearls and instead of a bouquet she carried a vellum-bound prayer book.[33] Showing their support for Violet's remarriage, her first husband's parents, Lord and Lady Lansdowne, attended the wedding. Continuing the low-key theme, there was no reception and after the wedding the couple left for a quiet honeymoon at Ford Manor, Lingfield.

The Astors had struck just the right tone, as showy weddings were considered inappropriate during the war. The prime minister's daughter, Violet Asquith's wedding to her father's private secretary, Maurice Bonham Carter, in November 1915 was particularly controversial. The Asquiths already had a bad reputation for maintaining their peacetime routine of weekday luncheon and dinner parties with house parties at the weekend. In June 1915 Maurice Bonham Carter wrote that Margot had not changed at all; instead of large dinner parties of twenty, she now had frequent ones of twelve, her clothes were still very new and her bridge playing expensive.[34]

However, at first it seemed that on this occasion Asquith and his daughter had decided to show some restraint. They claimed that they were going to have a quiet wedding with the minimum of ceremony and no reception. The prime minister even told his colleagues in the House of Commons, 'Wedding bells these days must ring in muffled tones'.[35] However, there was nothing subdued about the wedding when it actually took place. Margot Asquith was too insensitive to public opinion to scale down her grand style, even when the country was facing wartime austerity.

There were days of celebrations. First the Asquiths attended a reception in the Speaker of the House of Commons Library, attended by many Members of Parliament, where the bride-to-be was presented with a diamond sun brooch. The occasion was an opportunity for supporters of the prime minister to show their solidarity after the attacks led by Lord Northcliffe earlier in the year.[36] The day before the wedding, Miss Asquith was 'at home' at Downing Street where selected guests were invited to see the hundreds of wedding presents. The prime minister and his wife had requested that no list of the presents should be published, but details of the valuable gifts appeared in the newspapers. Occupying the place of honour among the jewellery was the gift from the king and queen of a diamond and enamel brooch with the royal cipher in diamonds on a background of blue enamel with a crown above. Queen Alexandra also gave a diamond brooch.

The ceremony, at St Margaret's Westminster on 30 November, rivalled a royal wedding. Crowds lined the streets as the prime minister and his daughter arrived by car from Downing Street. Inside, the church was packed with aristocrats, ambassadors and politicians. The wedding was staged like a theatrical show with no expense spared on the costumes. The bride wore a medieval-style wedding dress of ivory satin with long chiffon sleeves and a tulle veil down to her knees caught by the House of Commons' diamond sun brooch. Her two bridesmaids were dressed in Russian-style apricot chiffon ballet dresses under matching velvet full-skirted coats trimmed with skunk fur. To complete their outfits, they wore Russian hats in gold lace, fur and velvet and carried skunk fur muffs. To complement them, the four pages wore breeches and tunics in apricot velvet decorated with gold embroidery.[37]

As an acknowledgement to the reality of war, wounded soldiers formed a guard of honour as the bride entered on her father's arm, then the service began with the Archbishop of Canterbury and the Bishop of Southwark officiating. The public had been told that there was to be no reception, but most guests returned to Downing Street for a party afterwards. While most newly married couples behaved like the Astors and honeymooned in Britain during the war, the Bonham Carters enjoyed an enchanted fortnight in northern Italy. They had been lent a beautiful villa on the Italian Riviera with a garden which the newlyweds described as like a cross between Eden and Kubla Khan's Xanadu.

However, while they basked in the sun under the orange trees, there were repercussions at home.[38] The extravagance of the wedding was widely criticised at a time when economy was expected.[39] The socialist *Herald* ran an editorial entitled 'The Human Comedy: that Asquith Wedding' attacking the conspicuous display of wealth.[40] Ripples of discontent spread throughout the country. In the village of Great Leighs in rural Essex, the Reverend Andrew Clark recorded the disapproval of his parishioners. They resented the government calling on them to practise economy and telling them that extravagance was sinful when the prime minister had spared no expense on his daughter's wedding.[41]

Even Violet Asquith's sister-in-law, Cynthia Asquith, wrote in her diary, 'There is something terribly grim about a pompous wedding now. It seems so unnecessary and irrelevant, and one feels so remote.' However, she did recognise that it was hypocritical of her to say this as she had enjoyed a lavish pre-war wedding in 1910. She added, 'This is unkind [of me] because, if one were the bride oneself, no doubt one wouldn't feel one's glamour in the least impaired.'[42] Cynthia was more generous about the wedding of the Duchess of Rutland's son John to Margot Asquith's niece, Kathleen 'Kakoo' Tennant, in January 1916. Falling in love with Kathleen had been one of the reasons John had eventually given in to his mother's pressure and accepted that he would not fight at the Front. Cynthia described the couple, saying their vows as 'the most movingly lovely sight'. She explained, 'It made one cry to think they would ever be old or dead. John looked a glamorous, knightly figure with perfect technique: he held her hand and everything in the most inspired way.' Apparently Kakoo looked 'divine in the best wedding dress ever seen'.[43]

Unfortunately, not everyone was as delighted by this second Asquith wedding and it also caused resentment. Lloyd George's mistress and private secretary, Frances Stevenson, noted in her diary that both weddings had 'pained' the French. They could not understand the attitude of a prime minister who allowed such a display in his family at a time when everyone was preaching economy and sacrifice.[44] Once he was prime minister, Lloyd George was careful not to make a similar mistake when his daughter Olwen was married in June 1917. The wedding and reception were simple and the wedding cake was a cardboard imitation.[45]

It was not only wedding arrangements which needed to be handled with sensitivity during the war. Once the vows were said many newlywed couples had to negotiate their way through complicated emotions about the past. In the Astors' new life together, both husband and wife were aware of the need to prevent Violet's previous marriage overshadowing their present happiness. At first, John felt jealous of his wife's love for her first husband. Although Violet had remarried, Charles was never far from her thoughts. Two years after her second wedding she wrote to her former mother-in-law, Lady Lansdowne, 'Just a line of love as it is the fourth anniversary of our great sorrow. Although I have a very new life now old and wonderfully happy memories are never forgotten and the wound is far from healed.'[46]

When the Pearl Appeal was launched, Violet attended the first meeting, served on the general committee and in April she gave one of her jewels. Donating a pearl was a discreet way for Violet to remember her first husband while also giving thanks for her new one. By the time of the appeal she had another very special reason for thanksgiving. As she attended Lady Northcliffe's launch she was pregnant, and on 1 June 1918 John and Violet's first son, Gavin, was born.

However, reflecting the ever-present balance of joy and sorrow in Violet's life, a few months later in September 1918, as the 'big push' against the Germans came, John and his regiment came under heavy attack at Cambrai. John's right leg was shattered by a shell, gangrene set in rapidly and it was only the amputation of his leg in a field hospital that saved his life. John returned to England as a hero.

After his father's death, John and Violet inherited Hever Castle; the childhood home of Anne Boleyn was a romantic place to begin their married life. The couple had two more sons, Hugh and John, and as Violet's friends and family had hoped, her second marriage gave her the security she needed.

Blanche St Germans was not as lucky. The pearl her mother-in-law had donated with such high hopes for the future turned out to symbolise misfortune in marriage. Although Mousie had survived the war, in 1922 he was seriously injured in a riding accident while hunting. He went to South Africa to recuperate but died in Johannesburg on 22 March, he was 32 years old. With no sons to inherit, his title passed to his first cousin, Granville John Eliot. Aged only 25, Blanche and her daughters returned to her parents' home at Badminton. The effects of the tragedy on the young widow are captured in a photograph by the society photographer, Bassano, taken at this time. The countess, wearing a cloche hat, fur-trimmed coat and her long string of pearls, stares into the distance as though she is on the brink of tears.

NINE

THE PEARL
EXHIBITION

A striking poster advertised the Pearl Exhibition at the Grafton Galleries. It shows a statuesque Red Cross nurse standing serenely with a long skein of pearls held in her outstretched hands; one end of the necklace is draped around a red cross. Looking like a medieval damsel, the nurse's headdress is a white wimple, while a red cloak is draped around her shoulders and her long flowing white dress has a green girdle around the hips. The First World War was often portrayed in terms of a medieval conflict. The young men going off to battle were compared to gallant knights fighting for their country in a Crusade. Reflecting this perception, one pearl given by a donor who identified herself only as 'MFK' was sent 'in proud memory of a very perfect knight, George Alexander Geddie'.[1] The religious symbolism of pearls was also emphasised in the poster as the jewels were bound around the cross. By the end of June, well over 2,500 pearls had been donated to the appeal. From Saturday, 22 June to Monday, 1 July the public were invited to come and see them at the New Bond Street gallery.

Many of the people who visited the exhibition had been to the Grafton Galleries before. Stylishly refurbished in 1893 and located at the corner of New Bond Street and Grafton Street, it had a history of holding major exhibitions. In 1910, it had hosted critic and painter Roger Fry's landmark exhibition, 'Manet and the Post-Impressionists', which was largely devoted to the work of Manet, Cézanne, Van Gogh and Gauguin. Two years later, Fry returned with the Second Post-Impressionist Exhibition which included more English artists, notably Duncan Grant, Vanessa Bell and Frederick Etchells, alongside work by Henri Matisse and Pablo Picasso.

The first exhibition had caused outrage. Failing to appreciate the latest French art, some society ladies thought it was a sort of joke and giggled at the paintings. Others, who took it more seriously, believed this modern art would undermine the existing social order. It was seen as a foreign threat to native English art and morality.[2] The artist Philip Burne-Jones, son of Sir Edward, one of the leading lights of the Pre-Raphaelites, wrote to *The Times* describing the paintings as an 'egregious collection of canvasses' which disfigured the walls of the Grafton Galleries. Accusing the post-impressionists of shunning beauty and seeking their inspiration in the tavern and gutter, he attacked them for bringing about 'the anarchy and degradation of art'.[3] However, for the more avant-garde it marked the exhilarating start of a new era. Virginia Woolf claimed that at that moment human character changed. She saw the exhibition as symbolising the way European ideas imposed themselves upon the insular English consciousness. According to her, it altered attitudes to Englishness and the country's relationship with the Continent.[4]

During the war, the Grafton Galleries reverted to less challenging subject matter. In June 1916, an exhibition was put on which was in many ways a forerunner to the pearl one. A collection of John Singer Sargent's drawings were displayed as part of the Royal Society of Portrait Painters' Exhibition. Organised by the prime minister's daughter, Elizabeth Asquith, to raise money for the Art Fund, which helped actors, authors, musicians and painters, the forty-six drawings spanned twenty-six years. Like the pearls, Sargent's portraits and sketches were reminders of a pre-war culture that valued beauty and refinement.

In the Edwardian era, Sargent had been the high priest of British fashionable society. His portraits of languid women dressed in frothy pastels defined the look of the era and immortalised this generation for posterity. Between 1886 and 1907 he painted over 350 portraits and it became the ultimate status symbol to sit for the American artist in his Tite Street studio in Chelsea. Aware of the alchemy of his paintbrush, he was pursued by aristocrats and arrivistes who wanted him to transform them into modern icons.[5] Sargent's charcoal sketches grew out of this demand. Bored with painting endless portraits of society women which he described as a 'pimp's profession', the artist offered them a sketch as an alternative.[6] Instead of having to complete a time-consuming portrait he could do a charcoal drawing in an hour.

Gazing down from the walls of the Octagon Gallery at the 1916 Grafton exhibition were the prime minister's children, Elizabeth and Anthony 'Puffin' Asquith, next to Lady Diana Manners, her sister Marjorie and the pictures of Letty and Ego Elcho that marked their engagement. To see the image of her brother when the family were still waiting to know whether Ego was alive or dead was too much for Cynthia Asquith. She wrote in her diary, 'It is a real nightmare to see so many of one's friends so blatantly depicted staring at one from four walls.'[7]

Many of the reviews of the exhibition were critical; it was too 'pretty-pretty' for audiences who now faced the bleak reality of war. *The Scotsman* complained that Sargent's subjects were mostly 'stylish young women, and whether it is due to their sameness or to the limitations of the medium the effect is almost as monotonous as that produced by Lely's beauties at Hampton Court, and only slightly less insipid'.[8] The sketch of Lady Diana Manners came in for particular attack. *The Ladies' Field* claimed, 'You do not flatter a woman by drawing her like a doll.'[9] Like the world they represented, these sketches suddenly seemed outdated; they reflected the past, but the present demanded a grittier realism.

The Pearl Exhibition attracted a similar audience to the Sargent one. Many of the women who gave to the Pearl Appeal had been painted by the artist; then, their long strands of pearls were fashionable symbols of their opulence, now they had a new, more practical purpose. There was great anticipation about the Pearl Exhibition, *The Queen* claimed that it took 'easily the first place in social life in London that week'.[10] Before it opened to the general public, there was a private view by invitation only on Saturday morning from 11.30 a.m. until 1 p.m., for the royal family and women who had donated pearls. Reflecting the sombre nature of the event, many women were dressed in mourning. The queen, in a dark-blue gown of charmeuse with an overdress of georgette lightly embroidered in gold, arrived early with Princess Mary. Dressed in a black velvet gown with a sequined coat, Queen Alexandra came later with Princess Victoria, the president of the appeal. The royal party was greeted by Lady Northcliffe who, chic as ever, wore a black satin gown embroidered in Chinese blue with a splendid silver fox fur. By her side was the head of the Red Cross Finance Committee, Sir Robert Hudson.[11] He wrote enthusiastically to Lord Northcliffe:

> The opening of the Pearl Exhibition was an amazing triumph for your lady. The ease and naturalness with which she managed the Queens and half a dozen Princesses, talking to all of them in turn and keeping the ball going for nearly an hour, was a thing to be seen.[12]

As the elegantly dressed visitors walked into the cavernous Long Gallery, shafts of natural light from the ring of glass panels in the roof illuminated the nine cases displaying the pearls. The central one contained the royal gifts which were arranged like a family. Queen Mary's jewel was at the centre, while Queen Alexandra's pearl was arranged with Princess Victoria and the Princess Royal's gems on either side. Reflecting the way the Pearl Appeal had caught the imagination of people from all walks of life, a miscellaneous case filled with rings, brooches and tiepins given by people who had no necklaces from which to draw was close to some of the most valuable jewels in the collection. Among the curiosities was a large pink pearl weighing 16.4 grains and an even larger 'black' pearl which was dark grey, weighing 21.6 grains. A last minute addition to the display was a magnificent pearl presented by the Aga Khan.[13] However, the most emotive sight was the collection of pearls given 'in memory' or 'in honour' of men who had fallen; like the rows of white crosses in a war cemetery, there were too many to count.

Showing respect to the sentiment behind every gift, no attempt had been made to arrange the pearls according to their value. Instead, each pearl was treated the same. It was mounted separately and bore the name of its donor and a registered number. The pearls were suspended on royal blue silk strings and set on a background of cream velvet. An empty case was set aside for gifts which came in during the exhibition.

However, the pearls were not the only jewels to attract the public. Also on display was the great yellow Red Cross diamond. This stunning jewel, weighing 205 carats, was found at the De Beers Mines in South Africa in 1901.[14] It was presented to the Red Cross by the Diamond Syndicate and it had raised £10,000 at a Christie's auction in April.

Queen Mary spent a long time examining all the jewels and 'expressed again and again her delight at the generosity of the ladies who had given their flawless, perfect gems to this great cause'. At the end of their visit, each of the queens said to Sir Robert Hudson, 'You owe this to Lady Northcliffe.' He replied, 'Yes Ma'am we of the Red Cross are <u>well</u> aware of that!'[15]

Almost every visitor to the Grafton Galleries that day had experienced the loss of a loved one and it was an occasion when mothers and daughters supported each other. The Duchess of Rutland was there with her widowed daughter, Letty. Lady Sarah Wilson, whose husband had died at the start of the war, and Lady Lansdowne, mother-in-law of Violet Astor, also mingled in the crowd. It was an emotive occasion, and as they looked at the pearls no one could forget that each jewel represented at least one life changed forever by the war.

The horror of battle was reinforced by the large photographs in the gallery that loomed over the cases of pearls. Since May, the Grafton Galleries had been displaying the Australian War Pictures. During the war, several propaganda exhibitions of war photographs had been held in London. Two by the Canadians in December 1916 and July 1917, and two of 'British' photographs and war relics, which included Canadians and Australians, had already appeared at the Grafton Galleries and the Royal Academy.[16] The core of each exhibition was huge mural-sized panels which were up to 6m by 3m in size and artificially coloured. By displaying the war photographs at such distinguished galleries, it sent a signal that they were to be taken seriously, not just as a documentary record or propaganda but as art photography.[17]

The driving force behind these exhibitions was the Canadian newspaper owner Lord Beaverbrook, who worked closely with Lord Northcliffe at shaping public opinion. As head of the Canadian War Record Office and chair of the new Cinematographic Committee, Beaverbrook was well aware of the propaganda value of the photographs. He knew that to win the war it was vital that civilians were willing to endure to the end, but to inspire their steadfast support they needed to realise fully the conditions at the Front. He believed that the best way to bring the reality home to them was through photographs. Written descriptions of battles were harder for the mind to take in than the immediate visual impact of photographs. The war images had a realism that made them stick in the imagination. The idea was to make spectators at home feel as if they were on the battlefield itself.[18]

A gulf divided the experience of the soldiers from their loved ones. Often men tried to protect their families from knowing the full horror of the battlefield. Their letters were often couched in positive terms to reassure their readers. However, the risk of sparing their wives and mothers was that it put an unbridgeable emotional distance between them. To understand and come to terms with what was happening, the women at home needed to face the reality, because only then could they find their own ways of dealing with it.

In 1916, Lloyd George's mistress, Frances Stevenson, wrote in her diary about the effect of seeing the *The Battle of the Somme* film, a documentary filmed during the battle. It was a gruelling experience – 13 per cent of the seventy-seven-minute film was made up of shots of the dead and wounded.[19] There were pictures of the battlefield after the fighting and one particularly memorable shot showed a mortally wounded man being carried out of the communication trenches with a look of agony on his face. The caption read, 'British Tommies rescuing a comrade under shell fire. (This man died 20 minutes after reaching a trench.)' The film attracted large audiences and by October 1916 it had been booked by over 2,000 cinemas across the country, and it is estimated that 20 million people saw the documentary within a few weeks of its release.[20] It inspired mixed reactions. *The Times* and *The Guardian* received letters complaining about its explicitness while the dean of Durham described it as an entertainment which violated the sanctity of bereavement.[21] However, for many of the bereaved, including Frances Stevenson, it was cathartic. Frances' brother Paul had been killed earlier in the war and until she saw the film she had found it hard to imagine what his experience had actually been like, but having seen it she wrote that now she knew and would never forget. She compared it to the experience of ancient Greeks going to a tragedy – her mind had been purged through pity and terror.[22]

The photographs in the May 1918 exhibition at the Grafton Galleries were by Frank Hurley, who was already famous as an adventurer-photographer and cinematographer as the camera artist on the Australasian Antarctic Expedition and Ernest Shackleton's Imperial Trans-Antarctic Expedition. Hurley had been appointed official photographer with the Australian War Records Section in summer 1917. He was determined that his show should be even better than the Canadian exhibitions that had already been staged in London. His work provided an insight into the horrendous conditions men had to endure in modern warfare, while also recognising the vital role played by Australians in the war.

On 21 August 1917 Captain Hurley crossed the Channel to begin work in France and Belgium. Almost at once he was photographing the Third Battle of Ypres. Coming across ground covered with bits of guns, shells, bayonets and men, he described the scene as like hell. The most awful sight was of three decomposing corpses of German gunners in a mine crater. Recognising their humanity irrespective of their nationality, he thought it was a hideous end for men who had once been husbands, sweethearts or sons.[23] Visiting the ruins of the town of Ypres, he was moved by the shreds of clothing and fragments of toys which added pathos to the scene, reminding the onlooker that each item represented a tale of suffering and families destroyed.

War photography was dangerous work and Hurley soon won the respect of the Australian soldiers. In spite of heavy shelling by the Germans, he tried to take a number of shell-burst pictures. Many of the shells exploded only a few dozen paces away from him so he had to throw himself into shell holes to avoid splinters. Despite his dedication, Hurley soon clashed with the head of the Australian War Records Section, Charles Bean, because rather than recording events exactly as they happened he wanted to re-enact some scenes and use new photographic techniques. Hurley believed that composite printing, using two or more negatives to print a single photograph, was needed to capture the scale of the conflict. Bean disapproved and claimed that such methods would produce fakes or staged photographs. Hurley threatened to resign if he could not use composites, so eventually he was granted permission to make six combination prints for the Grafton Galleries exhibition.[24]

Due to this difference of opinion, in November 1917 Hurley was reassigned to Palestine and the Middle East to photograph the Australian Light Horse. As many of the key battles, such as the Charge of the Light Horse at Beersheba, had already taken place, Hurley persuaded the officers to re-enact the events. The brigades were very keen to have their photos taken and generals came from all over the country to take part. Hurley wrote that, compared to the hell of France, Palestine was like a holiday.[25] The experience was more like life back at home in Australia, the troops lived in the open air and there was less rigid discipline than in France.

In May, Hurley returned to London in time to curate the exhibition at the Grafton Galleries. It was a mad rush to get the pictures enlarged and displayed properly and he was worried that they would not be ready for the opening. With only two days to go there was still not a single picture hung, so Hurley and his team worked until 1 a.m. at the gallery to put up as many pictures as possible. However, some of the most important photographs were still not ready to be displayed and Hurley complained that the exhibition looked extemporised and unfinished. To register his disgust, he did not attend the official opening on 24 May.[26]

Once the problems behind the scenes had been sorted out and the final pictures were all in place, Hurley became more positive. He was pleased with the favourable criticism he received and felt that seeing his work admired by the masses was some recompense for the risks he had taken. One of Hurley's most famous images was captioned 'Death's Highway'. In it a soldier is surrounded by German artillery and shell bursts. Another picture, billed as the largest photograph in the world, was called 'A Raid'. Aiming to be cinematic, it shows two waves of men going over the top. 'Death the Reaper' suggested a spiritual dimension beyond the devastation by combining the image of the mud-splashed corpse of a German soldier with a shell burst.

The presence of beauty in Hurley's photographs was one of their most controversial aspects. Amidst the horror, Hurley had a sense of the sublime and he described the ruined town of Ypres as 'somehow wildly beautiful'.[27] His work helped to create the Anzac legend of the dashing Australian soldier who always achieved his objectives. Adding to this mythology, there was a romanticised quality in his photographs of the Middle East which drew on Biblical and medieval associations. Australian airmen were shown standing in landscapes of the Holy Land, suggesting that this was a modern Crusade in which they reclaimed the Middle East from the Turks and succeeded where Richard the Lionheart had failed in the twelfth century.[28]

A showman as well as a photographer, at the exhibition Hurley tried to create what would now be described as a multimedia experience. To add to the emotive atmosphere, a military band played throughout the day and a display of coloured lantern slides was put on depicting scenes of the Western Front, Flanders and Palestine. The audience were so moved that they applauded after every showing. There were also paintings by Australian official war artists, G.W. Lambert and H.S. Power, and Australia

House contributed war relics, including an Albatross DVA biplane, guns and uniformed mannequins.[29]

Officially the show closed on 22 June, but the 137 photographs were left in place during the Pearl Exhibition. Entering the Long Gallery must have been an almost overwhelming experience for many of the visitors. Wives, mothers and sisters had come to see the pearls, but were confronted with graphic images of exactly what their men at the Front faced. The photographs were on such an epic scale that they dwarfed the spectators. Enlargements meant that every gory detail was exposed, bringing to life elements of suffering that had previously been beyond the darkest imagining of civilians.

Although the experience was heart-breaking, most visitors spent a long time looking at the photographs. It was a haunting sight, but one they needed to see to remain close to their men. The photographs were a fitting backdrop for the pearls as they silently signified the need for such generous gifts.

The purpose of the exhibition was not only to display the pearls but also to fundraise; visitors were charged 2s 6d for admission on the first Saturday and then 1s 3d for the rest of the week. The interest in the exhibition was far greater than the organisers had imagined. While the royal private viewing was taking place, a large crowd gathered outside, keen to see the pearls for themselves. By the end of the first day more than 1,500 people filled the gallery, and over the following days more than 2,000 people a day attended, until by the end of the week 16,000 had visited the exhibition.[30]

Many women came with the intention to give pearls in person to the appeal. Some donors who had already given were so moved by the exhibition that they gave again. Typical of her family's unstinting sacrifice, on 28 June Lilian Kekewich, who had lost three of her sons, made her second donation of two pearls. By the end of the week nearly 300 additional jewels had been donated and the case that had been left empty to be filled with pearls was indeed almost full.[31]

TEN

THE PEARL POEMS

The culmination of the Pearl Exhibition was an afternoon concert held at the Grafton Galleries on Sunday, 30 June 1918. Showing the support of the musical and theatrical world for the Red Cross appeal, in the Long Gallery actors and musicians mingled with aristocrats and artists. The fundraising performance was opened by the tall, redheaded Australian violinist, Daisy Kennedy, playing Bach's 'Prelude in E Major'.

Equally adept as a recital artist and a concerto soloist, she performed regularly with leading orchestras under the conductors Sir Henry Wood and Sir Landon Ronald. Possessing a striking presence, all eyes in the audience were on Daisy as she was joined on stage by her husband, the Russian/Ukrainian pianist, Benno Moiseiwitsch. They then played together Franck's violin sonata. The romance of the Pearl Appeal was echoed in the choice of music, as the famous pianist then played three pieces by Chopin. Romantic music was Moiseiwitsch's forte, he was particularly identified with the works of Chopin, Schumann and his close friend, Rachmaninov.

Reflecting the international theme of the afternoon, the programme continued with the Scottish contralto, Carmen Hill, performing Hahn's 'D'une Prison'. A regular performer at the Promenade Concerts, she had recently sung the part of the angel in Sir Edward Elgar's 'The Dream of Gerontius' in cities throughout Britain.

A late addition to the programme was Henry Ainley reciting or, as he preferred to call it, 'telling', two patriotic poems: 'A Chant of love for

England' by Helen Gray Cone and 'The Irish Guards' by Rudyard Kipling. The distinguished Shakespearean actor had been appearing in silent movies since 1911, including *A Bachelor's Love Story* and *The Prisoner of Zenda*, but the stage was always his real home.

The most poignant moment of the afternoon came at the very end of the performance when Ainley read Maurice Baring's poem to his fallen friend, Julian Grenfell. First published anonymously in *The Times* on 5 June 1915, Baring wrote:

> Because of you we will be glad and gay,
> Remembering you, we will be brave and strong;
> And hail the advent of each dangerous day,
> And meet the last adventure with a song
> And, as you proudly gave your jewelled gift,
> We'll give our lesser offering with a smile,
> Nor falter on that path where, all too swift,
> You led the way and leapt the golden stile.[1]

Maurice had known Julian since he was a boy. Part of the Baring banking family, Maurice's brother, John Baring, Lord Revelstoke, was one of Ettie Desborough's long-term admirers. Inevitably, Maurice had also become ensnared in her web. They met in 1896 when Ettie was 29 and Maurice 22, and they were soon playing word games and sending flirtatious messages to each other. Maurice recreated Ettie and her world in his writing. Portraying her as a siren, his poem 'Circe' was published in a volume called *The Black Prince*, which was dedicated to her.[2] In his novel called *C*, which was one of the code names Ettie and his brother John used in their letters to each other, Maurice wrote about a young man 'C', who fell in love with a bewitching married woman called Leila. Capricious Leila had many lovers, but made each one think that they were the only one. 'C' died of love for her after he found out that her true love was his brother.[3]

Maurice drew on Ettie's character again in 1910 when he published his play, *Ariadne in Naxos*, in his *Diminutive Dramas*. Like Leila, Ariadne was an effusive femme fatale who played off Dionysius and Theseus against each other.[4] After the publication of this play there was a brief breach in Ettie and

Maurice's friendship, but their estrangement was only temporary. During the war years they drew closer as they shared a strong Christian faith and a similar perspective on the conflict.

The poem to Julian was a fitting way to end the concert. Its evocative lines reflected the initial concept of the Pearl Appeal, as the metaphor of a 'jewelled gift' was used to describe his sacrifice. It also emphasised poetry's importance in the First World War. Steeped in literature from childhood, many soldiers turned to verse to record their experiences. *The Times* estimated that it received about 100 poems each day in August 1914 and most of them were written in a patriotic or romantic tone.[5] Julian's own poem 'Into Battle', written four weeks before he died, marked the high-water mark of enthusiasm for the war. Unlike many later war poems, it showed no outrage against war; instead it portrayed conflict as the time when he felt most fully alive and at one with the natural world. It also showed an acceptance of death, if that was to be his fate. He wrote:

> And when the burning moment breaks,
> And all things else are out of mind,
> And Joy of Battle only takes
> Him by the throat, and makes him blind –
>
> Through joy and blindness he shall know,
> Not caring much to know, that still
> Nor lead nor steel shall reach him so
> That it be not the Destined Will.[6]

Julian copied out this poem, signed it and then sent it to his mother. Immediately after his death, Ettie had his poem published in *The Times*. This posthumous work made him famous and won the admiration of people who had never met him. The writer Henry James wrote to Ettie that, through these verses, he seemed almost to have known Julian. He added, 'What great and terrible and unspeakable things! But out of which, round his sublime young image, a noble and exquisite legend will flower.'[7]

As the war progressed, exterminating more and more young men, this positive line became increasingly hard to sustain. The novelist

D.H. Lawrence claimed that these young soldiers were 'in love' with death.[8] There was actually an element of truth in his analysis, as before the war young men like Raymond Asquith and Julian Grenfell had been searching for a purpose in their life. Julian's biographer, Nicholas Mosley, wrote that for the first time he had a proper function within society and he believed that it was doing what a conventional society should do by dissolving itself. He had no illusions about war and he was not surprised when it involved killing and getting killed.[9] Cynthia Asquith, who knew many of these young men well, saw it differently. She wrote:

> Their death was, in the fullest sense, sacrifice. Heaven knows, they had enough to lose! If some of them did feel, as I trust they did, that mystical joy in fighting immortally expressed in Julian Grenfell's poem *Into Battle*, they were equally alive to all the other aspects of war. But since the doom that had come on the world could not be shunned, and they were poets, most of them preferred to dwell upon whatsoever mitigated the horror of war – its livid splendour, and the human qualities it revealed – the fellowship, the heroism, the humour. To glorify the qualities that partially redeem war is not to vindicate war.[10]

The Pearl Appeal was based on a similar ethos that it was essential to focus on the positive in even the most devastating situations. This was not to ignore reality, but to try to bring some good out of evil. By involving the arts to raise funds for the Red Cross, it reflected the idea, so deeply embedded in the Pearl Appeal, that war could not destroy the finer aspects of civilisation. Although the war had released the most bestial elements of human nature, barbarism would not triumph.

By the summer of 1918, actors, poets and intellectuals were finding ways to contribute to the Red Cross fund in their own unique ways. However, the most unusual 'pearl' given to the appeal was not a jewel at all but a poem. The academic, Israel Gollancz, gave his translation of *Pearl*, a fourteenth-century poem written by a grieving father about his lost daughter. Describing his 'Pearl of price' as 'a fitting pendant to the Red Cross Necklace', Gollancz turned the symbolism of the fallen as precious pearls into verse. He wrote:

> Sunder'd from the shell they shine,
> Souls translucent, pearls of price;
> Yearning hearts their worth enshrine;
> Pearl of pearls is love's device.[11]

By linking the Pearl Appeal to poetry, Israel Gollancz had found an evocative way to raise money while offering consolation to the bereaved. Six hundred and fifty copies of *Pearl* were printed and 550 of the vellum-bound copies sold for £3 3s at Hatchards in Piccadilly.[12]

One of the leading scholars in early modern English and Shakespeare, in 1896 Gollancz had become the first university lecturer in English at Cambridge University. Nine years later, he was appointed to the chair of English language and literature at King's College, London. A charismatic professor, who inspired his students with his charm, enthusiasm and encouraging attitude, he had seen many of his brightest and best undergraduates go off to war never to return. Identifying the fallen of this generation with an earlier chivalric age, he set out the story of the *Pearl* in a preface.

The poem had been written 550 years ago, in the age of Chaucer, by a poet whose name was now forgotten but 'happily, Time has not destroyed the magic of his words'. Gollancz wrote, 'More wondrously than any previous English poet, he harmonized the quest for the beautiful, in imagery, word and music, with spiritual exaltation and moral purpose.'[13] Lost for centuries, *Pearl* was not published until 1864.

Its publication reflected the interest in medieval culture that was fashionable in the nineteenth century. In the poem, a man mourns for his jewel, which he has lost in a garden. He describes himself as 'greviously wounded by the power of my love for that pearl of mine'.[14] He then falls asleep and has a heavenly vision of his lost jewel. As he sees a girl elaborately dressed in pearl encrusted clothes and a crown, the reader realises that the pearl he is grieving for is not a gem but his dead daughter. Associated with the Virgin Mary, in medieval iconography, the pearls on her clothes symbolised purity and virginity. They were also a symbol of the soul – in the writings of St Augustine, Christ referred to the soul as 'the most splendid jewel'.[15] In her new incarnation, his daughter is transfigured; she has grown in wisdom and is able to teach her parent lessons. She comforts him and instils in him resignation by explaining that she is now safe among the blessed in heaven. Although she is transformed, she retains her individuality and is still her father's child. She remains his 'little queen' who is 'so small and sweetly slight'.[16]

Inspired by the image of the pearl in Revelations, the poet described visionary scenes of the New Jerusalem. Knowing the Bible, medieval readers and their Victorian descendants would have understood the many layers of meaning in the poem. It was not just about a man finding his daughter or 'pearl', it was about his spiritual quest for meaning in his life. Round and white, pearls were symbols of the bread/body of Christ in the Eucharist. The poem can be read as a metaphor about man having lost communion with his soul and finding consolation in the Eucharist, which is symbolised by the pearl maiden.[17]

Although the poem was overtly Christian, while Gollancz had been brought up as an orthodox Jew by his rabbi father, he believed that this poem 'transcends all questions of theology and dogma' because of its 'elemental and personal note'.[18] Gollancz had first published a translation of *Pearl* in 1891. He released this revised version in 1918 because his understanding of the poem had deepened and he felt it was particularly relevant for the war years when so many bereaved parents needed solace. By linking the present to medieval times, he hoped to provide a new perspective which would offer some comfort. Within the poem was the promise of immortality. He wrote:

In far-off days, in the midst of the incessant wars that harassed people in the reign of Edward III, an unknown poet placed on the grave of his little child a garland of song, blooming yet after the lapse of so long a time. In these latter days of stress and strain and tribulation, 'Pearl' still symbolises things of the spirit outliving the vesture of decay.[19]

As well as setting the First World War experiences in a medieval context, Gollancz's writing also reminded his readers of how the Victorians drew on their spirituality to deal with grief. In his 1918 edition, Gollancz prefaced the poem with a quotation from Alfred, Lord Tennyson. The late-Victorian poet laureate had sent him a letter praising the earlier translation of *Pearl* and acknowledging the importance of the poem to English literature. Tennyson wrote:

> We lost you – for how long a time-
> True pearl of our poetic prime:
> We found you, and you gleam re-set
> In Britain's lyric coronet.[20]

By alluding to Tennyson, Gollancz was subtly reminding his readers of another great poem of grief and eventual consolation. Tennyson's poem *In Memoriam A.H.H.* was written in memory of his beloved friend, the poet Arthur Hallam. Like many of those lost in the war, Arthur was an erudite young man. Educated at Eton and Trinity Hall, Cambridge, where he met Tennyson, Hallam was seen by many of his friends in the 'Apostles' as exceptional. In 1833, he died suddenly from a brain haemorrhage in Vienna at the age of 22. It took Tennyson sixteen years to complete the poem which is a meditation on the search for hope after great loss. The poem goes beyond the personal to the collective bereavement of his generation who found their Christian faith challenged by scientific discoveries. Tennyson's requiem explored these religious doubts. After going through the painful process of reassessing his deepest beliefs, he reaffirmed his faith from a new perspective. He believed that truth comes to us mediated through human love.[21]

Tennyson's poem had great resonance during the First World War. From their university days, Raymond Asquith and his friends had been fascinated by Tennyson's relationship with Hallam and considered that the Apostles were an amazing society.[22] No doubt they saw parallels between their own Oxford clique and the Cambridge circle of friends of a century before. However, Raymond was critical of *In Memoriam* and with his typical arrogance claimed that if he had been endowed with the gift of poetry he could have written as good or better.[23] His sister-in-law, Cynthia, admired the poem and, in her diary, mentions re-reading it after her younger brother Yvo's death. However, when she tried reading it aloud to her husband 'Beb', who was fighting at the Front, she noted, 'he wouldn't take much of it.'[24]

Maurice Baring drew on the Victorian verse and updated it for his own generation in his poem *In Memoriam, for A.H.* His 'A.H.' was his great friend Auberon 'Bron' Herbert, Captain Lord Lucas. This poem develops many of the themes Maurice first explored in his poem to Julian Grenfell. This was particularly appropriate as Bron was Ettie Desborough's cousin and his life was closely interwoven with Julian's.

Known for his integrity and courage, Bron was an inspirational figure for many of his contemporaries. His friend, J.M. Barrie, the writer of *Peter Pan*, analysed his attraction. He wrote that although Bron was the kindest of friends, 'he was still an elusive man, whom you often felt you knew well but could never quite touch, like a character in a book'.[25]

Maurice Baring first fell under Bron's charismatic spell at Oxford. They were part of a group that included the poet Hilaire Belloc and Raymond Asquith. After supper they often discussed literature, religion and politics late into the night. Their parties sound like precursors of the undergraduate antics recorded in Evelyn Waugh's *Brideshead Revisited*; guests would climb in through the window then syphons would be hurled across the room and butter would be thrown up to stick on the ceiling. Bottles of port were downed and then thrown about the room. They often ended the evening with practical jokes which sometimes backfired. One night, Bron pulled the master of Balliol's bath chair around the Quad, and the college took this so seriously that he was nearly sent down. However, what Maurice enjoyed best were long summer afternoons spent punting with Bron on the river. The punt would drift into tangled backwaters and they would doze or read aloud from *Alice in Wonderland* and Swinburne's poetry, then dive into the water for an impromptu swim. Maurice described this period as 'an interlude of perfect happiness'.[26]

After university, at the outbreak of the Boer War, Bron went to South Africa as a war correspondent for *The Times*. During the Relief of Ladysmith, he was shot through the thigh, gangrene set in and his leg was amputated below the knee. On his return to England, Ettie looked after him at Taplow Court. His courage influenced Julian and Billy Grenfell as they watched him overcome his disability through sheer will-power. He continued to ride or walk dozens of miles a day over challenging terrain and then returned to play cricket or lawn tennis. When Julian felt alienated by his mother's preoccupation with society, he turned to Bron for an alternative model of living. Although Bron loved Ettie, like Julian he loathed her parties, finding it impossible to have a proper conversation with her in such an artificial atmosphere. During his two-month stay with the Grenfells, he used to creep in and out of their house by the back door and was 'conducted to his bedroom by a servant holding a green umbrella before him to prevent his seeing or being seen' by any of Ettie's 'twittering' friends.[27] His friend, Raymond Asquith, described him as 'very black' against women at this time. He told him that his life was perfectly happy without them and only three things worried him – his sister being a theosophist, the prospect of inheriting a title and probably having a wife.[28]

A radical thinker, Bron had no interest in social rank or possessions. When he inherited Wrest Park, a country estate in Bedfordshire built like a French château, he loaned its art treasures to the National Gallery and leased the house out to the American ambassador. When the ambassador died the house lay empty until it was used as a hospital during the war.[29] Bron was a man who lived in the moment, not in the past, and was happiest pursuing an adventurous outdoor life unconstrained by society's demands.

After leaving Eton, Julian used to stay with Bron in Yorkshire. He wrote that he had the time of his life with his second cousin. Days were spent walking, shooting and fishing. The two men had much in common and what J.M. Barrie later wrote about Bron was equally applicable to Julian – he also was 'an untamed thing who no one ever flung a net over'.[30]

Once war was declared, many of this close-knit circle of friends joined up and were sent to France. In August 1914, Maurice was made a lieutenant in the Intelligence Corps attached to the headquarters of the Royal Flying Corps, which was housed in a château at St Omer. At this time, he did not know what the Royal Flying Corps was. As he wrote, air warfare was still 'in the gentleman-like stage'.[31] There were very few aircraft on both sides at the start of the war, and Britain had only about 180 planes. At first they were only used for observation, but from the summer of 1915 the first fighter aircraft took off, armed with automatic weaponry.[32]

In the early days of the war, like so many of his generation, Maurice saw the conflict in terms of a medieval Crusade. Ideas of chivalry had been instilled into Maurice and many of his contemporaries at school. At Eton, an ideal of patriotic service was romanticised for the boys through their Classical education combined with Pre-Raphaelite ideas of medieval chivalry. During services in Eton's chapel they were encouraged to focus on a Burne-Jones tapestry and a painting by D.C. Watts of Sir Galahad which provided the boys with an image of pure knighthood.[33]

When he first arrived in France, Maurice drew parallels between the modern British Army and the knights fighting at Agincourt. The battlefield was near to where he was stationed and he visited it with his old friend, Hilaire Belloc. In October 1914, he wrote about his pleasure in going to Mass in the cathedral at St Omer and listening to the same words, said in the same way and with the same gestures that Henry V and his 'contemptible little army' had heard before Agincourt. Standing beside a man in khaki, he wrote, 'History flashed past like a jewelled dream.'[34]

So many people Maurice knew were coming and going across the Channel that his pre-war social life continued in France, albeit in a slightly different form. In October 1914, he ran into Violet Asquith, who was visiting the Front. Dressed in a khaki Holbein coat trimmed with possum, Maurice was on a mission to buy lobster for the Royal Flying Corps when she spotted him. They travelled back in her car to headquarters through rolling green countryside, past large camps of horses.[35]

In March 1915, when Maurice heard that Julian Grenfell had been posted to France he went to visit him. He found Julian lying asleep in a barn on a large sheaf of corn, with his greyhound beside him. The sun was streaming in on him and he looked happy and radiant. As Maurice gently woke Julian up, the young soldier said jokingly, 'Shall I kill you?' Having decided against it, instead he took him to tea in the Mess and showed him the latest poem he had written. It was to be the last time he saw him.[36] Julian died in May.

As Maurice watched one after another of his friends killed, he wrote to Ethel Smyth:

> Life is a strain now isn't it; scaffolding falls about one daily, one's old friends, one's new friends are killed or disappear like flies; the floor of life seems to have gone and one seems to live in a permanent eclipse and a <u>seasonless</u> world – a world with no summer or winter, only a long grey neutral-tinted rainy chill limbo.[37]

Julian's death also had a profound effect on Bron. He wrote to Ettie that he was fonder of him than of any other living man and that a great part of his life had been torn from him by the loss. He added that Julian had brought fresh air into a stale, stuffy world.[38] Since Bron had inherited the title Lord Lucas in 1905, he had been an active member of the House of Lords serving as undersecretary of state for war, undersecretary for the colonies and president of the Board of Agriculture. However, in May 1915, after Julian's death, he left the Cabinet and gave up all political work to join the Royal Flying Corps. His action went beyond the call of duty because, with his disability and aged nearly 40, he could easily have avoided fighting, but he was determined to serve his country.

He compared his training to going back to public school. At first it felt strange, as he was 39 years old and most of his 'school fellows' were 18 or 19. However, his enthusiasm had an electrifying effect on all around him.[39] In the air, Bron was in his element and he adored flying. J.M. Barrie wrote, 'He came down a different man from the one who went up, and was different ever afterwards as if he had made a journey into the springtime of the world and brought back a breath of it.'[40]

In autumn 1916 Bron was sent to France. Once there, he met up with Maurice as often as possible. One evening they sat in the garden after dinner and talked until late. Bron was full of enthusiasm and although on a recent flight a bit of his propeller had been shot off, nothing could keep him out of the air. He described flying over the barrage as the most marvellous sight he had ever seen. The last time they met, as they walked across the aerodrome they were both struck by an unusual sunset. Beneath a large mass of drifting storm clouds the light was reflected on the horizon. Maurice wondered what it meant and said it was like a painting. Bron just laughed and said 'Yes'.[41] Maurice thought those weeks in France were the happiest in his friend's life; he felt young again as his disability was forgotten.

On 3 November 1916, Bron was flying over the German trenches of the Western Front when he was shot through the neck. Thinking of others even in his last minutes, he managed to land his plane safely before dying. The Germans buried him near Bapaume.[42] It was some weeks before his friends and family knew of his fate. At first, when he was described as 'missing' it was suggested that Bron's habit of preferring not to use his title might explain the absence of news of him from his captors.[43] However, by the end of the month it was confirmed that Bron had been killed. Maurice believed his friend's death was such a fitting 'crown' for his life that his own regret was lost in awe and wonder and his grief was silenced.[44]

When Bron's friend J.M. Barrie wrote a tribute to him in *The Times* under the headline 'Bron the Gallant', like Maurice, he focused on the idea of a glorious death. He wrote:

> Everyone who knew him will be glad that if he had to die he died in the air. It is an assurance to them that he was happy to the last, pursuing and pursued up there, exulting in it all, even in the last moment when he had the supreme experience.

Barrie believed the 'wonderful months' he had spent in the air 'were to him worth dying for'.

Still in its infancy, flying was written of in terms of chivalry. The modern airmen were portrayed as the medieval knights of the skies. It was as though they were superior, godlike beings. Barrie added:

> There was a touch of other-worldliness about him, even before he became an airman; after that I think it is there with all of them; you see it in the puzzled smile with which they regard those of us who live below.

Romanticising his friend's end, he believed that Bron would have felt no ill will to the German who shot him down and there would have just been 'a wave of the hand from one airman to another'.[45]

Developing Barrie's themes further, Maurice immortalised Bron in his poem *In Memoriam*. Comparing him to Homeric heroes and medieval knights, he portrayed his friend as the modern hero. Throughout the work, Maurice set his grief in a Christian context. He had been an agnostic, but he converted to Roman Catholicism in 1909. He wrote that it was the only action in his life that he was quite certain he never regretted.[46] His friends saw his conversion as the crucial action of his life. From when it happened, he used his writing to express his passionate conviction that belief in God could 'alone bring storm-tossed humanity into harbour'.[47] According to Maurice's friend, Laura Lovat, he developed a stoic ability to dismiss from his mind anything which would make life unendurable. In the face of sorrow and suffering he showed complete resignation. He wrote to a friend after a great bereavement, 'You must make up your mind whether you wish to live or die, you must now concentrate on living.'[48] Although he knew it was the most difficult thing in the world to do, he believed that a person had to accept sorrow for it to have any healing power.[49]

His poem *In Memoriam* portrays dying in battle as a redemptive act of sacrifice which promises immortality. In it Maurice imagined that, after death, Bron enters the heavenly city to be with those who have gone before him – befitting his heroism, he is with the Arthurian knights. Maurice wrote:

> Surely you found companions meet for you
> In that high place;
> You meet there face to face
> Those you had never known, but whom you knew;
> Knights of the Table Round,
> And all the very brave, the very true,
> With chivalry crowned.[50]

Although much of the poem explores his yearning for his lost friend, by the end he believes that there remains between them a perfectly realised friendship which transcends death. There is a reciprocal relationship between the living and the dead and the fallen are not forgotten by their friends who are inspired by their memory. He saw the dead warrior existing as a protective spirit for the living.[51] Emphasising his Christian faith by drawing on the language of Revelations, Baring wrote:

> They think of you, and when you think of them
> You know that they will wipe away their tears,
> And cast aside their fears […]
> That it is well with them because they know,
> With faithful eyes,
> Fixed forward and turned upwards to the skies
> That it is well with you,
> Among the chosen few,
> Among the very brave, the very true.[52]

Baring's *In Memoriam* was the culmination of his war poetry. It was widely admired. Writing to him several years after the war, T.E. Shaw (Lawrence of Arabia) told him that each time he read it, 'It takes me [...] absolutely by the throat. It is a lovely thing: and big, ever so big: and so simply sincere, and grievous and splendid.'[53] It put into words Maurice's Christian faith and the positive patriotic line. Through his poetry, he expressed his way of coming to terms with the loss of so many of the people he loved. His imagery of chivalry, heroism and sacrifice reflected his old friend, Ettie Desborough's attitude to the war. Attracted by romance and religion, they turned to the past when the reality of the present became unbearable.

ELEVEN

THE PEARLS IN PARLIAMENT

Although the pearls were steeped in symbolism, the appeal was for a very practical purpose – to raise money to help wounded soldiers. Lady Northcliffe never lost sight of this fact, and while she promoted the evocative stories of the jewels behind the scenes she was always planning how to maximise the profit they made. She knew that she had to get the timing just right if she was to make the most money for the Red Cross.

The response to the Pearl Appeal reflected the situation at the Front; when the soldiers' needs seemed greatest, the women of Britain responded by giving most generously. During the summer months, the situation had improved dramatically for the Allies. Repeated attacks had depleted German resources and their follow-up offensives gained little ground. In the middle of July, French troops supported by fresh American forces launched a ferocious counter-attack on the Germans in the Second Battle of the Marne. Now the weight of numbers had moved in favour of the Allies, not only were the Germans outnumbered, but Ludendorff's army was left exhausted by the battles of the spring. Seizing the initiative, France's General Foch and Britain's General Haig agreed that it was time to go on the offensive. On 8 August at the Battle of Amiens, British troops, joined by their allies, inflicted a decisive defeat on the Germans.[1] Recognising the importance of the battle, Ludendorff described it as 'the black day of the German army'.[2] Demoralised by their experiences on the battlefield and hearing about the dire situation at home in Germany where many civilians were close to starvation, German soldiers began to surrender in large groups.

However, although it was the beginning of the end, the war was not over and the fighting continued. During the Hundred Days Offensive, the Allies eventually pushed the Germans back to the position where they had been at the beginning of the year, but the Germans fought hard every step of the way and the pressure on the British armed forces was unrelenting. No one knew when the war would end and many people feared that the Germans would not be beaten until 1919. As one historian explains, the British soldiers were caught in an awful trap where they could see that victory was approaching but they knew that they might not live to see it. In an act of 'self-sacrifice on a grand scale', they fought on.[3]

Wanting to continue to show their support and to encourage their men to fight to the bitter end, British women gave more pearls. Over the summer the gems continued to pour in, so that by the end of July there were 3,300 pearls. Inundated with jewels, Lady Northcliffe and her committee had to make a decision about exactly what they would do with the hoard and when would be the best time to do it. Sir Robert Hudson wrote to Lord Northcliffe, 'Your lady's collection of Pearls is wonderful. But it is the devil to know what to do with them! They might fetch £100,000 if they were auctioned. They would bring in £1,000,000 if the Government would allow us to raffle them.'[4]

At a packed meeting at the Royal Automobile Club, it was decided that the jewels should be made into necklaces and raffled. Not only did this idea have the potential of raising the most money, it was also more egalitarian. If the pearls were sold in the open market or at auction the number of people who could afford to bid for them would be small. However, if tickets were sold at £1 it would allow more people from all walks of life to feel that they were part of this special tribute to the dead and wounded.

Unfortunately, there was one obstacle in the way of this plan – the law. Although raffles were 'doing a roaring trade', held at fundraising bazaars and village fetes throughout the country, it was actually against the law. Officially, any form of lottery was illegal as it was seen as promoting gambling. Although unofficially the police turned a blind eye and did not enforce the ruling, the law still stood. The Red Cross Pearl Committee faced a dilemma: if they held a raffle for the pearl necklaces it would be one of the largest the country had ever seen, but with such a high-profile project, supported by the great and the good, should they risk breaking the law? Never ones to be deterred, the powerful triumvirate of Lord and Lady Northcliffe and Sir Robert Hudson decided it was time to change an obsolete law. Lobbying their friends in high places, they persuaded Henry, 5th Marquess of Lansdowne, to bring the Lotteries (War Charities) Bill before Parliament in July and August of 1918.

Lord Lansdowne, was a controversial figure to pilot the Bill through Parliament. Before 1917 he would have been the ideal person to take on the task. He was a distinguished politician who had been Governor General of Canada and Viceroy of India. When he returned to Britain he held Cabinet office as secretary of state for war. Later, as foreign secretary, he signed the Anglo-Japanese Alliance in 1902 and the Entente Cordiale with France in 1904. Experienced in foreign affairs, in 1914 he was one of the senior politicians who pressed the government to send the British Expeditionary Force to the aid of France. However, his attitude to the war gradually began to change. On 31 October 1914 he received a telegram at his Berkeley Square home from the War Office. It stated, 'Deeply regret to inform you that Lord Charles Mercer Nairne Royal Dragoons has been killed in action yesterday Lord Kitchener expresses his sympathy.'[5] Charles was Lord Lansdowne's favourite younger son and the much-loved first husband of Violet Astor. His father never recovered from the loss. A year after Charles' death, on 28 October 1915, Lansdowne wrote to his wife Maud:

My darling,

You don't want to keep anniversaries and perhaps you are right, but, for all that, tomorrow will be a bitter day for both of us. All I will say now is that the past twelve months would have been unendurable but for your help and the courage with which you have faced them. I doubt whether they have really taken the edge off our sorrow. That will last as long as we last ourselves.[6]

A few days later, on their wedding anniversary, he wrote again to his wife, 'Our married life has been very happy until this dreadful war came to ruin everything.'[7]

Confronting his grief, Lord Lansdowne did what Ego Elcho had advised his parents to do; he invested all the love and hope he had had for his son in the next generation. Representing this shift, there is a heart-breaking photograph of an elderly Lord Lansdowne, dressed in army uniform, looking indulgently at his tiny grandson George, who is tightly holding his hand. The little boy is wearing a khaki soldier's uniform which is identical to his grandfather's and a scaled down version of the one his late father wore. Like Mary Wemyss and Ettie Desborough, Lord Lansdowne was determined his son should never be forgotten. Encouraged by his widowed daughter-in-law, Violet, he wrote a memoir about Charles for George. He explained, 'I have promised your mother to write, for your special benefit, a few notes about your father: the "Charlie" whom I loved so dearly, the "Daddy" whom you lost when you were two years old.' He wrote lovingly about his son:

> He had a keener and more delightful sense of humour than almost any of my acquaintances, a sense which led him to appreciate the brighter side of men and things and to find enjoyment even when the conditions did not promise to provide either, and although he never made light of the serious aspects of the case his temperament was essentially joyous and hopeful.

He described him as not only 'a wise councillor and a trustworthy comrade, but the brightest and most delightful of companions'.[8] As well as telling his grandchildren about the father they never knew, he revealed, 'His death well-nigh broke my heart.'

For a time after Charles' death, Lansdowne continued in politics. In 1915, he joined Asquith's coalition as a minister without portfolio. However, when Asquith fell from office in December 1916 and Lloyd George became prime minister, he decided to retire to his estate, Bowood. His personal experience and his shock at the scale of the slaughter made him increasingly critical of the war. As well as losing his son, six of his employees were killed and five wounded. At first, he voiced his fears in private, but in November 1916 he circulated a memorandum to the Cabinet which emphasised the terrible losses to the officer corps and argued that the best of the male population was being killed. He criticised any needless prolongation of the war. In October 1917, he wrote to his brother that he was 'more hopeless than ever about the war […] I don't believe that anything which we can accomplish at the Front will end the struggle – Meanwhile we are being financially ruined and stripped of the flower of our youth.'[9] A month later, in November 1917 he went public with his concerns, publishing what became known as the 'Lansdowne letter' in the *Daily Telegraph*. In it he called for Britain to negotiate a peace with Germany. He wrote, 'We are not going to lose this war, but the prolongation will spell ruin for the civilised world and an infinite addition to the load of human suffering which already weighs upon it.'[10]

Following the letter's publication, Lansdowne's view was immediately repudiated by the government and he was effectively excommunicated from the Unionist Party. In the aftermath of the Russian Revolution and America's entry into the war, his critics considered his intervention to be particularly ill-timed. Lansdowne's letter was misrepresented in the press as a call for 'Peace at any Price'. The Northcliffe press was particularly vicious in its attacks. *The Times* ran an editorial on the letter headlined 'Foolish and Mischievous'.[11] An article in *The Graphic* commented that in the face of the appalling attack on civilisation represented by the war, it was:

> … not astonishing that these doubts should arise in some minds. The wonder
> is that they do not occur with greater frequency, as they would do if human
> nature did not possess the gift of resiliency. To this diminution of resistance,
> this failure of resiliency is exactly what Germany counts upon.

The article ended defiantly, 'The peoples of the Allies have made up their minds that they will neither like it nor lump it. They know that there can be no terms with this pestilence.'[12]

Some observers were more sympathetic. The author of 'Motley Notes' in *The Sketch* attacked people who had criticised the letter without reading it. Instead, they had only read 'savage condemnations of it' under 'blood-curdling headings'. The journalist argued that it was 'a document of first-rate importance' which might prove to be 'the turning point of the war'.[13]

Some of the younger generation also saw the point of Lansdowne's argument. Duff Cooper wrote to Lady Diana Manners that he thought the letter was excellent and sensible.[14] Recent historians have also described Lansdowne's plans for an international organisation to arbitrate in future disputes, and reassurances to Germany that its enemies did not intend to crush them, as more sensible than the harsh terms which were eventually imposed after the war.[15]

Although his political career was over, Lansdowne remained a stalwart supporter of the Red Cross. Since September 1914, the orangery at his home, Bowood House in Wiltshire, had been a Red Cross Auxiliary Hospital for the wounded. From 1917 Lady Lansdowne had been commandant of the hospital with a staff of up to twenty nurses caring for sixty patients. The walled gardens were turned over to growing vegetables for the hospital. Any bad feeling between the Lansdownes and the Northcliffes after their difference in opinion over the controversial letter were put aside for the greater good of the Red Cross cause. As an experienced parliamentarian, Lansdowne was willing to use all his political skills in the battle over the pearls.

As the Bill was debated both inside and outside Parliament it was emphasised that the change in the law was hedged round with suitable restrictions. It would only legalise certain lotteries which promoted registered war charities and then only when the local police authorities had granted permission. It would be a temporary measure which would only remain in force during the war. It was argued that as lotteries were already taking place, it would be better to regularise the proceedings.

Lord Northcliffe threw the full weight of his newspapers behind the campaign to change the law. *The Times* was at the centre of the battle. On 29 July 1918, the newspaper made its allegiance plain, 'We hope and believe that it [the Bill] will meet with general approval', it was 'imperative' it was passed. The article explained that the needs of war charities were increasing and although the public's generosity to war funds had been 'great almost beyond belief', there were limits – not of desire or willingness to serve the causes, but of the 'sheer inability' of the same people to keep increasing the amount they gave.[16] New sources of revenue could be tapped by resorting to lotteries.

The anti-gambling lobby disagreed. In a letter to the editor from Farnham Castle, Surrey, on 2 August, the Bishop of Winchester sent 'a word of serious distress and grave protest'. He argued that those opposing the Bill were 'striving against what is avowedly one of the gravest moral evils in national life, the spirit of gambling and speculation'. If the law was changed, he was particularly concerned about the publicity the Red Cross Pearl Necklace would give to gambling. He was also horrified by the possibility that pearls might get into the wrong hands. With snobbish disdain, he exposed the threat it would pose to the established order. If 'a further sequel of newspaper paragraphs telling of the good luck of servants – maids or lads who have become possessed for a trifle of costly pearls, or a thousand pearls. The precedent would be deadly and far-reaching in effect.'[17] On 5 August, the Bishop of Norwich joined in the debate from his palace in Norfolk. Paternalistic in his tone, he wrote to the editor:

> I cannot but fear that the proposed policy will make it harder in the future to bring home to our less educated people the inherent wrong of the kind of gambling which ruins their positions and their characters (…) such things started in wealthier circles are quickly noted and discussed.[18]

The following day *The Times* published a letter sent by 'Common Sense' challenging the bishops' hyperbole. The anonymous author used a real-life example of how raffles worked in practice to show that most people who bought raffle tickets did it purely for the charitable cause. A young officer, home on leave, gives a cigarette case to a Red Cross bazaar in his village, the worse for wear because it had been dented by a German bullet, which it helped to prevent killing him. It is raffled, and 100 people buy half-crown tickets, of which £12 goes to the local Red Cross hospital. The old lady who wins the cigarette case 'shows no sign up to the present of starting on a wild career of gambling'. She exhibits the case proudly to her friends. 'Common Sense' asked, 'Is it seriously contended that anyone is the worse for this transaction? If so who? The pleased winner, the very contented losers, or the patients in the beds?' Nor could the writer believe that raffling the Red Cross Pearls would 'sap the morals of the race'. He wrote, 'The warm-hearted donors of pearls are concerned only that their gifts should realise as much as possible for Red Cross work.'[19]

Although Northcliffe's newspapers had influence, they did not have the power to change the law, only Parliament could do that. While the debate was taking place in *The Times*, an equally heated one was happening in Westminster. In the Lords, Lord Lansdowne emphasised the growing needs of the Red Cross. In the first year of the war their expenditure was £1 million; it was now considerably more than £4 million. More than £10,000 each day was needed. They spent £25,000 a week on medical, general and other stores destined for the theatres of war and £40,000 a week on comforts and different items that they sent to prisoners of war. He argued that this Bill would enable them to get money that they could not get in any other way.

The escalating argument split the Establishment. The Archbishop of Canterbury led the opposition in the Lords. He argued that the issue was of far-reaching importance and it was 'not really a little Bill' it had been described as, because a great principle was involved. If it was passed it would 'be opening the floodgates' to the growth of gambling. The archbishop added that a friend of his had come to him and asked whether it was really possible that those who had given pearls, as he had done in memory of someone who had lost his life, had given something which was going to be used for a purpose which the givers would deprecate. Although he would be pleased to see the Red Cross increase its income, he would not want to do it in a way which would 'compromise principles which I regard as of vital importance to our national life'.[20]

To the Red Cross Committee's relief, the Bill passed its second reading in the Lords, although the final hurdle would be to get it through the House of Commons. Drawing on skills honed over decades, the Northcliffes and Sir Robert Hudson were manipulating the situation behind the scenes. The Northcliffe press was used to applying persuasive pressure on politicians. As a former chief agent of the Liberal Party, Sir Robert also had many political contacts and was skilled in political manoeuvring. He wrote to Lord Northcliffe that the only way to get the Bill through the House of Commons was if it was given government backing and the home secretary, Sir George Cave, supported it.

However, the Northcliffe press had recently launched a populist campaign against Cave that might jeopardise his support. Northcliffe and many people in the country believed that Cave was not being tough enough on enemy aliens; they wanted immediate internment of all aliens of enemy blood. Stirring up a frenzy of anti-German and anti-Cave feeling by running a series of scare stories about enemy aliens, Northcliffe had driven Cave almost to the point of resignation. It was at this moment that Sir Robert reminded his co-conspirator:

> He [Cave] knows that it is a Bill to enable us to raffle those pearls. He knows your Lady collected the pearls. At present he is benevolent in the extreme. I want to keep him so. A couple of million pounds depends on his good will. By the time you see what is coming, and are probably saying 'Damn his

impudence', but nothing venture, nothing get. Couldn't certain papers give George Cave a rest for a fortnight?[21]

Northcliffe agreed to 'mark time for a bit', although he said that it would not be easy because there was a 'Niagara of public opinion' about enemy aliens.[22]

The plotting worked, and on 30 July Sir Robert Hudson wrote to Lord Northcliffe, 'I think I have today landed Cave with the entire charge of the Bill as a Government measure in the House of Commons.'[23]

In fact, the triumvirate only got part of what they wanted, the Bill did not get official government backing at this stage and instead had to rely on a free vote. However, the home secretary agreed to introduce the motion and it was promised that if it was carried it would be treated as a government measure in its remaining stages. On 1 August, Lord Northcliffe wrote to Sir Robert, 'Cave says that he has caved in, and it may not be necessary to prod him anymore, and I will remain quiet so long as he is good.'[24] Most importantly, the Bill was given the necessary parliamentary time before the summer recess. On 8 August, Parliament was adjourning for ten weeks so it was essential that the change in the law came quickly, in time for the Red Cross Pearl Appeal to benefit.

In the middle of the Bill's passage through Parliament, Lady Northcliffe wrote an effusive thank-you letter to Lloyd George rejoicing that it had passed the second reading in the House of Lords safely, but expressing anxiety about what would happen once it reached the House of Commons. She told Lloyd George that they would need all his help and support and she knew that she could count on it. Outside Parliament, her team were doing all that they could but they depended on the prime minister's sympathetic interest and practical help to achieve the result they required. With her customary charm, she finished by telling Lloyd George how grateful he had made her.[25]

This letter reflected the complex relationship between Lord Northcliffe and Lloyd George. The press baron had supported the Welsh politician for prime minister when Asquith was in power. However, there was an ambivalence in their feelings for each other. Once Lloyd George was prime minister, he was determined that his old supporter should not pull the strings. Lloyd George's mistress and private secretary, Frances Stevenson, was very critical of Northcliffe and did not want her lover to have too much to do with him. When there were rumours that Northcliffe might be made minister of air in 1916, she commented that if Northcliffe once got a position in government he would not rest until he was made dictator.[26] In April 1917 she recorded in her diary that the newspaper proprietor had been to see the prime minister and told him that his government was even more unpopular than the last one. Lloyd George put this comment down to the fact that he was doing things without consulting Northcliffe, which irritated the great man.[27]

Although Lloyd George's relationship with Lady Northcliffe's husband was becoming increasingly strained, it seems that the prime minister helped her on this occasion. However, the decision to give the Bill parliamentary time so late in the session caused controversy. When some MPs who opposed gambling heard what was happening just one or two days before the debate, they claimed that the government had taken them by surprise. They suggested that proponents of the Bill had an unfair advantage because they had known what was happening in advance. They complained that many members had already gone on holiday not knowing that the measure was being brought forward. Andrew Bonar Law, on behalf of the government, denied these suggestions but it created a bad feeling between the two sides in the run-up to the debate.

The atmosphere was tense on 6 August when Sir George Cave moved the second reading of the Bill in a late-night sitting attended by only a few MPs. He explained that the Home Office considered the present position was 'intolerable', as to enforce the law against raffles and tombolas for war purposes would run counter to the feeling of the great mass of the population. He added, 'Either the law must be enforced or it must be altered.'[28]

Passionate opposition was then expressed by anti-gambling MPs who were motivated by their religious or political principles. Theodore Taylor, a Lancashire woollen manufacturer, in moving the rejection of the motion, said he hoped he would not be seen as a 'kill-joy' or 'a skinny and disagreeable Puritan', but he accused Sir George Cave of putting 'a nasty thing in the nicest way'.[29] He then made a convoluted argument drawing parallels between Marie Antoinette's diamond necklace and the Red Cross Pearls, arguing that just as the diamond necklace had something to do with the French Revolution so the pearl necklace threatened the development of a revolutionary spirit in this country. How could Parliament permit titled ladies to gamble for the necklace and then send poor men to prison for other forms of gambling like playing pitch and toss?

At the heart of the debate was whether the ends justified the means. Was it worth risking an increase in gambling to boost funds for the Red Cross? Sir John Spear appealed to the House not to resort to illegal practices even to raise money for war purposes. While some Labour members raised valid concerns about the dangers of encouraging their working-class constituents to gamble, when every penny of their income was needed to feed and clothe their children, other opponents resorted to the same snobbish arguments as the bishops. Sir Stephen Collins asked, 'What is a workman's wife to do with that [the pearl necklace]? Put it round her neck?' He even criticised the donors of the jewels, commenting, 'If it had not been for the pearls we should have heard nothing of this lottery. If the good people who gave the pearls had only given money we should have heard nothing of this proposal.'[30] Continuing in a similar vein, Sidney Robinson claimed that the majority of people who bought tickets would be doing it to gamble rather than for the good of the cause. He asked, 'What good will a pearl necklace of great value be to a miner or a munition worker? Their wives would be anxious not to get the pearl necklace as such, but to convert it into cash. It is pure gambling, and it is nothing else.'[31]

Supporting a change in the law, Evelyn Cecil, who was a member of the Joint War Committee of the Order of St John and the British Red Cross, asked members what other more effective form of fundraising they could offer. He reminded them that voluntary, though illegal, efforts of this kind had been going on for some time in county bazaars and raffles held on behalf of the Red Cross. With heavy sarcasm, he commented, 'Estimable ladies have put their backs into it and done their utmost. I suppose they are all liable to be arrested and tried or imprisoned.'[32] The Chairman of the British Red Cross, Sir Arthur Stanley, who was actively involved in the Pearl Appeal, suggested that some of the previous speakers misunderstood the whole spirit of the enterprise and their words amounted to 'almost a sneer at the noble ladies giving these pearls'. He added:

> I would point out that many of these ladies are very far from rich. They gave that which to each of them was most precious, and they gave it in order to help what they felt was even more precious. They felt that they were giving

these pearls for the relief of suffering, which they themselves would willingly have laid down their lives to avoid.

Members were wrong to try to put a monetary value on the pearls because they were 'above all price'. Great trust had been placed in the Pearl Committee and it was their duty to find the best way to raise funds to help the suffering. Countering the more snobbish arguments of his opponents, he added, 'I own myself I should think that that necklace had been more properly and more worthily bought by the poor man who managed to pay the shilling [to a raffle] than by anyone who could afford to buy it.' He closed his speech by asking the members to let the Red Cross have 'a perfectly innocent incentive' for a generous public.[33]

When the free vote was taken late that night, to everyone's surprise, the Bill fell at the final hurdle. It was rejected by eighty-one votes to seventy-seven, a majority of just four. An unusual alliance of Establishment bishops, Nonconformist Liberals and anti-gambling members of the Labour Party had rebelled against the measure. 'Eve' in *Tatler* used humour to attack the antis, writing that they 'did us out, tiresome things, of the very toppingest topper-most gamble I've come across for years'.[34] However, other newspapers wrote more seriously about the implications. The defeat of the Bill caused widespread anger and a questioning of how well British democracy was actually working. The Red Cross' journal wrote sarcastically that two Members of Parliament, Mr Taylor who 'somehow' linked Marie Antoinette's necklace with revolution in this country, and Sir John Spear who declared that the House of Commons would be 'breaking the law' by altering the law, 'have something to learn in political history and constitutional law'.[35] *The Times* claimed that the effects of this decision were 'not pleasant to contemplate'. Parliament had gone against public opinion and the law would be hard to enforce. The police would now be expected to take action against all raffles, while other forms of gambling like betting on horseracing 'goes merrily on'. Not just the funds of the Red Cross would suffer, so would the work of the YMCA, St Dunstan's charity for the blind and other notable war charities. Stirring up its readers' emotions further, the article concluded, 'The sick and wounded men of our race will bear in their shattered bodies the marks of this example of the wisdom of the House of Commons.'[36]

Parliament's decision was a devastating blow to the Red Cross Pearl Appeal. They now had to find an alternative plan. The most unusual suggestion appeared in a letter to *The Spectator*. The author wrote:

Hundreds of pounds have been raised by exhibiting the pearls here. Could they not be sent round the world for exhibition until the war is over or a sufficient harvest has been reaped. Then let them be given to the countries Germany has outraged, to be worn by the wives of their rulers on State occasions in memory of those who died for them and us – notably on that great Thanks-giving Day which shall see their deliverance from Germany.[37]

A decision on the fate of the pearls needed to be made without further delay. If the pearls were to maintain their fundraising momentum they needed to be turned into money for the Red Cross within a few months. Eventually it was decided that an auction of the pearls should be held at Christie's on 19 December. It was estimated that between £100,000 and £200,000 would be raised by the pearls at auction, compared to between £1 million and £2 million if they had been raffled.

Despite the major setback in Parliament, Lady Northcliffe and her committee were not downhearted for long as the response from the public continued to amaze them. As the *Daily Mail* explained, the veto of 'bigots' in the House of Commons proved the best advertisement possible, and by arousing resentment and 'the fair and sporting spirit of the British public', even more gems came in.[38]

In the early autumn, many donations arrived from abroad. In Egypt, Lady Wingate's appeal collected 123 pearls and £3,500 in money. The wife of the high commissioner, Lady Wingate collected valuable gifts from many different nationalities and provinces. The pearls came from the sultan's family, local businesses and individuals. In South America, over 100 donors gave pearls through the British Ladies' Patriotic Committee in Montevideo. In Chile, gems including 100 small pearls from the ladies of Santiago were received by the wife of Britain's envoy extraordinary and minister plenipotentiary, Lady Stronge. Jewels were also sent from Singapore and India. Like the soldiers who had come from across the British Empire to fight for the motherland, the pearl necklace campaign reflected the patriotic spirit which reached far beyond Britain's borders.

TWELVE

THE KITCHENER RUBIES

No figure represented the ideals of Empire more than the secretary of state for war, Lord Kitchener. The conqueror of the Sudan and victor of Omdurman was a hero who, despite military setbacks, remained one of the most popular figures of the war. He embodied the patriotic spirit of the early years of the conflict. On 5 August 1914, Asquith appointed the military hero to be secretary of state for war with a seat in the Cabinet.

His first task had been to raise an army and make sure that raw recruits were effectively trained. An imposing figure at 6ft 2in tall, broad-shouldered and upright, his distinctive features, with the immaculate moustache and the slight cast in his right eye, became the face of the recruiting campaign. On posters across the country his finger pointed at young men as he told them, 'Your country needs you!'

In the final weeks of the Pearl Appeal, when it was decided that every necklace should have a clasp to hold the pearls together, a donor known only by their initials 'MFP' gave five rubies in memory of this national icon.

The jewels were from Lord Kitchener's sister, Frances Parker, who was known as Millie. She sent it with the message, 'Lest we forget. In Memory of Kitchener of Khartoum, June 5, 1916.' On that fateful day, Lord Kitchener had set sail from Scapa Flow to the Russian port of Archangel aboard the armoured cruiser HMS *Hampshire*. His mission was to advise the

Russians on military matters. A storm was raging but, impatient to get on with his task, Kitchener refused to wait until the gale died down. He was relaxing in his cabin when at about 7.45 p.m. there was an explosion. The ship had struck a mine that had been laid by a German submarine west of the Orkney Islands. The *Hampshire* lurched to starboard, the electricity failed and all the lights went out. Water gushed in through the enormous hole in her side and the ship began to sink. Hearing the commotion, Kitchener came onto the quarter-deck, showing no outward sign of nervousness. When the captain asked him to get into a lifeboat, he either did not hear or decided it would be useless.[1] In the violent storm there was little chance of survival; Kitchener, his staff and 643 of the 655 crew drowned or died of exposure.[2] Only twelve men reached the rocky shores of the Orkneys.

The sinking of the *Hampshire* was one of the most memorable moments of the war. Like the death of President Kennedy decades later, everyone remembered where they were when they heard the news. Margot Asquith rushed into a family christening at St Paul's Cathedral just bursting to tell everyone, she then insisted on talking loudly about it all through the ceremony.[3] Many ordinary people felt a personal sense of loss. Vera Brittain described how nearly everyone in England stopped what they were doing to stare into the incredulous eyes of their neighbour. Sad and subdued, she walked with her mother and brother beside the Thames at Westminster. Kitchener had such a powerful hold on their imagination that it felt as if the ship of state had sunk that night.[4] The king wrote to Millie Parker, 'While the whole nation mourns the death of a great soldier, I have personally lost in Lord Kitchener an old and valued friend, upon whose devotion I ever relied with the utmost confidence.'[5] Not since the death of Queen Victoria had there been such an outpouring of public grief. Stores closed, blinds were drawn and flags were flown at half mast.[6]

Lord Kitchener's sister used the Pearl Necklace Appeal to commemorate this key event in the war while also marking a very personal grief. Capturing the private man behind the public figure, accompanying the rubies were three pearls, given 'one for Ferby, one for little Marion and one from little Pet Evie'. This was one of the most unusual donations of the whole collection as it seems that it was made in the name of family pets. The whole Kitchener family were devoted to animals and Lord Kitchener adored dogs. Showing his sense of humour, he called his gun dogs Aim, Fire, Shot, Bang,

Miss and Damn.[7] As this donation suggests, relaxing with his family Lord Kitchener was very different from his tough image. After his death, his relatives were determined that the tender and affectionate man as well as the heroic figure should be remembered.

In November 1916, his first cousin wrote to her son wanting to share 'one of those little gleams of family affection which steals into the lives of even the greatest men'. In her letter she explained:

> You will read many histories of him and many biographies and they will all speak of his greatness but it will not be recorded, perhaps [because] it is known to few, how great too was this Kitchener of heart. It was in the rare glimpses of family life that his kindness could show itself.[8]

She recalled how 'Cousin Herbert', as a young 'stripling' gave his treasured stamp collection to her invalid brother, Tom. As he grew older, his 'grace, simplicity [...] and his total absence of guile' struck her. He often saw his cousin's family when he was on leave and during these visits he filled her house with his 'most delightful laugh'.[9] When he returned to the army, he left his beloved dog 'Bang' with them and gave the family another one called 'Bangle'.

No one knew better than Millie Parker the softer, generous side of her brother's personality. As Lord Kitchener never married or had children of his own, Millie's family were particularly important to him. He was godfather to her second son and paid for her daughter Frances' education at Cambridge. During the war, brother and sister had a ten-minute chat every fortnight. Early in the war, Kitchener told her that the Germans would take a great deal of beating and that the conflict would last three years, which was much longer than many people thought.[10] In their conversations, Millie often gave her forthright opinions, frequently criticising the 'red tape' of Whitehall which she believed was getting in the way of the war effort.[11]

When news reached Millie of the sinking of the *Hampshire* while she was at a charity bazaar in Essex, at first she could not accept her brother was dead. As his body had never been found, conspiracy theories and myths swirled around the tragic event. Some people believed that he had been kidnapped, others that he was in an enchanted sleep in a northern cave ready to reappear at Britain's moment of greatest danger.[12] Even the rational Raymond Asquith could not help suspecting that Kitchener would stroll back into the House of Lords, as strong and silent as ever, combing seaweed out of his hair.[13] For a time Millie believed that he was a prisoner in Germany. However, by July she was facing the reality, writing to a friend:

> It is a miserable time for all. What makes it more so for us is the mystery which is made over the loss of HMS *Hampshire* and the constant rumours which go on – Many will not believe Lord Kitchener is really gone from us – I personally have no hope and the reports are very trying entirely owing to our being given no information as to where the fault lay or the cause of the disaster.[14]

In reply to one of the many letters of condolence she received, she shared her feelings of loss, writing, 'No good life is wasted; the influence remains, but I feel victory without my brother will be very much saddened. So many of us will feel this, having lost so many of our loved ones.'[15] With no grave to grieve at, perhaps the donation of rubies and pearls was Millie's way of finally laying her brother's memory to rest.

As Kitchener had been such a lynchpin in the war it was appropriate that his rubies should form the clasp holding the pearls together. He was closely connected to many of the men who were commemorated in the Red Cross Necklace. Before the war he was a welcome guest of the Lansdownes at Bowood and the Grenfells at Taplow. A friend of Willie Grenfell since 1885, he always visited the family on his first Sunday back in England after his adventures abroad. He told Ettie Grenfell that he had no home, but when he came to their house it felt like home.[16]

During these visits, he developed a special rapport with Julian Grenfell. When they first met in 1899 the young boy had no idea who Kitchener was, but he readily accepted his invitation to come for a walk before breakfast. They then spent hours fishing and talking about Julian's dream of becoming a soldier. The older man became a role model for the boy, who admired his self-restraint and tremendous willpower and identified with his dislike of superficial social life. Kitchener told his young confidant that the two things he could not stand were state dinners and being photographed.[17]

Kitchener saw the Grenfell boys' potential, writing to Ettie, 'Much love to Julian and Billy, what splendid boys they are I expect one of them will have to be prime minister.'[18] With no son of his own, they, like his nephews and nieces, helped to fill the gap. He told Ettie that after Julian had been to college he should become a cavalry officer and he would make a first-rate soldier of him. After one visit to Taplow, Kitchener asked for a photograph of his protégé, it was the only picture he kept on his desk at the War Office.[19] When he heard that Julian had died he was deeply distressed.[20] He wrote to Willie Grenfell, 'I grieve with you both – I loved poor Julian and feel his loss badly – He was a splendid solider and served his country right well.'[21]

When, two months later, Kitchener heard the news that Billy had also been killed, it was the only time in the war that he broke down in office. He had to stop working for an hour to regain his composure.[22] He wrote to Ettie, 'You know how sincerely I grieve with you. It is sad for us, but not for them. You have given your country of the best, for they were both splendid and gallant soldiers and have done their duty nobly.' In his letter to his old friend he admitted to a degree of war weariness and self-doubt, writing, 'We all wish sometimes that the trumpet would sound for us, but we have to stick it out and do our very best until the release comes. I only wish I could do more, or rather that what I do was better work.'[23]

Although, the Kitchener rubies belonged beside the pearls given for his surrogate sons, there was an irony that they should be donated to an appeal headed by Lady Northcliffe. No man could have done more than Lord Northcliffe to undermine Kitchener. In May 1915, Northcliffe used the full weight of his newspapers to attack the secretary of state for war, claiming that he had starved the army in France of high-explosive shells and had sent instead shrapnel which was useless in trench warfare. An article in the *Daily Mail* on 21 May 1915, headlined 'The Shell Scandal: Lord Kitchener's Tragic Blunder', blamed his incompetence for thousands of soldiers' deaths. It urged that he should be dismissed.

However, Northcliffe's attack backfired as Kitchener was so popular. All day phones at the newspaper rang with protests from readers angrily denouncing the attacks on Kitchener and saying they would never buy the 'damned rag' again.[24] The *Daily Mail's* circulation dropped from 1,386,000 to 238,000 and special police had to guard its office at Carmelite House.[25] Copies of the paper were ceremonially burnt on the steps of the Stock Exchange. In railway compartments, if a *Daily Mail* was brought in the company would seize it, tear it into fragments and throw it out of the window.[26] As ever, Margot Asquith was vehement in her denunciation of Northcliffe, writing that he was pro-German and a wicked man. According to her, Kitchener was a much better fellow.[27] She wanted to see 'proper' censorship of the press and asked Kitchener why he did not have Northcliffe arrested.[28]

However, never one to surrender, Lord Northcliffe continued his onslaught. He told a colleague he was willing to take the personal opprobrium and it was better to lose circulation than lose the war. His pressure was partly responsible for Asquith re-forming his government as a coalition. Kitchener remained secretary of state for war, but all production matters were taken away from him and given to Lloyd George at the new Ministry of Munitions. Elements of Northcliffe's accusations proved to be true and Kitchener's credibility among his Cabinet colleagues was undermined, but he never lost the admiration of the public. Lord Northcliffe was one of the few not to grieve when he heard that the *Hampshire* had sunk. Instead he commented, 'Providence is on the side of the British Empire after all.'[29]

Magnanimously, in 1918 Millie Parker put aside any negative feelings she had towards the Northcliffes to help the Red Cross Pearl Appeal. She had already learnt to put the past behind her in her own family. Before the war her daughter Frances, known as Fanny, had been a suffragette. Both Fanny's mother and her uncle were disgusted by her involvement. It was particularly embarrassing for Lord Kitchener because he had paid for her to be highly educated at Newnham College, Cambridge. However, Fanny was more like her uncle than he would have admitted, because as a militant suffragette she showed the same sort of dauntless courage. Until 1913 she was the organiser of the Women's Social and Political Union (WSPU) in Dundee. She was imprisoned on several occasions for causing damage to property and her photograph was circulated to police around the country as one of the most 'wanted' suffragettes. In July 1914, she appeared in court in Ayr under the alias 'Janet Arthur'. Accused of trying to blow up Burns' Cottage at Alloway, she refused to enter the dock and would not recognise the court's jurisdiction. Instead she shouted quotations from Burns' poetry and accused the authorities of torturing women.

Fanny was taken to Ayr Prison, pending further inquiry. While in prison she went on hunger strike and refused food or drink for four days before she was transferred to Perth Prison where she was force-fed. Over the following days, force-feeding took place on seven occasions.[30] Fanny wrote about her horrific experiences in an article, which described how she was held down by six female warders and slapped in the face. The doctor tried to force her mouth open with a steel gag, and when that failed a nasal tube was forced down her nostril causing extreme pain. On another occasion, three female warders tried to feed her by the rectum. Fanny struggled against them and was screaming in agony. They later subjected her to 'a grosser and more indecent outrage'. The medical report by Dr Lindsay of Perth Prison indicated injuries consistent with an instrument being introduced into her vagina causing abrasions.[31] She described the experience as torture.

When her family heard what was happening her brother negotiated her release from prison to a nursing home, where she was examined and found to be in a state of collapse.

Within weeks, the war changed the whole political landscape for suffragettes like Fanny. In August 1914 the WSPU called a truce and offered to put their army at the service of the government. In return, suffragette prisoners were released. Fanny's case never came to trial because of this amnesty. However, not all suffragettes accepted this reconciliation. Sylvia Pankhurst and her new Federation of East London Suffragettes remained committed to pacifism. This group and the Women's Freedom League were the only suffragettes who continued to campaign for the vote during the war.[32]

Other suffragettes saw the war as a chance for women to prove themselves worthy of citizenship. Fanny threw herself into war work, becoming honorary organiser of the Women's Freedom League National Service Organisation, which put women workers in touch with employers to find the right work for them. She also served in the Women's Army Auxiliary Corps at Boulogne and was awarded an OBE for her dedication.[33] The co-operation of millions of women changed the attitude of many opponents of women's suffrage, including Lord Northcliffe. His newspaper, the *Daily Mail*, had first coined the term 'suffragette', using it to separate militant activists from less violent suffragists. Although it was intended as an insult, Emmeline Pankhurst defiantly accepted the label.

At the height of suffragette activity in 1912, Northcliffe promised Lord Curzon that his papers would do anything they could for the anti-suffrage cause.[34] However, by the end of the war the press baron used the Northcliffe press to reflect his change of heart. *The Times*, which had opposed the women's cause for almost half a century, now completely reversed its policy. The newspaper magnate himself talked to Prime Minister Lloyd George about granting women the vote. No doubt he was influenced by his wife's exceptional abilities when he wrote, 'The women are wonderful. Their freshness of mind, their organising skill, have been magnificent. Men are making too great a mess of the world and need helpers without their own prejudices, idleness and self-indulgence.'[35]

In 1918, the British Representation of the People Act, which enfranchised women over the age of 30, became law. It acknowledged the great sacrifice women had made during the war. However, it excluded many of the female munitions workers who were too young to vote and it deliberately kept women as a minority of the electorate.[36]

The war brought Millie and her daughter closer together. After several years of estrangement they were now both committed to the war effort. Millie had the same fighting spirit as her brother and daughter. During the war she was a leading campaigner for the temperance movement. At this time, there was a widespread fear that working-class women were using their separation allowances to buy alcohol and get drunk in public. In October 1914, the Archbishop of Canterbury wrote to Lord Kitchener that 'although it sounds horrid', his information showed that there was truth in this rumour. In response, a public meeting was held at Caxton Hall on 12 November 1914 calling for total abstinence during the war.[37] Millie did her bit by encouraging women to join the League of Honour, in which they pledged themselves to purity, teetotalism and prayer. She went around the country speaking out against alcohol. In Glasgow in 1915 she told a packed audience, 'My brother is trying to beat the Germans. It is not his place to try and beat drink; it is the place of every Britisher to back him up and stop this horrible, degrading and miserable state the country is in.'[38] At another meeting she described the alcohol trade as 'a vampire' and claimed that people who treated a soldier to a drink were 'not only fools but rogues. Every man who drank in this country was a thoughtless man.'[39]

Alcohol had become a major problem during the war; the government believed that it was undermining munitions-making and shipbuilding. Lloyd George claimed that drink was one of the greatest threats to victory. He started a campaign asking national figures to promise not to drink for the duration of the war.

In March 1915, the king agreed to set an example by promising that no alcohol would be drunk in the royal household until the war was over. It was an act of solidarity showing that George V did not expect his people to make a sacrifice that he was not willing to make himself. However, in private the king admitted he hated doing it. Knowing his feelings, when the royal cellars were locked up his servants placed a large wreath made of empty bottles and tied with a crepe ribbon outside the door with the word 'Dead' written on it.

His courtiers were equally unhappy to swap the finest wines for barley water and ginger beer. Ettie Desborough, who was one of Queen Mary's ladies-in-waiting, observed that the only cheerful person at court was Margot Asquith, who took copious swigs from a flask of brandy which she claimed was for 'medicinal reasons'.[40] The king later told Margot that he had been talked into heading the campaign on false pretences. He said that he had given up alcohol thinking that the government was going to pass drastic legislation on the issue. However, now he had committed to it he could not go back on his pledge.

It seems that Parliament was not as high-minded about drinking as it was about gambling. Members rejected the idea that the Commons and the Lords should become an alcohol-free zone. A heavy drinker himself, Asquith took little interest in his colleague's campaign. Churchill also thought this sacrifice ridiculous. There was also opposition to any form of prohibition in the country. In 1915 a pamphlet was published by 'The League of the Man in the Street', complaining that this was an assault on the drinking habits of the working man. 'Pump puritans' and 'killjoys' were attacked for interfering with ordinary people's rights and liberties. In contemporary cartoons, Lloyd George was satirised as a phony St George trying to slay the dragon drink.[41]

However, by the autumn, Lloyd George had made drink forbidden in pubs, restaurants and clubs unless served with a meal. The hours during which spirits could be bought were also decreased. Under the so-called 'beauty sleep order', clubs had to close by 10.30 p.m. However, this had the unplanned effect of increasing the number of underground nightclubs.

In November 1915, restrictions were placed on the sale of beer and spirits. Trying to end weekend binges that affected work in the factories on Monday, it was ruled that no beer and spirits could be bought on Saturdays and all alcohol sales were to be cash only. By May 1916 brandy was made unobtainable without a doctor's prescription.[42] Millie's temperance movement was gaining ground, but her aim remained to have total prohibition introduced. It seems that her donation of rubies and pearls represented not just one hero but a family of campaigners.

The Kitcheners were not the only ones to give precious jewels for the clasps. In total, nearly fifty rubies were donated. Mrs Hewitt sent one in memory of her husband, Rifleman F.J. Hewitt, with the message, 'More precious than rubies to his wife.'[43] While Mrs Arthur G. Hordern gave two rubies, 'In honour of our gallant Australians'.[44]

Another of the clasps also symbolised the importance of the Empire. Lady Wingate, who had organised the pearl collection in Egypt, gave a sapphire and diamond clasp to the appeal. Her husband, Sir Reginald Wingate, was Kitchener's successor as Governor General of the Sudan before becoming High Commissioner in Egypt. The two men had been old friends, serving together in the army for almost thirty years. Although Wingate was overshadowed by Kitchener's dominant personality, he worked very effectively as the leader's right-hand man behind the scenes. As a bachelor, Kitchener had no time for his married officers' attempts to maintain their family life. Wingate told his wife there was no point mentioning her to him as he always retorted that it was a mistake for officers to marry.[45]

While Sir Reginald governed the Sudan, Lady Wingate behaved as if she was the queen, even employing a personal umbrella carrier. The couple introduced official rituals and a rigid social etiquette which were largely their own creation. There were guards of honour, levees, durbars and illuminations. A Victorian virago, at the many formal dinners held at their palace Lady Wingate ruled that high-necked dresses should be worn by the ladies.[46] She also insisted that they wore white kid gloves when paying calls. Wielding her power with austere rectitude, she decided who should and should not be received, and as a strong Christian she gave a very cold reception to anyone who was having an affair. When her husband became High Commissioner of Egypt in 1917, a position which was second only to the Viceroy of India in responsibility and power, Lady Wingate became increasingly grand. She expected officials and their wives to pay court to her. After a visit to Egypt, Rudyard Kipling wrote to a friend that many army officers told him that *she* had governed the Sudan and that to get promotion in the Egyptian Army you had to conciliate her.[47]

During the war, Lady Wingate became president of the Cairo and Alexandria Red Cross Committee. Her collection of pearls and donation of the clasp was motivated by great personal loss. In March 1918, her adored youngest son Malcolm was killed on the Western Front. As a matter of conscience, he had left a safer staff post at General Headquarters because he thought a less able-bodied man should do his staff work and he ought to return to the firing line. After his death, Lady Wingate always blamed herself for not dissuading him. She never recovered from his death, making no secret of the fact that he had been her favourite child. In the corner of her drawing room a 'shrine' was made in his memory, but her pain remained so raw she would never allow his name to be mentioned. Every year after the war she visited Malcolm's memorial in France and when she died her own ashes were buried there.[48] The donation of the clasp to the Red Cross was her way of acknowledging a grief which was too deep for words.

However, like the pearls themselves, not every clasp represented loss. A historic diamond clasp from Lady Norbury symbolised transformation. The large rose diamond, surrounded by smaller diamonds, had belonged to the Duchess of Portland. Unlike some aristocrats, the Norburys openly embraced the wartime changes that were creating a more egalitarian society. During the war, Lord Norbury worked as a mechanic in a Surrey aircraft factory. The 53-year-old peer took on this role because he believed that every man should do what he could to help his country. He had a good knowledge of mechanics and internal combustion engines and hoped to be of use in accelerating the country's war output.[49] He told one newspaper:

> I am not altogether strange to work. I have had a lathe of my own for the past 35 years, and have been used to turning my hand to all kinds of mechanical jobs that wanted doing. I had intended at first to offer myself for shell work but when an advertisement appeared asking for mechanics for an aeroplane factory, I applied for a job and was taken on.[50]

In a Pathé newsreel, Lord Norbury was shown standing at a machine wearing mechanics' dungarees and a flat cap. He was then seen taking a break, standing by the door of the factory and wiping his hands on a rag. He was keen to be treated the same as other workers so he ate with them in the canteen and was paid 7d an hour for his labour. Unaffected and cheerful, he became very popular with his fellow workmen who nicknamed him 'Nobby'.[51] He found a new sense of purpose in his work, Lady Norbury explained:

Last week he was working until 3 o'clock in the morning and up again early and at his duty. He has no intention of giving up the work, which he thoroughly enjoys, and he is in excellent health notwithstanding that he is at the bench lathe or in the erecting sheds at 6am every day.[52]

While the Kitchener rubies commemorated a traditional hero suited to a different age, the Norbury diamonds were a donation that represented a modern man of the people. Lady Norbury was now the wife of a hardworking mechanic and, as the bishops and MPs had pointed out in the parliamentary debates about the pearls, what use had a working man's wife with fine jewels?

Lady Norbury wanted her valuable clasp to serve a useful purpose and raise funds for the war wounded instead of lying redundant in her jewellery box. Her diamonds symbolised a new spirit of egalitarianism and utilitarianism in the country. The old class divisions were decreasing.

Before the war, only about 2 per cent of officers had served in the ranks, by 1918 it was estimated that nearly 40 per cent of the officer corps came from lower and middle-class backgrounds. In the new more meritocratic system, a taxi driver and a schoolmaster commanded brigades while a coal miner, a railway signalman and a market gardener commanded battalions.[53] If the Red Cross Pearl Appeal was to be truly inclusive, it was right that it should represent both the old and the new cultures that vied for supremacy during the war.

THIRTEEN

PEARL MANIA

During the late summer and autumn, the Allies continued to press forward against the Germans. They were joined by more than half a million enthusiastic American troops who had arrived full of energy and eager to fight. From late September to early October, the Allies broke through the German Hindenburg or Siegfried Line in one of the most decisive victories of the war.

Ludendorff realised the seriousness of the situation: Germany had lost over 1 million men between March and July and a further three-quarters of a million in the following months, half of whom had been taken prisoner.[1] On 28 September, he informed his government that they would have to seek an armistice to allow Germany to draw breath and consider peace negotiations. The German Government then approached American President Wilson asking for an armistice based on the 'Fourteen Points' he had proposed in January 1918. However, when Wilson now suggested that the Allies should draw up the peace terms with military advice, Ludendorff withdrew his offer and advised a continuation of the war.[2]

Soon the German general would have little choice about the outcome of events. At home there were fears of revolution; at the Front the German Army was collapsing. Germany was also losing her allies. By the end of October, Bulgaria had surrendered and Turkey had conceded defeat, and early the following month Austria–Hungary also left the war. Faced with failure, on 26 October Ludendorff resigned.[3]

Watching international events closely, Lady Northcliffe and her committee realised that it was time for the Pearl Appeal to come to a close. The collection had begun when Britain was threatened with defeat, it was fitting that it should end as the country was on the point of victory. By the end of October, the pearls were ready to be turned into necklaces by the top jewellers. The original idea of collecting a few pearls for a single necklace had escalated and at the final count there was a treasure trove of 3,712 pearls, fifty rubies and several diamond and sapphire clasps, from which many necklaces could be created as well as several pearl rings, drop pearls and tiepins.

It was decided that the closing date for the collection of jewels should be on 24 October 1918, which was 'Our Day', the most important fundraising date of the year for the Red Cross, when flag collections and events were held across the country to raise money. The idea was that some people would like to commemorate the charity's special day by giving a final donation to the pearl necklaces.

Once the appeal officially closed, the jewels were handed over to the committee of jewellers who had been collecting the pearls. Mr Pearson from Garrard, Mr Ashwin from the Goldsmiths' & Silversmiths' Company and Mr Carrington Smith from Carrington & Company agreed to grade the pearls into necklaces. It was a time-consuming task. Before their work began, pearl stringers spent two days separating the jewels from the silk exhibition cords they had been suspended on at the Grafton Galleries. Then the three jewellers spent several weeks grading and re-grading nearly 4,000 pearls. They were first judged according to their natural beauty rather than size because it was intended that one as near perfect as possible necklace should be created. The necklaces were tentatively made up and then strung and restrung, as the connoisseurs' skilled eyes selected from one necklace a pearl that would go better in another. The experts knew that the careful matching of pearls in colour, size and shape would make a difference to the necklace's beauty and value. Eventually, after much painstaking work, forty-one necklaces were created.

Many of the jewellers who had been involved in the Pearl Appeal already had close links with the Red Cross, both in England and abroad. Since the time of Florence Nightingale, Garrard had made the medals awarded by the Red Cross to their members who had served with special distinction. From 1915 to 1918 the Royal Red Cross Medal was awarded to nurses who had gone beyond the call of duty. They were given a silver and enamel red cross on a bow ribbon, presented in the distinctive royal blue velvet and cream lining of the Garrard presentation box.

Tiffany was also closely connected to the Red Cross. The three favrile windows in the Board of Governors Hall of the American Red Cross National Headquarters building were commissioned from the Tiffany Studios in 1917. Reputed to be the largest suite of Tiffany windows created for a secular setting, they depict the theme of ministry to the sick and wounded through sacrifice. Although it was in memory of the heroic women of the American Civil War, its symbolism could equally be applied to the work of the Red Cross in the Great War.

The left window panel was inspired by Henry Wadsworth Longfellow's poem, 'Santa Filomena', which commemorated the work of Florence Nightingale, 'A lady with a lamp shall stand in the great history of the land, a noble type of good heroic womanhood'.[4] In the panel, St Filomena, who was noted for her healing powers, is surrounded by female attendants who provide compassion. One carries a shield bearing the Red Cross emblem. She is followed by Hope, carrying a banner with an anchor painted on it. Next to her is Mercy, bearing gifts. Beside her is Faith, who carries a torch, and Charity, who offers a healing drink. In the foreground, a mother holds her child, who has gathered flowers while, in the background, a young woman carries the Red Cross banner.

In the second window panel Tiffany drew on the imagery of chivalric knights representing modern soldiers. The central panel portrays an army of heroic knights on horseback as they set off for war. The central figure carries a large flag with a red cross in the centre. He rides a white horse with a jewelled saddle and bridle; these 'Tiffany jewels' are coloured glass stones. Near the feet of the horse lies a fallen soldier who is being fed by a loyal comrade. The window expresses the idea that even during the brutality of a battle, humanitarian behaviour still exists. The final panel portrays Una, wife of the red cross knight in Edmund Spenser's epic, *The Faerie Queen*. The story represents proper human behaviour – Una symbolises Truth, several maidens accompany her carrying a cross and a lamp of wisdom and behind her is a banner with a heart symbolising love.[5]

The themes of the Tiffany window shared much of the symbolism associated with the pearl necklaces. They too were things of beauty that represented the continuation of humanitarian values in the most barbaric situations. As the pearl necklaces were made up by the jewellers, another layer of symbolism was added. It was decided that all the pearls should become anonymous. In the final necklaces, no one would know whether a string was made up from a jewel from a queen or a young widow. This decision emphasised that each pearl, no matter what its monetary value, was of equal sentimental worth. As *The Times* explained:

> In this is a subtle justice to the generous donors, for a pearl from the necklace of a woman with few jewels, though it might not be as valuable, was often a greater sacrifice than a jewel that was intrinsically more valuable presented by a woman with many jewels.[6]

Like each soldier who had given his life in the war, it was not the rank that counted but the human sacrifice. During the war, class barriers had been broken down as the owners of great estates lived side by side with their men, sharing the camaraderie and the squalor of the trenches. Similarly, in the hospitals, titled nurses had become firm friends with other nurses from different classes. As the Pearl Auction catalogue wrote, 'The pearls themselves have sunk their identity in the privilege of ministering to the sick and wounded, the prisoner, the disabled and the incurable.'[7]

Anonymity added an air of mystery to the pearl necklaces. It was hoped that the most perfect necklace, composed of sixty-three of the finest pearls and Lady Norbury's diamond clasp, would attract the attention of the world's major buyers. However, it was also emphasised that there were many others strings of great beauty. One was a necklace composed almost entirely from fine pearls sent from Lady Wingate's collection in Egypt, the other was a 'specially beautiful' necklace of 'straw-coloured' pearls, which were much sought after by Continental buyers.[8]

The jewellers knew just how much money pearls of this quality could fetch. During the Edwardian era, pearl mania had swept across Europe and America. Since the reign of the French King Louis XIV, diamonds had commanded the highest prices among precious stones. However, around 1900 pearls became more popular and pearls of 100 grains became scarcer than diamonds of 100 carats. The largest pearls were worth four times as much as diamonds of equal weight. Until the middle of the nineteenth century there were very few diamonds weighing 100 carats or over, but once the African mines opened in 1870 the number of large diamonds had increased at a much greater rate than the number of large pearls, and consequently prices of pearls soared.[9] After 1900, whenever a perfect pearl was found in the Persian Gulf the European pearl trade was put on a state of alert. The boom in pearls even affected financial markets. It altered rates of exchange and caused alarm in the banking world because these jewels introduced an unquantifiable element.[10]

Many of the most valuable pearls were sold at auction at Christie's in London. In 1902, Earl Dudley's rose-coloured drop pearl sold for $67,500 while his pearl necklace of forty-seven pearls reached $111,000. In 1907, Mrs Lewis Hill's strand of 229 pearls was auctioned for $83,500, while Mrs Gordon-Lennox's five strands of 287 pearls realised $127,500. To put the results of these sales in perspective, pearls were commanding similar prices to the most expensive paintings. In 1910, J.M.W. Turner's painting 'Rockets and Blue Lights' was auctioned in New York for $129,000.[11]

Cartier, Tiffany and Chaumet were the most important firms in the international pearl market. In 1910 Cartier New York made newspaper headlines by selling a necklace made up of thirty-nine pearls with diamond roundels for a record price of $570,000. The buyer was the urbane American Nancy Leeds, one of Cartier's most regular customers, who was a great collector of pearls. When Edward VII was shown a perfect black pearl by Pierre Cartier in Paris, the king could not make up his mind whether he wanted to buy it, only to learn that in the meantime it had been sold to Mrs Leeds. When he discovered that he was staying at the same Paris hotel as her, he sent a message through Cartier that he would like to see her pearls. Evidently, the meeting went well because afterwards the king asked Cartier to present Mrs Leeds with his dog Caesar's silver collar, which was inscribed, 'I belong to the King'.[12]

The turbulence of war did not deter pearl collectors. In the spring of 1918, a necklace of forty-nine pearls sold at Christie's for more than £17,000. A notable feature of Christie's sales during the Great War was the immense sums spent on jewels. Many of the finest diamonds found their way into the hands of German and Austrian financiers, who invested in jewellery to avoid the fluctuation in their fortunes caused by the falling exchanges. There was also a ready market in smaller, less valuable jewels which were bought by businessmen who had turned their factories into munitions works and preferred to buy jewellery rather than putting their profits into War Loan Stock.[13]

Pearls were aspirational jewels not just for the rich. As society became less hierarchical during the war, it was not only the elite who bought pearl necklaces. In 1918 editions of *The Queen* there were adverts for 'Sessel pearls', 'the finest reproductions existing', made by 'a secret and scientific process which imparts to them the same delicacy of tone, texture and durability as Genuine Oriental Pearls'.[14] Intruding on the territory of the old established jewellers, the Sessel shop in New Bond St, London, offered 'beautiful' necklaces with a gold clasp for £4 4s, or a string with a diamond, ruby, sapphire or emerald clasp from £3 3s. In *The Queen's* 'Dress and Fashion' section, an article promoted the merits of this new type of jewellery:

> Few of us can afford to give the enormous amount of money demanded for real pearls. But there is no reason why we should deny ourselves the very charming addition to our personal jewellery, for there is one kind of imitation pearl which is so perfect as to baffle even experts until the gems are actually handled.[15]

Lady Northcliffe's fundraising efforts had tapped into the aspirational appeal of pearls. The public fascination with every stage of the Red Cross Pearl Necklace Appeal showed no sign of waning as the gems were transformed into necklaces.

This exceptional level of interest was captured in a novel written by the Australian mystery writer, Arthur J. Rees, who had moved to Britain in his twenties. He became a journalist on *The Times* during the war and, judging by his detailed knowledge of the Pearl Appeal, it seems likely that he wrote many of the detailed articles on the jewels which promoted Lady Northcliffe's fundraising. In *The Hand in the Dark*, published in 1920, there is a scene where an international pearl expert, Vincent Musard, held his listeners spellbound at a country house party while he discussed the Pearl Appeal. 'If you admire pearls you should see the collection which is being made for the British Red Cross,' he told his fellow guests, adding, 'I had a private view the other day. It is a truly magnificent collection.' The ladies then eagerly asked him questions, even Miss Garton, a lady journalist and an 'advanced woman', who had campaigned for sex equality was as interested in the pearls as 'the most frivolous members of her sex'. Musard explained that under ordinary circumstances it could take years to match pearls to make a faultless necklace, but because the experts making them up for the Red Cross had such a variety to choose from their task had been comparatively easy. He claimed that although all the pearls were supposed to be anonymous, it would be a simple matter for a trained eye to identify a number of the most distinctive individual pearls. He finished by explaining the enduring allure of historic jewellery like the Red Cross Pearls:

> All great jewels have [...] dual histories. Their careers as cut and polished gems is only the second part. Infinitely more interesting is the hidden history of each great jewel, from the discovery of the rough stone to the period when it reaches the hand of the lapidary, to be polished and cut for a drawing room existence. What a record of intrigue and knavery, stabbings and poisoning [is] connected with some of the greatest jewels.[16]

It was this hidden history of the Red Cross Pearls that made them so precious. With the fashionable world's obsession with pearls showing no sign of ending, as the jewellers put their final touches to the pearl necklaces there was great anticipation about who would buy them and just how much money they would make.

Before sending them to Christie's, the jewellers packed the pearls in specially designed cases of royal blue velvet with a white lining, on the top was shown a red cross. Connoisseurs were unanimous that a finer collection of pearls had never been offered for auction in London.

FOURTEEN

PEARLS OF PEACE

At the eleventh hour of the eleventh day of the eleventh month in 1918 guns were fired across London to mark the signing of the armistice. A vast crowd gathered outside Buckingham Palace waiting for the king and queen to come out. When they appeared on the balcony looking like two tiny dolls, they were given a spontaneous ovation that was so loud and continued for so long no one could hear a word that the king said. For the rest of the day, a good-humoured crowd swarmed through the capital shouting with joy that the war was finally coming to an end. Adding to the noise was the hooting of horns from cars crammed full of excited passengers. According to Cynthia Asquith, it was a pleasure to see the wide grins on the soldiers' faces and elderly couples dancing in the street.[1]

However, although there was great relief that the fighting was over, there were mixed emotions. For many it was more a day for remembering the loved ones who would never return than rejoicing at the victory. Having lost two sons in the war, Mary Wemyss wrote in her diary:

> It is their Victory – it is also the <u>saddest</u> peace and except for a few Babies in their teens, <u>no one</u> can be light of heart and to most of us almost the hardest part is now beginning. <u>We miss our shining victors in the hour of victory.</u>[2]

As they had done throughout the war, Mary and her closest friend Ettie Desborough supported each other through this emotional time. While the jubilant crowds partied in London, they stayed quietly at their homes, Stanway and Taplow, where they felt closest to their lost sons. Without saying a word, they both knew what the other was going through. Ettie told Mary that the thought of her had 'burnt in her innermost heart' all day. She echoed her friend's words, writing, 'Victory and we look in vain for our Victors.'[3] For once, Ettie admitted to feeling a sense of emptiness and sadness. Friends noticed that the war years had changed her. She had become more beautiful, but it was a fragile beauty and her face showed that she had suffered deeply. She frequently quoted a line from Maurice Baring's elegy to her cousin Bron Lucas, 'Something is broken which we cannot mend.'[4]

However, no matter how broken she felt inside, on the surface Ettie put a positive gloss on events. Perhaps to convince herself as much as her friends, she wrote in November 1918:

> They died for the needs of grace and for the hope of glory, and it has not been in vain – the cause has triumphed that they all sprang out to serve and it is their Peace. I feel as if they were all so proud and glad, and not counting the cost – and that the pain is only ours, still held in mental bondage.[5]

As usual, Mary sensitively avoided getting into a potentially divisive debate with her friend about their sons' sacrifice by replying simply, 'Darling, I was not going to say anything of all the thoughts and agonies that are surging through our shattered, glory-crested lives – because I hope to see you soon.'[6]

Typically selfless, both Mary and Ettie immediately thought of others rather than themselves. When the armistice was declared, Mary wrote to her daughter-in-law Letty Elcho, knowing how difficult it would be for her that her husband Ego would not be returning. Ettie also tried to console the young widow by drawing on her faith in an afterlife. Expressing more grief for Letty than she would for herself, she wrote:

> Oh darling how the thought of you has ached at my heart all through these days […] Only my Letty, I just cannot bear to think of you although I know how nobly you are bearing these days, as you have borne all – Ego must feel so triumphant over you, that look in his eyes that was only there for you – and you know that he is waiting for you, beautiful and young for evermore.[7]

Lacking Ettie's Christian certainty, members of the younger generation struggled to come to terms with the slaughter of so many of their contemporaries. On the brink of a brief nervous breakdown, Mary's daughter Cynthia Asquith wrote in her diary:

> I think it [peace] will require more courage than anything that has gone before. It isn't until one leaves off spinning round that one realises how giddy one is. One will have to look at long vistas again, instead of short ones, and one will at last fully recognise that the dead are not only dead for the duration of the war.[8]

The armistice changed the situation for the Red Cross Pearl Necklace as well as for the women who had given to it. The appeal came to completion at the same time as the cessation of the war. In these changed circumstances, it was important to keep the public interested in the fate of the pearls if they were to make as much money as possible for wounded soldiers returning from the war. In a letter sent out to local and national papers on 25 November, Princess Victoria and Lady Northcliffe explained that the Red Cross' need for funds was as great as ever:

> Let no one think that the signing of the armistice brings with it the instant evacuation of our hospitals. Treatment and after-care for thousands of wounded men must be continued for months, and alas! In many cases for years. The public may rest assured that the money which the pearls yield will be applied faithfully to the care of the wounded and to the all-essential task of fitting these gallant sufferers to face the life which lies before them.[9]

Emphasising the historic interest of the pearls which had been 'offered with such glad self-sacrifice' by so many women, they hoped that at the auction the public would come forward and 'give not merely what the necklaces are worth, but what the occasion and the cause demand'.[10]

The pearls now became part of one of the first post-war acts of remembrance. The jewels were on display for three days at Messrs Christie, Manson and Woods' King Street salerooms. There was a private viewing on 16 December when the price of admission was 5*s* including a copy of the auction catalogue. At the private view, most of the visitors were women. According to the *Daily Mail*, 'Many of them wore magnificent pearls. But it was notable that even the women with the finest pearls looked wistfully at some of the Red Cross Necklaces.'[11]

Admission was free on 17 and 18 December to make sure that the pearls could be seen by as many people as possible. By 10 a.m. on the opening day, crowds were eagerly waiting outside the doors of Christie's. Describing the scene, *The Queen* wrote, 'The thoroughfare was literally besieged; people who had never been in a crowd before waited and jostled with more or less good humour.'[12] In the first hour, 300 people inspected the pearls, and throughout the rest of the day the crowd was never less than three deep around the showcases. The pearls were simply displayed in sombre, oblong, black boxes. Prospective buyers asked saleroom officials to take out the necklaces so that they could be more closely examined. Schoolgirls back for the Christmas holidays admired the 'young' necklaces made of smaller pearls. However, nearly everyone was speculating about how much money Lot No. 101, the finest pearl necklace with the Norbury diamond clasp, would make. One lady said:

> Whatever it fetches will not matter to the buyer. […] It will be historic as the jewels of Marie Antoinette; it will be an heirloom more famed than the Hope diamond. Other pearls came from the sea. These pearls came from human hearts, and human tenderness and gratitude will run up their purchase price.[13]

The first day was busy but the second day was even more crowded. Soon after 10 in the morning, the queue became so long that it wound around the outer room and stretched down the stairs across Christie's' reception hall and out into the street. The crowds continued all day long and, as so many people patiently and persistently awaited their turn, inspection of the pearls could only be tantalisingly brief. On the final day the crowds were greater than ever and included people of every rank in life. Servicemen, home on leave, and their wives regarded the collection as one of the sights of the town.

The Pearl Necklace Auction was not the first sale held by Christie's for the Red Cross. Since 1915 the auction house had been putting on sales free of charge to raise funds. Like other businesses, Christie's had been greatly affected by the war. When the conflict began, one of the partners, Captain Victor Agnew, and many of the male staff volunteered to fight. In the first months of the war, work for the auction house was in short supply. After the last sale of the summer season in July 1914 not a single work of art came onto the market and the business looked like closing down temporarily.

However, then Christie's' fortunes changed.[14] Many people who could not afford to send money to the Red Cross started sending gifts instead, the fundraisers asked Christie's to auction them and Alec Martin, the firm's managing director, generously agreed to give their services and the use of their staff and salerooms free of charge. The auction house received and acknowledged all gifts as well as cataloguing the lots, publishing the catalogues, storing the lots, taking the sales, taking payment from successful bidders and then packing the lots in readiness for them to be taken away with their new owners.

The first Red Cross sale held in April 1915 was an experiment. Running for twelve days, it generated a great deal of interest. Under the headline 'Selling Household Goods for Charity', the *Illustrated London News* ran a full-page painting of the first day of the auction.[15] In the picture, ladies in plumed picture hats or elegant toques are crammed into the auction room with men in glossy top hats and bowlers. Beside the elegant auctioneer on the rostrum, a man in a cloth cap and tweeds holds up a seventeenth-century sporting rifle which had been donated by the king to be auctioned. Pencils in hand, ready to mark their auction catalogues, the keen bidders are all straining to get a view. The newspaper reported that as the bidding began there was a round of applause and after seven bids this unusual lot sold for 350 guineas.[16]

The king's gun was one among an eclectic range of 1,867 lots on offer. Another royal donation was a life-sized bust of the artist James Abbott McNeill Whistler made out of terracotta by Princess Louise, Duchess of Argyll, which sold for 75 guineas. One of the most poignant donations were two Irish silver potato rings belonging to a young flying officer, Samuel Pepys Cockerell, who had been killed in Egypt. They were bought for 1,000 guineas by Lord Newlands, who immediately returned them to the officer's parents in memory of their son. Although the artist John Singer Sargent had abandoned portrait painting, he was persuaded to do one more as a donation for the Red Cross Auction. Sir Hugh Lane paid £10,000 for this portrait. However, the question of the sitter had not been decided at the time and Sir Hugh died just a month later in the sinking of the *Lusitania*. It was finally agreed by his trustees that the portrait should be of the American President Woodrow Wilson.[17]

The most flamboyant figure at the auction was the wealthy widow, Lady Wernher. Over the next few years she became known as the heroine of the Red Cross sales. At the first one held in 1915 *The Sketch* recorded:

> Lady Wernher marked her Christie catalogue with much more spirit than most other women can muster when they make a book for Punchestown or see their programmes filled at a country dance. She treated the great sale as if it were the sporting event of the week, took any number of risks and enjoyed herself despite the somewhat gloomy company surrounding her.[18]

When her neighbour asked if she was interested in the next lot, she said with a laugh, 'Do you think I *really* want anything?'

The question needed no answer. As the widow of Sir Julius Wernher, the South African financier and gold and diamond mining magnate, Alice (known as Birdie) had more than enough of everything. Partly of Polish origin, Birdie was petite, bright-eyed and blonde. Famous for her glamorous pre-war parties, her lavish tastes had always been indulged by her husband. She rushed into events like a human dynamo, swathed in furs over her Worth gowns and magnificent jewels. Although with her husband's business she could have worn the finest diamonds in the world, she often chose to wear pearls.

During the Edwardian era, the Wernhers lived in considerable style in Bath House, a mansion on Piccadilly, opposite the Ritz Hotel, and at their Bedfordshire estate, Luton Hoo. Famed for its grand belle époque interiors, semi-Palladian exterior and its Lancelot 'Capability' Brown park, Luton Hoo was more a palace than a country house. On their estate, the Wernhers employed fifty-four gardeners, twenty or thirty house servants and ten electricians. Every aspect of their lifestyle was on the grand scale, in their conservatory alone there were 4,000 potted carnations.[19]

The Wernhers' opulence was criticised by some as vulgar and materialistic. After dining at Bath House, the Fabian and socialist Beatrice Webb wrote that there might just as well have been a goddess of gold erected to overtly worship.[20] She described Birdie as badly bred and too talkative. Although Beatrice conceded that her hostess was a clever woman, she complained that she was too aware of her wealth and talked of nothing except her possessions. The socialist even criticised Birdie's style, disliking the extravagance of her jewels and her clothes. She considered her to be 'essentially ugly', both in her person, manners and speed, because she was always frenetically rushing from one place to another.[21]

In fact, Birdie had far more depth than Beatrice imagined. A talented pianist, she invited the leading musicians of the era, Feodor Chaliapin, Richard Tauber and the Menuhins, to play at her musical soirees. Both husband and wife were avid art collectors. Sir Julius had one of the finest collections of medieval ivories, Renaissance jewellery and bronzes, as well as some superb old master paintings by Rubens, Titian and Reynolds. Many of his pictures were of the Virgin and Child and it is thought that these were bought largely to please his wife. Birdie's own collection of English porcelain, which began as a hobby, grew into an obsession until it was rivalled only by the royal family and the Victoria and Albert Museum. Although Sir Julius was born in Germany, during the Edwardian era, he became a well-respected member of British society who was known for his probity and philanthropy. Unaware of Beatrice Webb's attacks on his wife, he gave generous donations to her pet project, the 'Charlottenburg Scheme', which became the present-day Imperial College of Science and Technology.[22]

In 1912 Sir Julius died leaving more than £11 million, which was the largest South African fortune on record. At first Birdie was too bereft to attend her husband's funeral. However, she gradually acclimatised to widowhood. She was left an exceptionally wealthy widow; Luton Hoo and Bath House went to her for her lifetime, she also received income from a £1 million trust.[23] Making the most of her new independent status, Birdie reinvented herself. She dyed her hair, keeping a distinctive, stylish white streak down the middle and even daringly wore trousers to play tennis.[24]

Although, Birdie did not need, or even really want, any of the items on sale at the Red Cross Auction, she was determined to raise as much money as possible for the cause. Whenever the price of a valuable lot needed hoisting she started bidding large amounts to encourage others. One of the most prized donations was a Stradivarius violin from Lord Newlands. Birdie bought it for £2,500, then she called out, 'Be quick! Tell the auctioneer to offer it again.' Auctioned for a second time, it raised another £1,400 for the charity. She did not stop there, later in the day she also bought a manuscript chapter from Charles Dickens' *The Pickwick Papers* and a Jane Austen manuscript which she gave to the British Museum.[25]

As less exciting items came up, she went on buying. 'Heavens, its mine!' she would say to her neighbour as the hammer fell. No doubt she had visions of Luton Hoo piled with packing cases full of bric-a-brac, but she did not mind.[26] Her enthusiasm energised the atmosphere at Christie's, as *The Sketch* explained, she showed 'a genius for seeming extraordinarily gay over endless unnecessary additions to the already endless list of her superfluous possessions'.[27] Her liveliness was so essential that when she left her place for just five minutes a gloom fell over the auctioneer on the podium and her neighbours seated near her. Their spirits flagged until her return.

It was generous benefactors like Birdie that made the 1915 sale a success. The final sum raised at the auction was almost £38,000. Recognising how much the charity owed her, the former librarian of the House of Lords and poet, Edmund Gosse, who had been sitting next to her at the auction, felt she should have a memento of the sale. 'Your catalogue is shabby,' he said to her. 'I'm going to buy you another and bind it in morocco – red morocco.' With her usual charm, she replied, 'And write in it,' acting as if this was the greatest gift she had ever received.[28]

When Birdie encouraged an encore of the Red Cross Auction at Christie's the following year, the gossip columnists described her as 'nothing less than heroic'.[29] Perhaps she spotted an opportunity to recycle some of the unwanted items she had bought in the previous sale by donating them to the 1916 auction, however, she also gave some valuable items from her own collections. She donated exquisite pieces of old lace, silver, jewels and a seventeenth-century enamelled badge with views of castles, flowers and the Cross of St John of Jerusalem in white on a blue background on one side and a male saint and angels on the other.[30]

Her gifts to the Red Cross were just one of the ways she did her bit for the war effort. When the war was declared, Luton Hoo became the 3rd Army Headquarters. However, Birdie was not happy with the arrangement. She wrote to the king's private secretary, Lord Stamfordham, complaining that she felt like a guest in her own house. She said that she had only stayed on to make sure everything was done properly. She provided the Officers' Mess with fruit, game, cigars, wine and flowers, but there were complaints that she kept too many rooms for herself and had removed many works of art and rugs from the rooms the army were using.

As well as writing to Lord Stamfordham, she also contacted Lord Kitchener. Her concerns were listened to and within a fortnight her beautiful home was returned to her. Later in the war, Luton Hoo became a convalescent home for officers and Birdie contributed £1,000 to the running costs.[31] She also donated £500 to a base hospital in France and occasionally opened her London home for fundraising events for war charities. However, when she was offered an OBE for her war work she refused, saying that it would be criminal to own Bath House and not give parties.[32]

Birdie was not the only person who raided their possessions to support the Red Cross. Soon, thousands of gifts were flooding in for the 1916 auction. However, as Christie's were once more busy with their own work, at the same time as coping with a depleted staff, the Red Cross decided that they would collect the goods themselves. To accommodate all the items, they set up a depot at 48 Pall Mall and several subcommittees were formed to deal with the different types of gifts. Lady Northcliffe volunteered to help in the china and furniture department. She was to use the experience she gained, encouraging contributions, sorting out the donations and then cataloguing them, two years later in the Pearl Appeal. As *The Sketch* noted, she was particularly suited to the task as she had 'long been known to have the flair for serendipity in the world of curio-shops: on motor journeys with her husband hers has always been the eye that singled out the likely showpiece in the likely shop, in the likely village'.[33]

In the run-up to the sale, the Red Cross volunteers were inundated. Thousands of gifts came pouring in at the back and front of the depot. The parcel post was always at the door and vans were constantly arriving and unloading. Grand ladies slipped in, quietly left their valuable gifts and disappeared again.

Poorer people were just as ready to contribute to the Red Cross auctions as the rich. However, the public's generosity caused some problems. The Red Cross privately reported:

> The deluge of almost valueless things, dear to their owners but almost useless as money-makers, threatened at one time to overwhelm the willing assistants at the depot. It is a mistake, therefore, to invite the population to turn out their old drawers and cupboards and send the contents to the Red Cross for a Christie's Sale.[34]

At the depot, all donations were recorded before being sent to Christie's in King Street. Inevitably, mishaps occasionally arose. One list read:

2416. Lady Glitterham, a diamond tiara.
3750. Miss Smith, a cup and saucer.

When the tiara could not be traced, a frantic search took place at the depot. Finally it was rediscovered, but it turned out to be not an aristocratic heirloom but a paste bangle. The second entry passed unnoticed until someone asked, 'What do you think of the Sèvres écuelle?' Miss Smith's 'cup and saucer' was in fact a piece of priceless porcelain.[35] There were also some bizarre gifts, as a *Times* journalist asked, 'What was an already overworked staff to do with a live goat which presented itself one day at the office demanding to be sold by auction at Christie's?'[36]

The sale scheduled to be held in April 1916 lasted for fifteen days and, on this occasion, raised nearly £64,000. For the second year running, *Punch* magazine donated a cartoon done especially for the event. In 1915 the cartoonist F.H. Townsend had drawn a cross between Britannia and Lady Diana Manners in a Roman toga with the St John and Red Cross emblems on her front. She stood with her empty hands outstretched waiting to receive gifts, above the caption, 'For the Wounded'. In 1916 the same figure made a second appearance, this time with her hands holding back the curtains as if she is on a stage. Representing the return of the Red Cross Auction, the caption reads, 'Recalled'. It was bought by a member of the Red Cross Committee, who presented it to Christie's as a token of the charity's appreciation of the auction house's generosity.

Christie's had created just the right atmosphere for the sales. They had 'the ideal auctioneer' in their senior partner, Lance Hannen. His encyclopaedic knowledge of art values and his 'finish and finesse' made him perfectly suited to his task. Once he entered the rostrum, he never orated but simply introduced 'Lot One'. As he looked over his half-rimmed spectacles, assessing potential bidders, his style and timing were faultless. As one columnist noted, 'The drop of the eyelids, somebody said the other day is very like the Lord Chief Justice's [...] only the King Street L.C.J. is a trifle more blasé.'[37]

In the run-up to the third great Red Cross sale in 1917, conditions in the labour market had become very difficult. Christie's' staff was reduced to a minimum as men had been replaced by untrained girls. The printers who produced the catalogue were also short staffed, and paper was growing scarce. Knowing the constraints Christie's were working under, the Red Cross Committee tactfully tried to obtain a smaller number of gifts of greater value for this year's auction. However, the desire to give did not decrease and 2,132 items came in.[38]

Red Cross volunteers did everything they could to reduce the pressure on the auction house and Birdie Wernher was more involved than ever behind the scenes. As *The Sketch* journalist wrote, she was 'head over heels in a hundred little responsibilities' connected with the auction.[39] This year she had a particularly personal reason for being so active. During the war all three of her sons fought for their country. Her youngest son Alex insisted on leaving Eton when he was only 17 to join the army, however, at first he was refused a commission on medical grounds because he had poor eyesight. Disappointed, but determined to do his bit for the war, he worked with the Red Cross, then he went to Rouen as an interpreter before finally getting a commission in the Royal Bucks Hussars in 1915. The following year, he transferred to the Welsh Guards and fought with them at the Front. His family knew that he would never be happy until he had served in the trenches.

In September 1916, he was injured in the leg during the Battle of Delville Wood. Left in no man's land for a time, he was being dragged back to an ambulance when he was shot by a sniper in the head. He was 19 years old when he died.[40] Just a few months later, Lady Wernher contributed £2 million to the government's war loan in his memory. As one newspaper commented, drawing on all the hyperbole it could muster, this was 'the greatest loan that any private individual has ever made out of pure love of country in the history of the world'.[41] Helping at the Christie's sales was another way for Birdie to commemorate her son and distract herself from her grief.

The auction in March 1917 raised nearly £72,000. Birdie was under the rostrum in King Street for the twelve days it ran, 'gingering up other bidders and generally setting the pace in scores of small deals, ranging from 10 shillings to a thousand pounds a piece'.[42] At this sale, she bought a Fred Walker painting, 'The Plough', for £5,400 and then donated it to the nation. Perhaps the most unusual lot at the sale was the original 'golliwog', and the drawings and manuscripts of the eleven golliwog children's books, presented by the artist, Florence Upton. The shy creator of the much-loved books came to the auction to hear the final speeches. Although she knew Lady Northcliffe and Sir Robert Hudson, who were also in the room, she described the event as a terrible trial for her nerves. As her name was mentioned she felt panicky and soon left Christie's with trembling legs and stiff muscles.[43] However, Florence was delighted with the result, her creations raised £1,995. The book with the, to modern ears, contentious politically incorrect title *The Golliwog Fox Hunt*, was presented to the London Museum, while the golliwog dolls went on loan to the prime minister's country residence, Chequers. The proceeds from this quirky donation were used to buy and equip an ambulance which went immediately to France. On each side of the vehicle, beneath the Red Cross sign, was printed in large letters, 'Florence Upton and the Golliwogs gave this ambulance'. No doubt the inscription would have amused many of the young soldiers who had grown up on the golliwog books.[44]

The fourth Red Cross sale, held in April 1918, made the most money, realising £150,000. Perhaps this was because unlike the first auction three years before which had been like a white elephant stall, this time it was more like a 'young museum'. There was Hepplewhite furniture, Persian carpets, sable coats and a unique tortoiseshell birdcage on sale. Lord Kitchener's family donated scimitars and pistols from his collection. The artists Frank Dicksee, John Lavery and William Orpen all agreed to paint a portrait for the highest bidders.

When Max Beerbohm offered to do a caricature of the Christie's auction, Birdie Wernher could not resist buying it and then presenting it to Christie's as an enduring reminder of their support for the Red Cross. The atmosphere at these auctions was captured in Beerbohm's cartoon. Beneath the elegant portraits, the saleroom is dominated by rather grotesque men of all shapes and sizes in top hats and bowlers. They include the writers J.M. Barrie, Joseph Conrad and Edmund Gosse, the actor Gerald du Maurier and the Red Cross champion and politician, Lord Lansdowne. The only woman present is the imposing fur-clad figure of Birdie.

The Red Cross auctions altered the way the art world was perceived. The image of it as an elitist and self-indulgent clique was broken down as Christie's and many artists gave their services for free, and wealthy art collectors donated their much-loved treasures. The element of sacrifice involved impressed the public. Instead of being enjoyed by only the privileged few, luxury items were now used as a type of currency to redistribute wealth to be spent on those who most needed care.[45]

The earlier Red Cross auctions paved the way for Lady Northcliffe's sale of the pearls. It drew on many of the same principles and people. However, one of the main differences between the Pearl Necklace Auction and the other Christie's sales was that this time the auction was a uniquely female tribute to the war heroes. With an emotive story behind each pearl, it promised to be the most poignant Christie's sale of all.

FIFTEEN

THE PEARL NECKLACE AUCTION

On the day of the Pearl Necklace Auction, London was preparing to show its pride in its heroes. At 1 p.m. on Thursday, 19 December 1918, Field Marshall Sir Douglas Haig and his generals arrived in the capital for a victory parade. Escorted by a fleet of aeroplanes, they had travelled from Dover by special train to Charing Cross Station where they were greeted by the Duke of Connaught, on behalf of the king, and the past and present prime ministers, Asquith and Lloyd George. They then travelled through Trafalgar Square, Piccadilly, Hyde Park and along Constitution Hill to lunch with the king and queen at Buckingham Palace. Thousands of people lined the route and, as the carriages passed, those standing on balconies showered flowers on the victors.

However, the parade was not staged as a full-blown military pageant because the official welcome was reserved for 'when the men come marching home'. Haig was determined that nothing should rob his 'comrades', the rank and file of servicemen, of their share of the glory.[1] As this parade was more a personal and spontaneous demonstration of gratitude rather than a formal, organised event, Haig's homecoming had a special quality. One newspaper commented, 'We who are the most emotional people in the world, and most habituated to the control and repression of our emotions prize the spontaneous expression most. It is only when we do let ourselves go, as did the cheering crowds yesterday, that our real warmth appears.'[2]

The clamour had hardly died down before some members of the patriotic crowd rushed off to Christie's for the Red Cross Auction. Haig's arrival had only been announced a few days before and, knowing that many people would want to attend both historic events, at the last minute, Lady Northcliffe and her team postponed the auction by half an hour.

It was only a short walk from Haig's parade to Christie's in King Street. As supporters of the Red Cross gathered in the auction house's impressive red-walled saleroom beneath historic portraits and paintings, there were many more women present than at most sales. Many members of the committee were there, hoping that all their hard work would now pay off. Joining Lady Northcliffe and Lady Sarah Wilson was Alice Keppel. The auction had all the cachet of a society event. The former prime minister's daughter, Elizabeth Asquith, was there with her fiancé, Prince Bibesco, while Birdie Wernher had brought along her daughter-in-law, Lady Zia Wernher. Zia added to the glamour of the occasion.

The daughter of Grand Duke Michael of Russia and a descendant of Catherine the Great and Pushkin, she had married Birdie's second son, Sir Harold Wernher, the previous year in the most fashionable wedding of the season. The alliance had been widely discussed in the newspapers. Inheriting much of his father's fortune, Harold was one of the richest bachelors in England. In the past, Zia had been a social butterfly but as her family had been ruined by the Russian Revolution she now needed to settle on a wealthy husband. The more uncharitable gossip columnists described it as a marriage of convenience. 'Eve' in *Tatler* snobbishly commented on the 'topsy turvy world' of 'these democratic days' when the son of a self-made millionaire could marry the daughter of a Russian Imperial Highness.[3]

However, the couple were well-matched. Zia had never cared much about status and according to one observer had 'practically revolted before the revolution'.[4] Rushing around London in her Calthorpe motor car, she was involved in fundraising for war charities. With her sister, she had come up with the idea of launching an appeal for a million gloves and mittens for the British Expeditionary Force. In response, many of their grand friends got their knitting needles out, creating an odd assortment of garments which the girls then sorted and packed to be sent to the front line.

Harold was not just exceptionally rich, he was also a courageous soldier. He had an impressive war record, having been mentioned three times in Despatches for his bravery while fighting in France.[5] By the time of the auction, the Wernhers had much to celebrate as their first son had been born on 22 August 1918.

When the auction began at 1.30 p.m. the atmosphere at Christie's was highly charged as the auctioneer, William Burn Anderson, entered the Chippendale rostrum. Antique ivory-headed hammer in his hand, he addressed the crowded room explaining that previous Red Cross sales had been held under the clouds of a terrible war, while the present sale was taking place after the great and glorious victory of the Allies. The cessation of hostilities did not mean that the Red Cross' work was finished – far from it. They still needed money to tend to the wounded, and he appealed to his audience to keep that thought in their minds as they bid for the pearls today. He added that those who bought the jewels would receive 'something which is not only of intrinsic value, but also of considerable historic interest; for these Red Cross Pearls have become historic'.[6]

When the first lot, a brilliant pave ring, was put up, Mr Anderson read a letter which had been received that morning from the entrepreneur and philanthropist, Sir Francis Trippel. Offering £1,000 for the first four lots, he wrote that if they fell to him they should be put up for auction again, as he only wished to give, not to buy. His letter gave advice to other bidders: 'Give till your sides ache, so that the financial success of the sale may be worthy of the Red Cross, the most deserving and the most humane of war charities.'[7]

Before the forty-one pearl necklaces were auctioned there was the sale of other pearl jewellery, including earrings, pearl pins, brooches and rings. Many of the early jewels realised high prices. Among the buyers was Frank Partridge, an art dealer whose saleroom was based in Bond Street, near Christie's in King Street. He bought a brooch set with five pearls and diamond scrolls for £75. Partridge had a particular reason to give thanks. In 1915, he had visited New York to open an office on Fifth Avenue. Although warnings had been given out that any ship crossing the Atlantic flying the British flag was liable to be destroyed by the Germans, in May 1915 Frank decided to take the risk and return to England. He had been invited by eight dealer friends to join them aboard the *Lusitania*. However, the night before they sailed Frank became apprehensive, fearing that the ship would sink. Weighing up the options, he decided to go but he told a friend that he was going to sit on deck each night with a lifejacket on.

His fears were realised when the *Lusitania* was torpedoed by a German submarine off Kinsale, Ireland. The ship sank within eighteen minutes and out of the 1,959 passengers, only 761 survived. Frank was the sole member of his party of nine not to drown. The sinking of the *Lusitania* was seen as a new low point in Germany's conduct of the war. The Germans argued, correctly, that the ship had been carrying ammunition and that Britain was also guilty of violating the freedom of the seas by enforcing its blockade of Germany. However, the Royal Navy had not sunk ships without warning and they had not deliberately killed citizens of neutral countries.[8] The *Lusitania* had many women and children aboard and their loss particularly horrified the British and American public. A recruiting poster appeared calling on all patriots to 'Remember the *Lusitania*'. It had no picture, just text describing how a mother had been thrown into the sea with three of her children. She tried to hold onto them until a lifeboat arrived but her attempts to save them failed. By the time the rescue boat came her children were all dead. With her hair streaming down her back and shaking with sorrow she gently took each of her children from the rescuers and placed them back in the sea. Lord Northcliffe took the tragic story a stage further, and under the headline 'British and American Babies Murdered by the Kaiser', the *Daily Mail* published a shocking photograph of dead children.[9]

Frank saw his survival as a miracle and thanked God for having spared him. As a dealer he had regularly attended Christie's auctions for many years. However, after his fortunate escape, he sometimes bought items for sentimental rather than commercial reasons. The Pearl Auction was not the first time he had 'lifted bidding into the plane of honour'. The art dealer was a friend and advisor on Chinese porcelain to Lord Kitchener, who was a keen collector. Just a few days before he set sail on HMS *Hampshire*, the secretary of state for war had sent for Frank to ask him to buy on his behalf an enamelled bowl decorated with 'The Eight Immortals' at a Christie's sale. Days after Frank received the shocking news that Lord Kitchener had drowned, he attended the Chinese porcelain sale held on 22 June 1916 at the auction house, determined to honour his friend's last request. As Lot 165 came under the auctioneer's elegant hammer, Frank bid £241 10s for the decorated ceramic bowl. No doubt the sinking of the *Hampshire* revived painful memories of being aboard the *Lusitania* the previous year because Frank then donated the so-called 'Kitchener bowl' to the London Museum as 'a little tribute to the memory of the great dead'.[10]

The real excitement at the December 1918 sale began when the pearl necklaces were auctioned. At 3.30 p.m. there was a flutter of anticipation as Lot 95, the first of the strings, was brought out and shown to the audience by one of Christie's young women attendants. It sold for £2,200. The tension increased and there was a sense of drama as the lights went up and Mr Anderson introduced 'the necklace of necklaces', Lot 101, the most perfect pearls with the Norbury diamond clasp. The first bid was £20,000 then, with his encouraging smile, the auctioneer looked for nods around the room. Bids rose in steps of £500 until the necklace was sold to Mr Carrington Smith with his bid of £22,000. Carrington Smith was one of the jewellers who had served on the Red Cross Jewellery Committee and had helped to receive and grade the pearls.

Before the auction, *The Times* expressed a hope that the necklaces would be bought by private collectors rather than by dealers 'who might not properly appreciate the sentimental value attached to them'.[11] In fact, several dealers were buying that afternoon. Mr Carrington Smith was the most prolific, with S.J. Philips and Max Mayer also acquiring jewels. A Hatton Garden diamond merchant, Mayer, who was a world-renowned expert on pearls, bought two relatively modest lots: a scarf pin for £105 and a pair of drop pearls for £370.

Perhaps his restraint was due to his unfortunate experience with pearls five years earlier. In the summer of 1913 Mayer had sent a string of sixty-one flawless oriental pearls of 'a fine, warm, rosy tint' with a diamond clasp to a potential buyer in Paris.[12] The pearls had taken ten years to collect and the necklace was known as 'The Mona Lisa of Pearls' because of the lustre and quality of the gems, which were perfectly matched and graded. Considered the finest pearl necklace in existence, it was insured by Lloyds Underwriters for £150,000. Unfortunately, the prospective buyer chose not to purchase the pearls and the necklace was returned by registered post in a wooden box, wrapped in blue linen and sealed with seven large red seals. When the parcel arrived back in London, Mayer broke the intact seals and opened the box to find that the necklace was missing. Bizarrely, in its place were sugar lumps and a section of a French newspaper. Not wanting to make the huge insurance pay-out, Lloyds offered a reward of £10,000 for the necklace's return. After a short investigation, the police arrested Joseph Grizzard, a well-known jewel thief, but the pearls were still missing. Two weeks later, they reappeared after a member of Grizzard's gang panicked and dropped the pearls, which were wrapped in a small brown parcel, into a gutter in Highbury. A passer-by saw him do this and after opening the intriguing packet he handed one of the priceless pearls to a street urchin, who then played marbles with it. He gave the rest to the police and received the reward. Max Mayer never tried to sell the pearls as a single piece again. Instead, they were divided. By the time of the Christie's Pearl Auction it seems his pearl collecting was on a less ambitious scale.

Although more women bought items at this auction than was usual at Christie's sales, the male professionals still bought the vast majority of the lots. Journalists claimed that few women had the 'courage' to bid beyond the sum of £50 at auctions and many were 'overawed by those plain-clothes policemen of the collecting world – the dealers'. The amateur females were deterred by the self-assurance of the 'top-hatted gentry of the trade' who were backed by commissions. Apparently, these ladies often went to auctions intending to bid but ended up watching the items they wanted fall for less than they would have paid to the 'unperturbed Amors and Andrades [dealer] of St James's Street and the neighbourhood', their feminine 'fluttering hesitation' ending in misses.[13] Birdie Wernher was one of the few women with the confidence and independent income to compete on equal terms with the men. At the Pearl Auction she bought two necklaces, however, rather than keeping them for herself she gave them back to be sold again.

Reflecting a changing society, where financiers, war profiteers and entrepreneurs had more readily available money than ancient aristocratic families, Lady Wernher was one of the few titled bidders of the day. The only other person with a title to buy pearls was Lord Rowallan. Born Cameron Corbett, he was a property developer who bought Rowallan Castle in Kilmarnock, Scotland, as his country estate and he was created a baron in 1911. Known for his strong social conscience and as a generous benefactor, he bought a pearl necklace composed of seventy-one pearls with a ruby clasp for £1,400. His wartime experience reflected the mixed emotions of sorrow and thanksgiving that lay behind so many of the pearls' stories. During the war, all three of his children, including his only daughter Elsie, served their country. As a widower left to 'hold the fort' on the Rowallan estate, he was lonely. However, he made no attempt to dissuade them. His eldest son, Godfrey, wrote, 'He knew the grave threats our small country faced from the mighty German war machine, and as a Corbett he was committed to the philosophy of service and sacrifice.'[14]

It was no surprise that Elsie wanted to play her part in the war like her brothers. Her upbringing had filled her with unconventional ideas and ideals. Several of her late mother's friends had been militant suffragettes and they influenced her. She had always longed to be a doctor and as a child she used to play with a toy Red Cross hospital while her brothers played with toy soldiers. Before the war she had little outlet for her potential. A gauche young woman, the balls and shooting parties that were part of the social season left her unsatisfied. As soon as war was declared, she could not wait to be actively involved. Aged 21 she became a Red Cross nurse and went to Serbia.

From May to August 1915 she worked in a children's fever hospital. She then moved to a surgical hospital where, along with other members of the unit, she was taken prisoner by the invading enemy when Austria–Hungary and Germany launched an offensive against Serbia in the autumn. With characteristic sangfroid, in a letter to her father she assured him that she was well and receiving considerate treatment. She explained, 'Being taken prisoner is not nearly so exciting as it sounds.'[15] She wrote that both friends and foes in Serbia always respected the Red Cross and so she never experienced anything other than 'the most wonderful helpfulness'.[16]

Elsie and her comrades were held prisoner for four months before the Germans agreed to repatriate them. In February 1916, she returned to England looking tired and haggard. However, she was undeterred by her experience and a few months later she went back to work with the Scottish Women's Hospital's Motor Ambulance Column. Frequently facing enemy fire, Elsie would drive her ambulance car through rain and snow as fast as she could in the mountains, along treacherous roads with hairpin bends and unfenced precipices. Sometimes the patients she had collected would be screaming out with pain from their wounds in the back of her ambulance, but Elsie was undeterred. On one occasion, the pin in the brake pedal suddenly broke and she bounced to the end of a cart track before coming to rest. However, armed with her new skill in mechanics, Elsie soon sorted it out and was on the road again. She called her ambulance car 'Diana' because she jumped like a hunter over any obstacle.[17]

Camping out in tents, Elsie loved the exhilaration of her Serbian life. She admitted that in spite of the language difficulties she found conversation much easier with the different nationalities she came across than with the young men she had hunted and danced with at home.[18] Her dedication was recognised when she was mentioned in Despatches for her 'conscientious and hard work in the evacuation of the wounded'. During one year alone she had driven 9,153 miles and carried 1,122 patients.[19] As she wrote in her memoirs, 'Such danger and hardship as we did encounter were things that I would not have changed for almost anything else life might have brought me.'[20]

Both of Lord Rowallan's sons also took great risks for their country. His youngest son, Arthur, could not wait to leave school and train for the Royal Flying Corps. He became engrossed in building model aeroplanes and was completely calm and cheerful at the thought of active service. Knowing the dangers involved in flying, he showed a fatalism typical of his generation. Shortly after he first took to the air in 1916 he was shot down and killed.

The peer's eldest son, Godfrey, had a luckier escape than his younger brother. He had fought with the Ayrshire Yeomanry at Gallipoli in 1915 before transferring to the Grenadier Guards and serving on the Western Front. In March 1918, his battalion experienced one of the heaviest bombardments of the war in the German Spring Offensive. He was trying to dig out wounded soldiers who were half buried when he heard a swish and a thud and then felt himself being thrown up in the air and bombarded with clods of soil. He tried to pull out his left leg and found that he could not bend it above the knee. He recalled that it felt 'funny and unreal' as if it was floating. Soon his whole body was incredibly painful and he felt as if he was going far away. People were running past and he tried to follow but he could not move. His comrades said they would come back later and help him, so Godfrey was left lying in limbo, passing in and out of consciousness for several hours before four soldiers rescued him and took him on a stretcher to a first aid post.[21]

At the time of his injury, Godfrey was engaged to Gwyn Grimond, whose father founded the jute industry in Dundee. They met at a cousin's wedding and Gwyn first really attracted his attention when she played tennis in daring black stockings. At first he had held back from proposing to her because he felt it was wrong that a young girl like her might soon become a war widow, but on his next leave he could not resist asking her. She readily agreed and a date was set for their wedding in June.[22] When he was injured, his first thought was of the wedding. He was sent to a specialist femoral hospital at Étaples and when a doctor came to see him, Godfrey's initial question was, 'When will I get home?'

He said, 'Oh in about 6 weeks.'

Godfrey argued, 'I can't possibly wait as long as that. I'm getting married next month.'[23]

However, he had no choice; the wedding had to be postponed and when it finally took place in St Andrews on 14 August 1918 it was a day of even greater celebration. All of the couple's family and friends knew what they had been through. Godfrey had been awarded the Military Cross for his valour.

The local newspaper described it as one of the most popular weddings that had ever taken place in the town.[24] Recognising Godfrey's injuries, the Bishop of St Andrews kept the ceremony brief, the whole service lasting only fifteen minutes, and it was agreed that the groom should not kneel down.

The pearls bought by Lord Rowallan at Christie's were a symbol of new beginnings. After the wedding, he handed his Scottish estate over to his son, making Godfrey the laird of 6,000 acres. The following year, Godfrey also became a father when Gwyn gave birth to their son. Elsie never married, instead she spent the rest of her life living with Kathleen Dillon, a fellow VAD who had been her constant companion in Serbia. We do not know whether Lord Rowallan bought the Red Cross Pearl Necklace for his daughter-in-law or daughter, but either lady would have been a deserving person to receive it after the challenges they had faced during the war.[25]

After Lord Rowallan's necklace, there were a further twenty-nine lots. Reflecting the wide variety and quality of pearls on offer, prices paid during the afternoon ranged from £22,000 for the Norbury necklace to £30 for the children's necklaces. Bidding in the auction lasted for three and a half hours. As the hammer fell on one lot after another, Mr Anderson's smile never wavered as he sought, found and inspired members of his audience to compete with one another and bid higher.

The whole event was carried out with the understated professionalism expected of Christie's. As one newspaper explained, 'A Christie's auctioneer is not like other members of his profession. He is not garrulous, he never jokes, he never describes his lots in unnecessary detail.'The journalist added that if the imperial crown should come up for sale at the auction house, 'the dignified gentleman with the hammer would describe it dispassionately as "lot so and so", and leave it at that'.[26] The Red Cross Pearl Necklaces needed no hyperbole, their beauty spoke for itself.

At the end of the afternoon, the final sum raised was £85,290 12s 4d, and by the time donations and money raised at the Grafton Galleries and Christie's exhibition were added the total was nearly £100,000. This was a vast amount of money, given that a gardener working for one of the women who donated to the appeal would be paid about £24 a year in 1918 and the top salary for a chef was £150.[27] As Sir Arthur Stanley for the Red Cross told the audience, everyone involved should be proud of the result.

The money was much needed, and *The Times* wrote:

> It may be more than a fancy that the money given for these sacred things will do more than other money could do for those on whom it will be spent. The guns are silent, the trenches are empty, but the victims of the guns and of the trenches are still with us in their thousands, still needing care and sympathy. It will be long indeed before we whom they have saved will have paid our debt to them; and then only will the tears be dried, the memories purged of all bitterness.[28]

SIXTEEN

PEARL RIVALS

The Red Cross Pearl Auction marked the end of an era and the beginning of a challenging new one. With the war over, the Red Cross hospitals at home and abroad began to close. The money raised was now needed for the rehabilitation of returning soldiers.

The women who had given their pearls, worked in the hospitals and served on fundraising committees would now return to their peacetime roles. However, after their wartime experiences the world could never be the same again. The romantic idea of heroic knights riding off into battle to fight a holy war had died on the fields of Flanders; it could not survive in the brutal reality of modern warfare. The world had also changed for pearls, no longer would they remain the exclusive possessions of the elite; in the post-war world there would be new types of pearls, new fashions and different women wearing them. The Red Cross Pearl Necklace Auction was one of the last times when natural pearls would reign supreme. Soon, cultured and artificial versions would rival their supremacy. The traditional values they represented, of chivalry, piety and patriotism, would be equally challenged in the coming decades.

The formal end of the Pearl Necklace Appeal was on 23 May 1919. Lady Northcliffe went to Marlborough House to present a cheque to her friend and colleague, Princess Victoria who, after thanking those who had given so generously, handed it to Sir Robert Hudson, chairman of the Joint Finance

Committee of the British Red Cross Society and the Order of St John of Jerusalem.

Although the reporting of this final meeting was bland, it concealed a secret love story that was one of the keys to the Pearl Necklace Appeal's success. Lady Northcliffe and Sir Robert Hudson had been in love with each other for years. Molly Northcliffe had first met the widower in 1908. Over the next decade a complicated love triangle developed between Lord and Lady Northcliffe and Sir Robert. Divorce was not an option because Northcliffe still relied on his wife and no one wanted the scandal it would have caused, so compromises had to be made. As the years passed, Northcliffe accepted Hudson as a friend, not a rival. Although they were opposites in character and political beliefs they respected each other.

Throughout the war they had worked together on *The Times* Red Cross Fund. No newspaper had ever worked so closely with a charity. All gifts of money, large or small, received by the Red Cross were acknowledged in the newspaper and treated as being part of *The Times* Fund. The organisation estimated that 2,000 columns of *The Times* had been placed at their disposal as a free gift to their cause. With uncharacteristic modesty, Lord Northcliffe explained, 'All a newspaper can do in such a movement is to act as a constant reminder, and a faithful seconder.'[1] However, Sir Robert and his Red Cross colleagues knew the incalculable value of this free publicity, declaring, 'Without the constant help of the Press our needs could never have been made known to the vast scattered public from whom we have drawn our support.'[2]

By the end of 1918 the amount raised in the fund had reached more than £14 million. Acknowledging the achievement, King George wrote a letter of thanks emphasising, 'the value of the help thus rendered to our own sick and wounded cannot be estimated'.[3]

Over the war years, the relationship between Northcliffe and Hudson went beyond the professional to become personal. When Northcliffe travelled on his war mission to America in 1917, he had a premonition he would not return so he asked Robert to look after his wife.[4] The following year, working together on the Red Cross Pearl Appeal brought the love triangle even closer. While Molly headed the campaign, Robert, as head of the Red Cross finances, was often by her side, joining her at the exhibition and the auction. However, her husband also played a vital role, providing the publicity which helped to make the appeal such a success. The two men and Lady Northcliffe worked brilliantly as a team, as was evident during the attempt to change the lottery law in Parliament in August 1918. One member of the triumvirate would follow up on the other's earlier move, using their different skills and contacts to achieve the best result for the Red Cross.

Once the war was over, Molly and Robert no longer had the excuse of the Pearl Appeal to bring them together. However, rather than ending their relationship, their love affair developed further. Hudson became a permanent member of the Northcliffe household, joining them wherever they travelled. When Northcliffe went on his world tour in 1921 he was happy to leave his wife in his friend's care. While he was away, the press baron thought a great deal about his wife and kept three pictures of her in his cabin.[5] It seems that both men genuinely loved Lady Northcliffe and were willing to share her. They wrote solicitous letters to each other about Molly's wellbeing and both openly expressed their admiration for this remarkable woman. Although it seems that Hudson spent the most time with her, he was always tactful, writing to her husband about 'your lady'. Hudson's biographer believed that Northcliffe felt genuine affection for his wife's admirer and his trust in him amounted almost to dependence.[6]

This strange dynamic was played out with long-lasting consequences during Northcliffe's final illness. Bizarrely, in 1922 Northcliffe, the scourge of the Germans, decided to tour Germany. It seems that he was already suffering from persecution mania as, during the visit, he went under an alias and carried a revolver for self-protection because he claimed the Germans were after him. After a short while behind 'enemy lines', Northcliffe began to question his own sanity, writing to Hudson that he thought he was going mad. At the time, Robert and Molly were staying at Évian-les-Bains with a well-known doctor, so the ailing peer decided to meet them there. Tensions within the *ménage* à *trois* mounted as Northcliffe became dangerously ill. Raving and suffering from delusions, he shouted abuse at Molly who was driven from his room in tears. However, he wanted his wife's lover to be constantly with him, so for days and nights on end Robert only left his side to snatch short intervals of sleep. Writing to a friend, describing the nightmare situation that all three were trapped in, Robert said that he feared Northcliffe's madness would drive them all insane.[7]

When the patient was able to travel he was brought back to London by Robert and Molly in a special train arranged by the French premier, Raymond Poincare. During his final weeks, Northcliffe was confined at 1 Carlton Gardens with a team of doctors and male nurses. On the verge of a nervous breakdown, Lady Northcliffe retreated to her house in Sussex, leaving the Harmsworth brothers in charge of her husband. Diagnosed as having septic endocarditis, Northcliffe's blood had become infected with streptococcus which caused periods of delirium, he was often irascible and occasionally violent. When one of his physicians, Sir Thomas Horder, who had recently been knighted by the Lloyd George coalition, came to examine him, Northcliffe called him 'one of George's bloody knights', and pulled a pistol from underneath his pillow as if he was going to shoot him.[8]

According to some newspaper reports, when Northcliffe was dying, he called in his wife and her lover and, joining their hands across his sickbed, made them solemnly promise to marry after his death. He died on 14 August. On the wall facing his bed was an illuminated portrait of his wife, apparently she had put it there to remind him of her.[9]

When Robert and Molly married only eight months later in a quiet ceremony, it caused much controversy. While one American newspaper described their love as 'one of the most beautiful romances of modern times', some unkind observers claimed Hudson was marrying Molly for her money.[10] In fact, he was a wealthy man in his own right and due to a peculiar twist in her late husband's will, she forfeited most of her inheritance if she remarried. When Northcliffe was in his final illness he signed another will leaving everything to his wife to use as she chose under Robert's guidance.[11] However, the rival will led to a dispute between Molly and the Harmsworth family. Eventually, to prevent a scandal, a compromise was reached in which Molly received £27,000 a year, free of income tax, and a quarter of a million pounds in cash.[12]

For Sir Robert and the new Lady Hudson, the Red Cross Pearls symbolised happiness in marriage. The couple had waited patiently for fifteen years to be together and they were determined to enjoy their married life to the full. They went to Italy for their honeymoon and as a wedding gift Robert bought his new wife an ancient Italian villa. An authority on architecture, he drew up plans for its restoration. After the capricious outbursts Molly experienced with her first husband, she thrived in the harmonious atmosphere of her second marriage. As they had discovered while fundraising together, Robert and Molly were very compatible, sharing similar tastes in politics, art and philanthropy. As she now held the same Liberal political beliefs as her new husband, it was even rumoured that Molly might run for Parliament.[13]

However, their 'serene companionship of mature minds and interests' was all too brief. After a few idyllically happy years together, Robert died of pneumonia in 1927.[14] Molly lived on until 1963, dying when she was about 95 years old. In later life, she preferred talking about her second husband than her first.[15]

The success of the Pearl Necklace Appeal was a lasting memorial to this very unusual *ménage à trois*. The sale of the pearls had raised £96,033, and once the expenses for administration, printing, stationery, advertising and stringing of the pearls had been paid £94,044 remained.[16] It was a magnificent achievement. To put the amount in perspective, it cost £9,585 to run all the Red Cross convalescent homes in France and Belgium from October 1918 to December 1919.[17] During the same period, the expense of housing relatives of the wounded in hostels in France and Belgium was £8,122.[18] Funding the enquiries for the wounded and missing cost £3,047, while the cost of caring for the war graves was £1,538.[19] However, the real purpose of the Pearl Appeal had been to help former soldiers rebuild their lives, and one use for the money was to provide provisional artificial limbs for soldiers who had lost one or both arms or legs. By the end of the war, many men were waiting for long periods for permanent artificial limbs to be fitted, and in the meantime they needed temporary substitutes. To help fill this gap the Red Cross began supplying provisional artificial limbs made of plaster or fibre pylon – by 1919, they had given out 11,750 limbs.[20]

During the war, the Red Cross had already started to run rehabilitation projects. In 1915, Sir Arthur Stanley, chairman of the Joint War Committee, who was a major supporter of the Pearl Appeal, recognised the urgent need for suitable accommodation for men disabled during the war. At this time, the Red Cross had received many letters from hospitals explaining that they had been given orders to discharge paralysed patients, but they had no place to send them except the work-house infirmary.[21] Queen Mary shared Sir Arthur's concern about the long-term welfare of these servicemen, and they agreed that something must be done to help.

In the autumn of 1915, the Auctioneers' and Estate Agents' Institute raised money to buy the historic Star and Garter Hotel in Richmond,

Surrey. Dominating the skyline on Richmond Hill, the turreted hotel boasted spectacular views over the Thames as it snaked towards Windsor. The Victorian hotel had once been the height of fashion, Charles Dickens had celebrated the publication of *David Copperfield* there, while William Makepeace Thackeray had used it as a setting for a scene in *Vanity Fair*, but it closed in 1906 and was now almost derelict.

Once the money was raised to buy the Star and Garter, it was given to Queen Mary who asked the Red Cross to equip and run it as a 'permanent haven' for disabled ex-servicemen. Donations poured in from across the world. The British women in Nyasaland sent £562, while the Chinese community of Jamaica donated £100. People could also sponsor a room or a bed. Typically, Molly Northcliffe was one of the first to help this Red Cross project and soon 'the Lady Northcliffe Bed' could be found beside 'the Canton British Women's Memorial Bed' and a 'Women of Umtali Bed'.[22]

By January 1916 the home was ready to receive its first sixty-five residents. Their average age was 22 and all of them had been paralysed by being shot through the spine or brain. They had been released from hospital because it was thought that nothing more could be done to improve their condition. However, the staff at the Star and Garter were not willing to give up on them. Although out of 112 admissions, twenty deaths occurred in the first year, in the caring environment many of the young men improved.[23] Everything was done to make them as comfortable as possible. The ballroom was converted into a ward and, with its elegant arched colonnades, grand piano and aspidistras still in place, there were echoes of pre-war hotel life – with immaculately dressed nurses in the place of the waitresses.

The day ran to a rigid routine: breakfast was served at 8 a.m., followed by lunch at 12 noon, tea at 3.30 p.m. and supper at 7 p.m. All patients had to be in bed by 9 p.m. unless they had been issued with a special late pass, and only one pass was allowed each week. No gambling, wine or beer were allowed, and so when several patients were caught drunk or fighting they were expelled for misconduct. However, genteel entertainment was provided. Concerts were held three times a week and there were day trips on the river to Sunbury. Occasionally there were even sports days where the 'sports' included a 'smelling competition', 'needle threading and button sewing' and 'an obstacle race'. After careful nursing, by the end of the first year eighteen men had improved enough to move back to their homes or nearer their families, while five were able to walk out of the front door. Taking pride in their work, the staff never ceased to boast about this 'famous five'.[24]

Although the old building had character, by 1919 it was decided that a new purpose-built home would better serve the needs of its residents. Like the Pearl Appeal just a few years before, the money for the rebuilding and equipping of the home was provided by contributions from the women of the Empire through the British Women's Hospital Committee. Just like the pearls, it became a women's war memorial which was to alleviate the suffering of the men who had sacrificed so much.

While the new home was built, the seventy veterans were moved to Enbrook House, near Sandgate in Kent, which became known as the 'Seaside Branch'.[25] Giving his services free of charge, the architect, Sir Edwin Cooper, created 'a building of beauty combined with every facility for the rapid and easy movement of disabled men'.[26] One newspaper claimed that with the combination of red brick and Portland stone and Doric colonnades, the new building 'has the dignity and charm' of Hampton Court Palace.[27]

The new Star and Garter Home was opened by the king and queen in July 1924. Although the home had become an independent charity, many of the people who had been involved in the Red Cross Pearl Appeal were at the opening. Sir Arthur Stanley, now chairman of governors of the home, welcomed the king and queen, while Sir Robert Hudson and his new wife were also in the party.

Levels of care were of a high standard in the new home, with the 180 patients cared for by sixty members of staff. The aim was to give patients as much freedom as possible, with the use of 'self-propelling' wheelchairs and plenty of space to move around in the spacious grounds. To entertain the men, a cinematograph hall and gymnasium was set up and social events were put on. As well as therapy, training was provided and, under the guidance of skilled professionals, many of the ex-servicemen became proficient craftsmen. They took pride in their work and produced high-quality goods for sale. One year they embroidered an altar frontal for St Paul's Cathedral and to thank them for their hard work they were sent a large case of tobacco and cigarettes. From 1924 an annual exhibition and sale of their work was held which was visited by prestigious guests, including the Duchess of York, later Queen Elizabeth.

However, not everyone believed that an institution like the Star and Garter Home at Richmond was the best place for disabled soldiers. One critic, Leonora Scott, wrote to *The Times*, commenting that no matter how well designed the Star and Garter was, it could not be as good for them as their own home where they could enjoy 'in some degree, the natural life'. Describing even the best institutions as 'gilded prisons', she also queried whether sending men from other parts of the country to Richmond to live was best for them. As an alternative, she proposed that disabled soldiers should be given the choice between a sheltered 'home' or a pension which would be enough to pay a relative or friend to look after him and pay for a daily visit from the parish nurse. She explained, 'What I plead for is variety in the offers which the nation is to make, so that, as far as may be, each man may have the kind of assistance which will best promote his happiness.'[28]

After the war, Red Cross branches across the country tried to do this. Paralysed discharged soldiers who were no longer under the care of the War Office were passed on to Red Cross county branches, who contacted the local military hospital to arrange for patients to be transferred as close to home as possible. The local branches also ran orthopaedic clinics for disabled people. King Manuel of Portugal became the representative for these clinics and visited each one as it was set up throughout the country. He championed the importance of 'curative work', making sure that part of the recovery process involved men being trained in a craft of their choice which ranged from electrical engineering to shoemaking. The Military Orthopaedic Hospital, Shepherds Bush, became a model for other centres. The Red Cross provided £10,000 for them to set up treatment departments including operating theatres, hydrotherapy, electrotherapeutic massage and plaster departments.[29]

The returning soldiers were coming home to a very different world to the one they had left behind. Although some of the class barriers broken down by the war were soon built up again, the old, rigidly hierarchical pre-war order seemed outdated. In his War Book, Lord Northcliffe had predicted that the bravery and camaraderie of the officers and men had altered class feeling forever. He wrote:

Our millions of men abroad are changed communities of whose thoughts and aims we know but little [...] so will the men I have seen in the trenches and the ambulances come home and demand by their votes the reward of a very changed England – an England they will fashion and share; an England that is likely to be as much a surprise to the present owners of Capital and leaders of labour as it may be to the owners of the land.[30]

Northcliffe was right – power and property were changing hands. Following the Representation of the People Act in 1918, Britain was becoming more democratic. From 1918, men of all classes over the age of 21 had the vote and thus a say in who governed Britain.

The journey made by the Red Cross Pearls symbolised the change in British society. They had been emblems of the privileged pre-war world, but nearly all the pearls sold at the Christie's auction had gone outside aristocratic circles. The splitting of heirloom necklaces to give to the charity foreshadowed the breaking up of aristocratic estates after the war. The conflict had weakened the social and political influence of the great landowners and they now faced increased taxation and death duties.

Many of the women who gave pearls watched as, after the war, their husbands sold swathes of land that had been in their family for generations. In 1919 the Earl of Rothes put Leslie House, twenty farms and 3,552 acres on his Fife estate up for sale.[31] By the end of that year, more than 1 million acres of English and Welsh land had been auctioned. It altered the balance in the countryside because, in many cases, these sales allowed tenant farmers to own land for the first time.[32]

Things were changing in London, too. In 1920 the first of the great private palaces, Devonshire House, was sold off by the Duke of Devonshire to two businessmen for 1 million guineas. It was demolished five years later and replaced with an eight-storey block of flats.[33] In 1927, Grosvenor House, where Bendor and Shelagh the Duke and Duchess of Westminster had lived so lavishly, was sold. In its place, another block of flats and an American style hotel were built.[34]

The Times was one of the first newspapers to analyse what was happening. In May 1920, it announced that 'England is changing hands' and grand houses were being bought by war profiteers or turned into schools or institutions. However, the article added that this was a quiet revolution:

For the most part the sacrifices are made in silence […] the sons are perhaps lying in far away graves; the daughters secretly mourning someone dearer than a brother, have taken up some definite work away from home, seeking thus to still their aching hearts, and the old people, knowing there is no son or near relative left to keep up the old traditions, or so crippled by necessary taxation that they know the boy will never be able to carry on when they are gone, take the irrevocable step.[35]

Although selling estates that had been in the family for hundreds of years was demoralising, the aristocracy's loss of property could not compare to the loss of their sons. As Mary Wemyss wrote to Ettie Desborough, after what they had been through, houses and material possessions mattered so much less. Their whole perspective on life was different, she explained, 'Everything looks the same and everything is different, everything is changed – because we are different, we shall never be the same people again.'[36]

The pearl necklaces were also entering new incarnations. In early 1919, the most famous Red Cross Necklace, Lot 101 with its perfect pearls and Norbury diamond clasp, made a new appearance. Arranged in the shape of a heart, and set within a gold frame complete with rococo scrolls and the Royal Coat of Arms with 'By Appointment' strategically placed beneath, it starred in an advertisement for Carrington & Co. in the *Illustrated London News*. Not one to hide his benevolence, Mr Carrington Smith had written beneath, 'The Red Cross Pearl Necklace purchased at Christie's for £22,000. By Carrington and Co. Pearl Merchants and Jewellers to Their Majesties the King and Queen.'[37] No doubt Mr Carrington Smith was hoping to entice customers into his shop to buy either this necklace or some of the other pearls he had bought in the auction. The advert informed readers that they could view the Red Cross Pearls at Carrington & Co. in Regent Street. Such blatant self-promotion was a reflection of the post-war climate, where jewellers like Carrington could no longer rely on an exclusive clientele. In the modern world, they had to appeal to a mass market, and after all the publicity of the Red Cross Appeal few jewels could be more alluring than the most famous pearl necklace in the world.

However, even the historic necklace could not turn the tide for the natural pearl market. During the next decade cultured pearls and costume jewellery would compete with natural pearls for a place round the elegant necks of the most fashionable women in society. From the 1920s, large numbers of Japanese pearls flooded the market. The finest of these cultured pearls came from the Japanese entrepreneur Kokichi Mikimoto's pearl farms. His whole life was devoted to his passion for pearls and for several decades he had been trying to produce them. Early in Mikimoto's career he pledged himself to protect and raise the stocks of Akoya pearl oysters, which had been depleted by decades of overfishing, and to grow pearls using the oysters on Ojima Island at Toba. Finally, after facing years of financial difficulties and a 'red tide' of algae blooms that destroyed his oysters, in 1893 he succeeded in developing a technique which created semi-spherical pearls.[38] This was a historic moment because it was the first time that pearls had been produced from an oyster with human intervention. By 1904 Mikimoto had produced 24,000 of these half pearls on his oyster farms.[39]

At the same time, a scientist, Tatsuhei Mise, and an enthusiastic amateur, Mikimoto's son-in-law, Tokichi Nishikawa, were separately working on techniques to create spherical gems. Mise and Nishikawa's methods were similar: the Mise-Nishikawa technique involved grafting a piece of mantle from a donor oyster into the reproductive organ of a receiving oyster, then a bead was introduced which encouraged a spherical pearl to grow. Recognising the superiority of this formula, Mikimoto negotiated a financial agreement which allowed him to use the Mise-Nishikawa technique. In 1905, he succeeded in cultivating a perfectly spherical pearl. By 1914 he had 50 square miles of water under cultivation, with the water varying in depth from 5 to 15 fathoms and women divers used to collect the pearl harvest.[40] Two years later the process was industrialised, allowing more pearls to be produced.[41]

In 1919 Mikimoto started to sell spherical cultured pearls in Europe. When they first appeared on the market they caused shockwaves among pearl dealers across the Continent and soon a debate was raging about whether these cultured pearls could really be called pearls or whether they were frauds. Dealers in London confidently claimed that the cultured pearl could be detected in a moment by any expert.[42] A French connoisseur agreed, adding, 'The difference between them and the real pearl is that between an ancient work of art and a modern imitation.'[43] Panicking about the impact these Japanese intruders would have on the natural pearl market, French dealers suggested various actions, including an embargo on cultured pearls. The controversy led to a lawsuit which became known as the 'Paris Trial' in which the French Association of Commerce and Industry tried to prove that cultured pearls were fakes. After many scientific tests and much deliberation, leading experts including Professor H. Lyster Jameson of Oxford University and Professor Louis Boutan of Bordeaux University testified that 'there is no fundamental difference between natural and cultured pearls in terms of their formation and structure'.[44] Following this conclusive evidence, in 1924 a French Court of Justice ruled that 'cultured pearls do not differ from natural pearls at all'.[45]

In 1927 Mikimoto received a further endorsement which turned him into a household name overnight. During a tour of Europe and the United States he met the famous inventor Thomas Edison in New York. When Edison saw the exquisite Japanese pearls, he was so impressed that he told Mikimoto:

> This isn't a cultured pearl, it's a real pearl. There are two things which couldn't be made at my laboratory – diamonds and pearls. It is one of the wonders of the world that you were able to culture pearls. It is something which is supposed to be biologically impossible.[46]

Edison's remarks were reported in the *New York Times*, which immediately reinforced Mikimoto's credibility with American pearl collectors.

During the interwar years, Mikimoto's pearls revolutionised the world of jewellery. Costing a fifth or even a tenth of the price of natural pearls, these cultured gems made pearls an affordable luxury. However, there was some snobbery attached to making beautiful jewels more easily obtainable. Believing that trying to pass off cultured pearls as natural ones was a vulgar type of deception, Loelia, Duchess of Westminster, Shelagh's successor, argued that no woman should wear more cultured pearls than her husband could have afforded if they were natural. Not many women had such stuffy scruples; many embraced the new gems with enthusiasm and some even considered that the smoothness and sheen of the Japanese pearls made them more desirable than natural ones.[47]

By 1936, Mikimoto's pearl fisheries were producing 60 per cent of the world's pearl supply.[48] The so-called 'Pearl King of Japan' planted 3 million oysters on his pearl farm each year and more than 1,000 men and women were employed in pearl cultivation. Every oyster planted was numbered, every pearl carefully registered while it was growing and every worker strictly accountable for a given number of pearls and oysters. The finest pearl ever produced on Mikimoto's farm held the record for being the second largest pearl in the world. It was kept locked away in a specially built and guarded safe.[49]

Following in Mikimoto's footsteps, other Japanese entrepreneurs also began to culture pearls. However, some of these new entrants produced inferior jewels which threatened to damage the reputation of Japanese gems on the world market. Determined to maintain the quality of cultured pearls, Mikimoto publicly burnt large quantities of these second-rate jewels on a bonfire in front of international journalists.[50] This sacrifice of inferior versions was just one of the ways the 'Pearl King' demonstrated his commitment to creating the finest pearls possible. Throughout his life he had treated pearls as sacred objects which had to be nurtured and treated with respect. Reflecting his reverential attitude, according to contemporary newspapers, in 1936 he held a unique memorial service for the spirits of more than 100,000 pearl oysters which had been killed during the past twenty years at his pearl farm. At the unusual event, more than fifty priests took part in the rites in front of about 10,000 guests.[51]

The other man who inadvertently helped to end the reign of natural pearls, was Bendor, Duke of Westminster. While his former wife Shelagh had given pearls to the Red Cross Necklace, and his third wife, Loelia, tried to maintain the status quo for natural pearls, his gift of pearls to his mistress was to inspire innovative jewellery. In 1923, Bendor met the fashion designer Coco Chanel in Monte Carlo. The yards of pearls he lavished on his new mistress became her fashion signature. Revelling in her refusal to be bound by convention, Chanel found new ways of wearing jewels. On Bendor's yacht or on the beach in the South of France she garlanded herself in a myriad of jewels and no one could be sure whether they were the real thing or fakes. As she said, nothing looks more like a fake jewel than a beautiful jewel.[52] Like Queen Elizabeth I before her, Chanel used her pearls to symbolise feminine power. She covered herself in pearls when she wanted to exude confidence and her jewels became a talisman. She once told her assistant she would not go up to her ateliers until she had her pearls around her neck.[53]

Coco encouraged other women to follow her lead. As one of the first designers to commission distinctive pieces of costume jewellery for her collection, her timing was perfect. The sophisticated rich wanted something different from the precious stones of the past because conspicuous displays of wealth through wearing ostentatious jewellery had become associated with the nouveau riche wives of profiteers during the war. Working with the jewellery designer Augustine Gripoix, Chanel gave them the ideal alternative. Gripoix's first collection for Chanel introduced many colourful Byzantine-influenced jewels modelled on the emeralds, rubies and sapphires given to her by Bendor. However, it was the pearls which turned Chanel into the leading lady of costume jewellery. By 1925 'everyone in Paris' was wearing ropes and ropes of Chanel's Gripoix pearls.

The craze for these carefully crafted gems soon spread across the Atlantic.[54] The golden lustre of Chanel's fake pearls, worn at just the right length to elongate the silhouette, became an essential part of the art deco image. During the twenties, pearls were worn in imaginative new ways. Inspired by her visits to Bendor in England, Chanel created what became known as her 'English look'. Over loose woollen cardigans her models wore strands of faux pearls, similar to her gifts from the duke.[55] To enhance her streamlined shift dresses, Chanel encouraged women to cascade long ropes of pearls down their backs.[56]

The smartest women on the French Riviera would even don a strand with their bathing suits and wear them to the beach. In Scott Fitzgerald's *Tender is the Night*, the heroine, Nicole Driver, lies on the sand with her swimsuit seductively off her shoulder, her creamy pearls setting off to perfection her fashionable tan.[57] Never precious about jewellery, Chanel suggested that the American girls she saw swimming at the Venice Lido should dip their pearls into the sea, returning the gems to the element from which they first came.[58] She took this idea a step further while having a heated argument with Bendor aboard his yacht about his flirtation with a younger woman – rejecting his peace offering of a priceless pearl necklace, she threw it into the ocean.[59]

As well as looking chic, the finest costume jewellery made a statement. For women who had experienced their first taste of independence during the war, this new fashion signified that they were not willing to return to their old roles. Whereas the outrageously expensive natural pearls of the past were often gifts from men, women could afford to buy the fake strands for themselves.[60] They no longer wanted costume jewellery that masqueraded as the real thing; instead, *Vogue* encouraged its readers to wear Chanel's pink, grey, almond and blue pearls as large as possible so that no one could imagine they were real gems.[61]

Fashions in jewellery come and go, but the emotional appeal of the Red Cross Pearls is timeless. Like religious relics from a previous age, they symbolise devotion and commitment to humanitarian values. A century after they were collected, they retain their enigmatic essence, they served their purpose and until now they have discreetly vanished from public consciousness. It seems likely that many of their twenty-first-century owners do not know the poignant history of the strands they wear around their necks. Yet, although the pearls are now scattered, the spirit of philanthropy they represent still survives. In 1993 the International Fundraising Committee of the British Red Cross ran 'The Pot of Gold' appeal. After an elderly widow donated her wedding band to the charity, the fundraisers appealed for jewellery. Valuable gems flooded in and when they were auctioned at the Savoy they raised £2 million. Ten years later, in December 2003, the committee held another successful auction of donated jewels at Christie's called 'Jewels for Life'. One hundred years after the Pearl Appeal, dedicated men and women are still giving freely of their time and money, drawing on their connections and organising events for the British Red Cross. Their fundraising supports humanitarian causes in Britain and abroad. Through their altruistic actions they are following in the pearl-wearing, well-heeled footsteps of Lady Northcliffe and her friends a century ago.

DRAMATIS PERSONAE

MARY NORTHCLIFFE. Known as 'Molly', Lady Northcliffe was the wife of the press baron Alfred Harmsworth, Lord Northcliffe. She was chairman of the Red Cross Pearl Necklace Appeal and led the call for donations of jewels.

LORD NORTHCLIFFE. Born Alfred Harmsworth, Lord Northcliffe had founded the *Daily Mail* and now owned *The Times*. He threw the full weight of his newspapers behind the Pearl Appeal to make it a success.

SIR ROBERT HUDSON. Sir Robert was chairman of the Red Cross and St John's Ambulance Joint Finance Committee. He was an intimate friend and admirer of Lady Northcliffe. He worked closely with her and her husband in the Pearl Appeal.

PRINCESS VICTORIA. The daughter of Edward VII and sister of George V, Princess Victoria was president of the Pearl Appeal.

NOËL, COUNTESS OF ROTHES. A survivor of the sinking of the *Titanic*, the countess donated two pearls that she was wearing on that fateful night to the Red Cross pearl collection.

MAXINE ELLIOTT. Maxine was an American actress and the lover of the Wimbledon tennis champion Anthony Wilding. During the war she took a barge to Belgium to support civilians who had been displaced by the fighting.

VIOLET, DUCHESS OF RUTLAND. When she was first married, Violet was known as Lady Granby but after her husband inherited the dukedom she became the Duchess of Rutland. She was a member of the 'Souls' circle of friends. Her children were John, Marjorie, Diana and Letty Manners.

LETTY ELCHO. Born Violet Manners, the daughter of the Duke and Duchess of Rutland, she was known as 'Letty'. When she married Hugo (known as 'Ego') Charteris, Lord Elcho, she became Lady Elcho. She was left a young widow with two children when her husband was killed in the war.

MARY WEMYSS. When Mary was first married, she was known as Lady Elcho but after her husband inherited his father's title she became the Countess of Wemyss. She was a leading light in the 'Souls'. Two of her sons, 'Ego' and 'Yvo' were killed in the war.

ETTIE DESBOROUGH. Born Ethel Fane, she became Ettie Grenfell on her marriage to Willie Grenfell. When her husband received his title, she became Lady Desborough. She was a key member of the 'Souls' and a society hostess. She lost two sons, Julian and Billy, in the war.

LILIAN KEKEWICH. Lilian married into a well-known Devon military family. During the war her brother-in-law, a Boer War hero, committed suicide and three of her sons were killed. She made several donations to the Pearl Appeal.

KATHERINE MacDONALD. Known as 'Maudie' or 'Christy', Katherine was a Canadian nursing sister who nursed in France. She was killed in May 1918 when the Germans bombed her hospital. A pearl was given in memory of the heroism of the nurses killed that night.

CONSTANCE EDWINA, DUCHESS OF WESTMINSTER. Known to her friends as 'Shelagh', the Duchess of Westminster was unhappily married to one of the richest men in Britain, Hugh Grosvenor, Duke of Westminster, known as 'Bendor'. The couple divorced. During the war she found a new sense of purpose and romance working in the Red Cross hospital she had set up in France. After the war she married James Fitzpatrick Lewis.

BLANCHE, COUNTESS OF ST GERMANS. Born Lady Blanche Somerset, she was known as 'Linnie' to her friends. In 1918, she married 'Mousie', Earl of St Germans. Her husband had been badly injured during the war and died in 1922 following a riding accident.

VIOLET ASTOR. Born Lady Violet Elliot-Murray-Kynynmound, daughter of the Earl of Minto, her first husband was Lord Charles Fitzmaurice (later Mercer Nairne). Charles, the youngest son of the Marquess of Lansdowne, was killed in the war. Left a widow with two young children, Violet found new love with her second husband, John Jacob Astor.

FRANK HURLEY. Adventurer, photographer and cinematographer, Frank's photographs of battles were on display at the Pearls Exhibition held at the Grafton Galleries in June 1918.

ISRAEL GOLLANCZ. Professor of English literature and language at King's College, London, Israel contributed his translation of *Pearl*, a fourteenth-century poem, to raise funds for the Red Cross Appeal.

MAURICE BARING. A writer and poet, Maurice wrote poems to his friends Auberon 'Bron' Herbert and Julian Grenfell. He was a close friend of Lady Desborough.

HENRY, 5TH MARQUESS OF LANSDOWNE. Lord Lansdowne was a former Governor General of Canada, Viceroy of India and Foreign Secretary. His son Charles, the first husband of Violet Astor, was killed in the war. Lord Lansdowne piloted a Bill through Parliament that would have allowed the pearls to be raffled. Unfortunately for the Red Cross, the Bill was defeated.

FRANCES PARKER. Known as 'Millie', Mrs Parker was Lord Kitchener's sister. In memory of her brother, she gave rubies to make a clasp for the pearl necklaces.

BIRDIE WERNHER. Alice (known as 'Birdie') Wernher was the widow of the South African financier and gold and diamond mining magnate Sir Julius Wernher. She lost her youngest son, Alex, in the war. She was a great supporter of the Red Cross auctions at Christie's.

POSTSCRIPT

The story of the Red Cross Pearl Appeal has a relevance for the present as well as the past. In Autumn 2017 I attended a meeting of the International Fundraising Committee of the British Red Cross in London. After I had given a talk about my book, the head of the committee, Maria Shammas, approached me, saying that she was inspired by the evocative story to launch a new Pearls for Life Appeal to mark the centenary of Lady Northcliffe's fund.

Since then, many of the inheritors of the original participants have got together. In March 2018 the book was launched at Christie's King Street saleroom. No venue could have been more appropriate because it was on the same site, 100 years ago, that the Red Cross Pearl Auction was held. At the launch there were many of the descendants of the women I had written about: the grandchildren and great-grandchildren of Lady Desborough, Lady Wemyss, Violet Astor and the Duchess of Westminster were all there. Once I had finished my speech, Maria Shammas spoke, launching the new Pearls for Life Appeal.

Over the next few months some amazing jewellery once again poured in to support the work of the Red Cross. Among the donations this time were a pair of pearl earrings from Dame Judi Dench, which she wore when she collected her Oscar; earrings from Dame Darcey Bussell, which were worn on *Strictly Come Dancing*; and jewellery from Dame Kiri Te Kanawa. Some of the jewellery houses that were involved in the appeal a century ago also donated: Boucheron gave a jewel-encrusted brooch, Fabergé designed an exquisite ring, while Tiffany and Chanel gave pearl necklaces. Perhaps the most poignant donation was an ethereal enamelled dove of peace brooch, with ruby eyes and holding a drop pearl. It was made in 1910, shortly before the peace of the Edwardian era was shattered forever. The auction of the jewellery was held at the Savoy Hotel in July. It was a glamorous occasion, with models dressed in ballgowns modelling the jewellery during dinner. After dinner the auction was once again done by Christie's for the Red Cross. It raised £275,000, which will be used to help in crises both at home and abroad.

As well as the London gala, the Devon Red Cross committee also put on a memorable event at Powderham Castle in November 2018 to mark the centenary of the armistice. Once again, several descendants of the original donors were present. In the castle's great hall a wall of poppies had been created and a local jeweller had designed a pearl and ruby poppy necklace, which was auctioned to raise funds for the Red Cross.

There have been other exciting developments. After a review of *Pearls Before Poppies* appeared in *Country Life*, I was contacted by Tony Powell, who is a great-grandson of Lilian Kekewich. Lilian's story was one of the most tragic stories I came across when writing about the experiences of the women who donated, as she lost three of her sons in the Great War. Through talking to Tony, I discovered that the tradition of remembering the sacrifice made by the soldiers who gave up their lives was continued down the generations. His mother, Rosemary, who was Lilian's granddaughter, sold poppies with her mother when the first Poppy Appeal was launched in 1921. She continued supporting the appeal for the rest of her life and was honoured in 2018 by the queen for being the longest-serving poppy seller. When I wrote *Pearls Before Poppies*, one piece of the jigsaw was missing, and ever since the book was launched people have asked, 'What happened to the pearl necklaces?' For months we appealed for anyone who owned one of the forty-one necklaces to come forward. We also checked in every possible archive, but we got nowhere. Then, in autumn of 2018, after an article appeared in a magazine, I received a thrilling email. A lady, who wished to remain anonymous, contacted us and said that she had one of the necklaces in its original box. When I saw the necklace for the first time, it was a very special moment for me. The pearls were so large and lustrous and, reflecting their history, they were all slightly different colours. The dark-blue velvet box, with a cream silk lining and a discreet red cross on the lid, was also perfectly preserved. When a jewellery expert at Christie's saw the necklace he confirmed that the pearls were the finest quality natural pearls and of great value. Although the owners did not wish to be identified, they kindly allowed their priceless pearls to be displayed at Christie's in December 2018 to mark the centenary of the auction.

When I first saw that one line about the Red Cross Pearls at Port Eliot in 2014, I could never have imagined where the story would take me. I just knew that it was a story that I had to tell, and one that would not let me go. I discovered, Like Lady Northcliffe did a century ago, that the Red Cross Pearls have a momentum all their own, and now, as then, they gathered like-minded people together through the timeless hold they exert on the imagination.

NOTES

INTRODUCTION

1   Paul Cornish, *The First World War Galleries* (London: Imperial War Museum. 2014) p.234.
2   William Shakespeare, *Richard III*, Act 1, Scene 2, Line 154.
3   Matthew 13: 45–46.
4   Revelations 21:21.
5   'Memories and Tears', *The Times*, 2 December 1918, p.11.

CHAPTER ONE

1   Mary Wemyss' Diary, 1 January 1918. Wemyss Papers.
2   Adrian Gregory, *The Last Great War: British Society and the First World War* (Cambridge: Cambridge University Press, 2008) p.214.
3   *Ibid.*, p.213.
4   Lyn MacDonald, *To the Last Man: Spring 1918* (London: Viking, 1998) p.xxii.
5   Niall Ferguson, *The Pity of War* (London: Penguin Books, 1999) p.276.
6   Vera Brittain, *Testament of Youth: An Autobiographical Study of the Years 1900–1925* (London: Virago, 1978) pp.401–04.
7   Paul Cornish, *The First World War Galleries* (London: Imperial War Museum, 2014) p.213.
8   Gregory, p.213.

9 The Pearl Necklace Appeal was in aid of both charities which were working together during the war. However, for brevity throughout this book I will refer to it as the Red Cross Pearl Appeal. For similar reasons I will refer to the Red Cross when describing the work of the British Red Cross.

10 Information from Sir Arthur Stanley's speech at the launch of the Pearl Appeal, reported in *The Queen, The Lady's Newspaper*, 30 March 1918.

11 Gregory, p.148.

12 Gregory, pp.148–49.

13 'Letters of Eve', *Tatler*, 16 January 1918, p.72.

14 Jeremy Paxman, *Great Britain's Great War* (London: Penguin, 2014) p.93.

15 Tom Clarke, *My Northcliffe Diary* (London:Victor Gollancz, 1931) pp.200–01.

16 Reginald Pound and Geoffrey Harmsworth, *Northcliffe* (London: Cassell, 1959) p.224.

17 *Ibid.*, p.225.

18 *Ibid.*, p.225.

19 'Here and There', *The Sketch*, 17 April 1918.

20 Niall Ferguson, *The Pity of War* (London: Penguin Books, 1999) p.244.

21 Pound and Harmsworth, p.518.

22 Gary S. Messinger, *British Propaganda and the State in the First World War* (Manchester: Manchester University Press, 1992) p.154.

23 Pound and Harmsworth, p.510.

24 Pound and Harmsworth, p.621.

25 Frances Dimond, 'PrincessVictoria (1868–1935)', *Oxford Dictionary of National Biography* (Oxford: Oxford University Press, 2004–14).

26 Diana Souhami, *Mrs Keppel and her Daughter* (London: St Martin's Press/Hachette, 2013).

27 *Ibid.*

28 'Lady Sarah Wilson and the Red Cross', BlenheimPalace.com.

29 Tom Clarke, p.102.

30 Michael and Eleanor Brock (eds), *Margot Asquith's Great War Diary 1914–1916:The View From Downing Street* (Oxford: Oxford University Press, 2014) p.149.

31 Paul Ferris, *The House of Northcliffe: The Harmsworths of Fleet Street* (London: Weidenfeld and Nicolson, 1971) p.201.

32 'Life-Saving Pearls', *The Times*, 13 March 1918, p.9.

33 'Pearls for the Red Cross', *The Queen*, 30 March 1918, p.363.

34 Niall Ferguson, p.243.

CHAPTER TWO

1   'The Countess of Cromer', *The Queen*, 30 March 1918, p.1.

2   'Pearls for the Red Cross', *The Queen*, 30 March 1918, p.363.

3   Beatriz Chadour-Sampson and Hubert Bari, *Pearls* (London:V&A Publishing, 2013) p.103.

4   Beatriz Chadour-Sampson and Hubert Bari, p.115.

5   *Ibid.*

6   'Princess Mary Sets the Fashion', *Yorkshire Evening Post*, 13 June 1913, p.6.

7   Jane Mulvagh, *Costume Jewellery in* Vogue (London:Thames and Hudson, 1988) pp.22, 37.

8   Peter Hart, *1918:A Very British Victory* (London:Weidenfeld and Nicolson, 2008) p.104.

9   Lyn MacDonald, p.274.

10 For a full account of the situation in 1918 see Jeremy Paxman, pp.252 -54.

11 Quoted in Paul Cornish, p.214.

12 'Crowns Coronets Courtiers', *The Sketch*, 20 March 1918, p.246.

13 For a full description of that fateful night see Angela Young's article 'Titanic's Secret Saviour', *You* magazine, *The Mail on Sunday*, 12 April 2015, pp.44–47.

14 Quoted in Stephanie Barczewski, *Titanic One Hundredth Anniversary Edition: A Night Remembered* (London:A&C Black, 2011).

15 Walter Lord, *A Night to Remember* (Open Road Media. 6 March 2012).

16 'Countess of Rothes to Visit Fraserburgh', *Aberdeen Journal*, 19 July 1915, p.4.

17 *Fife Free Press and Kirkcaldy Guardian*, 2 April 1927.

18 *Dundee Courier*, 10 August 1915, p.7.

19 A. Wallis Myers, *Captain Anthony Wilding* (London: Hodder and Stoughton, 1916) p.5.

20 *Ibid.*, p.237.

21 'Tea Table Talk', *Sunderland Daily Echo*, 14 June 1916, p.4.

22 'Literary and Dramatic Notes', *Western Daily Press*, 17 January 1914, p.7.

23 Catherine Bailey, *The Secret Rooms:A Castle Filled with Intrigue,A Plotting Duchess and a Mysterious Death* (London: Penguin, 2013) p.161.

24 Catherine Bailey, p.350.

25 Diana Forbes-Robertson, *My Aunt Maxine:The Story of Maxine Elliott* (New York:The Viking Press, 1964) p.234.

26 A. Wallis Myers, p.240.

27 Diana Forbes-Robertson, p.237.

28 *Ibid.*, p.238.

29   *Ibid.*, p.243.

30   A. Wallis Myers, p.262.

31   *Ibid.*, p.286.

32   *Ibid.*, p.290.

33   *Ibid.*, pp.290–92.

34   *Ibid.*, p.2.

35   *Ibid.*, p.294.

36   Letter from the Countess of Grosvenor to Mrs Wilding. Quoted in A. Wallis Myers, p.295.

37   A. Wallis Myers, p.298.

38   Adrian Gregory, p.44.

39   Max Pemberton, *Lord Northcliffe: A Memoir*, quoted in Adrian Gregory, p.47.

40   'American Actress', *The Sketch*, 27 January 1915, p.71.

41   'The Letters of Eve', *Tatler*, 10 February 1915, p.172.

42   Diana Forbes-Robertson, p.259.

43   *Ibid.*, p.261.

44   'Red Cross Necklace', the *Daily Mail*, 28 March 1918, p.4.

45   'Crowns Coronets Courtiers', *The Sketch*, 20 March 1918, p.246.

46   'In England-Now!' *Bystander*, 8 May 1918, p.232.

47   'Femina', *Bystander*, 6 March 1918, p.529.

CHAPTER THREE

1   *The Times*, 1 April 1918, p.7.

2   For a full discussion of the 'Souls', see Angela Lambert, *Unquiet Souls: The Indian Summer of the British Aristocracy* (London: Macmillan, 1984).

3   Quotation from Wilfrid Blunt, in Claudia Renton, *Those Wild Wyndhams: Three Sisters at the Heart of Power* (London: William Collins, 2014) p.99.

4   Jane Ridley and Clayre Percy (eds), *The Letters of Arthur Balfour and Lady Elcho 1885–1917* (London: Hamish Hamilton, 1992) p.viii.

5   Angela Lambert, p.79.

6   Diana Cooper, *The Rainbow Comes and Goes* (London: Rupert Hart-Davis, 1958) p.18.

7   *Ibid.*, pp.51–52.

8   For a full discussion of the Duchess of Rutland's attitude, see Catherine Bailey.

9   Diana Cooper, p.144.

10   Catherine Bailey, p.300.

11   *Ibid.*, pp.222–31.

12 Marjorie Anglesey to Ettie Grenfell, Desborough Papers, Hertfordshire Archives and Local Studies: DEX789C46.

13 For a full discussion of Violet's intervention, see Catherine Bailey.

14 Catherine Bailey, pp.344–45.

15 *Ibid.*, p.134.

16 Cynthia Asquith, *Haply I May Remember* (London: James Barrie, 1950) p.135.

17 For a detailed description of Haddon's death, see Catherine Bailey.

18 Catherine Bailey, p.120.

19 Diana Cooper, p.13.

20 *Ibid.*, p.18.

21 *Ibid.*, p.95.

22 Cynthia Asquith, *Remember and Be Glad* (London: James Barrie, 1952) p.198.

23 John Joliffe (ed.), *Raymond Asquith: Life and Letters* (London: William Collins, 1980) p.18.

24 Raymond Asquith to H.T. Baker, 6 October 1898, in John Joliffe, p.51.

25 Raymond Asquith to H.T. Baker, 21 April 1902 in John Joliffe, p.92.

26 David Cannadine, *The Decline and Fall of the British Aristocracy* (London: Penguin, 1990) pp.82–83.

27 Diana Cooper, p.151.

28 Cynthia Asquith, *Haply I May Remember*, p.14.

29 Mary had three sons, Ego, Guy and Yvo (Colin had died in 1892), and three daughters, Cynthia, Mary and Irene ('Bibs').

30 Mary, Countess of Wemyss, *A Family Record* (London: The Curwen Press, 1932) p.156.

31 Diana Cooper, p.79.

32 Mary, Countess of Wemyss. *A Family Record*, p.156.

33 Cynthia Asquith, *Remember and Be Glad*, p.10.

34 Letty Elcho to Ego Elcho, undated, Wemyss Papers.

35 Letty Elcho to Ego Elcho, 13 May, Wemyss Papers.

36 Letty Elcho to Ego Elcho, 14 May, Wemyss Papers.

37 Letty Elcho to Ego Elcho, undated, Wemyss Papers.

38 Letty Elcho to Ego Elcho, undated, Wemyss Papers.

39 Letty Elcho to Ego Elcho, undated, Wemyss Papers.

40 Cynthia Asquith, *Haply I May Remember*, p.169.

41 Ego Elcho to Letty Elcho, September 1914, Wemyss Papers.

42 Ego Elcho to Letty Elcho, 9 April 1914, Wemyss Papers.

43 Mary, Countess of Wemyss, *A Family Record*, pp.256, 264.

44 Letty Elcho to Mary Wemyss, 18 May 1915 in Mary, Countess of Wemyss, *A Family Record*, p.270.

45   *Ibid.*, p.363, Ego Elcho to Mary Wemyss, 22 January 1916.

46   Mary, Countess of Wemyss, *A Family Record*, pp.305–06.

47   Cynthia Asquith, *Lady Cynthia Asquith: Diaries 1915–18* (London: Hutchinson, 1968) p.91.

48   Letty Elcho to Mary Wemyss, 23 October 1915, in Mary, Countess of Wemyss, p.349.

49   Ego Elcho to Mary Wemyss, 25 October 1915, in Mary, Countess of Wemyss, p.351.

50   *Ibid.*

51   *Ibid.*

52   Letty Elcho to Mary Wemyss, 12 March 1916, in Mary, Countess of Wemyss, p.366.

53   Ego Elcho to Letty Elcho, 1 February 1916, Wemyss Papers.

54   Mary, Countess of Wemyss. *A Family Record*, p.372.

55   *Ibid.*, p.393.

56   Jeremy Paxman, pp.276–77.

57   Alfred Harmsworth Northcliffe, *Lord Northcliffe's War Book* (New York: George H. Doran, 1916) p.239.

58   Mary Wemyss to Evelyn de Vesci, undated, de Vesci Papers, Somerset Archives and Local Studies Service (South West Heritage Trust): DD/DRU/87.

59   Letty Elcho to Mary Wemyss, 3 May 1916, in Mary, Countess of Wemyss, p.374.

60   Cynthia Asquith, *Lady Cynthia Asquith: Diaries 1915–18*, p.183.

61   *Ibid.*, p.184.

62   Cynthia Asquith, *Diaries*, p.188.

63   Lord Wemyss to Mary Wemyss, July 1917, in Mary, Countess of Wemyss, p.404.

64   Cynthia Asquith, *Diaries*, p.188.

65   Letty Elcho to R. Smallbones, 2 January 1917, in Mary, Countess of Wemyss, p.403.

66   Mary, Countess of Wemyss, *A Family Record*, p.36.

67   Violet, Duchess of Rutland to Letty Elcho, undated, Wemyss Papers.

68   *Ibid.*

69   Mary Wemyss to Letty Elcho, 19 August 1916, Wemyss Papers.

70   Mary Wemyss to Letty Elcho, 22 October 1916, Wemyss Papers.

71   Mary Wemyss to Evelyn de Vesci, 23 July 1916, de Vesci Papers, Somerset Archives and Local Studies Service (South West Heritage Trust): DD/DRU/87.

72   Mary Wemyss to Violet, Duchess of Rutland, 13 July 1916, Wemyss Papers.

73   Letty Elcho to Evelyn de Vesci, 29 August 1916, de Vesci Papers, Somerset
      Archives and Local Studies Service (South West Heritage Trust): DD/
      DRU/87.

74   Jeremy Paxman, p.276.

75   Cynthia Asquith, *Diaries*, p.188.

76   Letty Elcho to R. Smallbones, 2 January 1917, in Mary, Countess of
      Wemyss, p.402.

77   Mary Wemyss to Evelyn de Vesci, 26 September 1916, de Vesci Papers,
      Somerset Archives and Local Studies Service (South West Heritage Trust):
      DD/DRU87.

78   Letty Elcho to Mary Wemyss, 1 October 1916, Wemyss Papers.

79   Nicola Beauman, *Cynthia Asquith* (London: Hamish Hamilton, 1987) p.181.

80   Letty Elcho to Mary Wemyss, 27 December 1916, Wemyss
      Papers.

81   Letty Elcho to R. Smallbones, 2 January 1917, in Mary, Countess of
      Wemyss, p.402.

82   *Ibid.*, p.403.

83   Mary Wemyss to Arthur Balfour, April 1917. Quoted in Jane Ridley and
      Clayre Percy (eds), p.346.

84   Mary Wemyss to Letty Elcho, 15 September 1917, Wemyss Papers.

85   Letty Elcho to Mary Wemyss, 5 July, Wemyss Papers.

86   Violet, Duchess of Rutland expressed this belief in a letter to her brother,
      Charlie. Quoted in Catherine Bailey, p.236.

CHAPTER FOUR

1   *The Times*, 1 May 1918, p.8.

2   'Lady Desborough with her Sons', *Tatler*, 11 August 1915.

3   Cynthia Asquith, *Remember and Be Glad*, p.53.

4   *Ibid.*

5   Richard Davenport-Hines, *Ettie: The Intimate Life and Dauntless Spirit of
     Lady Desborough* (London: Weidenfeld and Nicolson, 2008) p.7.

6   Cynthia Asquith, *Remember and Be Glad*, p.51.

7   Richard Davenport-Hines, p.2.

8   Richard Davenport-Hines, p.81.

9   Raymond Asquith to Ettie Grenfell, April 1916, in Ethel Anne Priscilla
     Grenfell, *Pages from a Family Journal 1888–1915* (Eton College: Privately
     Printed – Spottiswoode, Ballantyne & Co. Ltd, 1916) p.358.

10   *Ibid.*, p.99.

11   Nicholas Mosley, *Julian Grenfell* (London: Persephone Books, 2014) p.234.

12   Julian Grenfell to Ettie Grenfell, 1909, in Ethel Anne Priscilla Grenfell, p.148.

13   *Ibid.*

14   Julian Grenfell to Ettie Grenfell, July 1910, in Ethel Anne Priscilla Grenfell, p.185.

15   Billy Grenfell to Ettie Grenfell, October 1909, in Ethel Anne Priscilla Grenfell, pp.158–59.

16   Julian Grenfell to Ettie Grenfell, 1909, Ethel Anne Priscilla Grenfell, p.140.

17   Ethel Anne Priscilla Grenfell, p.99.

18   Billy Grenfell to Ettie Grenfell, 1 August 1913, in Ethel Anne Priscilla Grenfell, p.309.

19   Julian Grenfell to Ettie Grenfell, 6 August 1914, in Ethel Anne Priscilla Grenfell, p.452.

20   Julian Grenfell to Ettie Grenfell, 17 October 1914, in Ethel Anne Priscilla Grenfell, p.472.

21   Julian Grenfell to Ettie Grenfell, 15 October 1914, in Ethel Anne Priscilla Grenfell, p.470.

22   Julian Grenfell to Ettie Grenfell, 3 November 1914, in Ethel Anne Priscilla Grenfell, p.480.

23   Julian Grenfell to Ettie Grenfell, 28 October 1914, in Ethel Anne Priscilla Grenfell, p.477.

24   Ethel Anne Priscilla Grenfell, p.549.

25   Angela Lambert, p.186.

26   Julian Grenfell to Ettie Grenfell, 14 May 1915, in Ethel Anne Priscilla Grenfell, p.546.

27   *Ibid.*, p.550.

28   *Ibid.*, p.553.

29   *Ibid.*, p.554.

30   *Ibid.*, p.556.

31   Nicholas Mosley, p.400.

32   Ethel Anne Priscilla Grenfell, p.556.

33   *Ibid.*, p.557.

34   *Ibid.*

35   Billy Grenfell to Norah Lindsay, June 1915, in Ethel Anne Priscilla Grenfell, p.124.

36   Billy Grenfell to Anne Islington, 11 July 1915, in Ethel Anne Priscilla Grenfell, p.595.

37   Billy Grenfell to Con Manners, June 1915, in Ethel Anne Priscilla Grenfell, p. 594.

38   Mary Wemyss to Ettie Grenfell, 5 June 1915, Desborough Papers,

Hertfordshire Archives and Local Studies: D/ERVC477/37.

39   Mary Wemyss to Ettie Grenfell, 20 May 1915, Desborough Papers,
     Hertfordshire Archives and Local Studies: D/ERVC477/34.

40   Mary Wemyss to Ettie Grenfell, 29 May 1915. Desborough Papers,
     Hertfordshire Archives and Local Studies: D/ERVC477/36.

41   Ettie Desborough to Mary Wemyss, 3 June 1915, Wemyss Papers.

42   Mary Wemyss to Ettie Grenfell, 5 June 1915, Desborough Papers,
     Hertfordshire Archives and Local Studies: D/ERVC477/37.

43   Ettie Grenfell to Mary Wemyss, 3 June 1915, Wemyss Papers.

44   Mary, Countess of Wemyss. *A Family Record*, p.289.

45   11 June 1915, Cynthia Asquith, *Diaries*, p.41.

46   27 July 1915. *Ibid.*, p.59.

47   4 August 1915. *Ibid.*, p.62.

48   Richard Davenport-Hines, p.199.

49   Ettie Grenfell to Evelyn de Vesci, undated, de Vesci Papers, Somerset
     Archives and Local Studies Service (South West Heritage Trust): DD/
     DRU103.

50   Richard Davenport-Hines, p.19.

51   Ettie Grenfell to Evelyn de Vesci, undated, de Vesci Papers, Somerset
     Archives and Local Studies Service (South West Heritage Trust): DD/
     DRU103.

52   Ego Elcho to Mary Wemyss, 25 October 1915, in Mary, Countess of
     Wemyss, p.351.

53   Mary Wemyss to Ettie Grenfell, 23 October 1915, Desborough Papers,
     Hertfordshire Archives and Local Studies: D/ERVC477/43.

54   Mary Wemyss to Ettie Grenfell, 23 October 1915, Desborough Papers,
     Hertfordshire Archives and Local Studies: D/ERVC477/43.

55   Angela Lambert, p.169.

56   Raymond Asquith to H.T. Baker, 4 October 1899 in John Joliffe, p.61.

57   15 January 1918, Cynthia Asquith, *Diaries*, p.396.

58   20 October 1915. *Ibid.*, p.91.

59   Nicola Beauman, p.157.

60   Mary Wemyss to Evelyn de Vesci, 23 July 1916, de Vesci Papers, Somerset
     Archives and Local Studies Service (South West Heritage Trust): DD/
     DRU103.

61   Ettie Grenfell to Evelyn de Vesci, 3 July 1916, de Vesci Papers, Somerset
     Archives and Local Studies Service (South West Heritage Trust): DD/
     DRU103.

62   Mary Wemyss to Ettie Grenfell, 3 December 1916, Desborough Papers,
     Hertfordshire Archives and Local Studies:
     D/ERVC477/50.

63 Mary Wemyss to Ettie Grenfell, undated, Desborough Papers, Hertfordshire Archives and Local Studies: D/ERVC477/51.

64 Mary Wemyss to Evelyn de Vesci, 22 March 1916, de Vesci Papers, Somerset Archives and Local Studies Service (South West Heritage Trust): DD/DRU87.

65 Mary Wemyss to Evelyn de Vesci, 4 September 1916, de Vesci Papers, Somerset Archives and Local Studies (South West Heritage Trust): DD/DRU87.

66 17 August 1916, Cynthia Asquith, *Diaries*, p.206.

67 20 November 1916, Cynthia Asquith, *Diaries*, p.236.

68 Claudia Renton, p.346.

69 16 December 1916, Cynthia Asquith, *Diaries*, pp.245–46.

70 Mary Wemyss to Letty Elcho, undated, Wemyss Papers.

71 Mary Wemyss to Arthur Balfour, September 1914 in Jane Ridley and Clayre Percy (eds), p.313.

72 Mary Wemyss to Arthur Balfour, 22 December 1915 in Jane Ridley and Clayre Percy (eds), pp.331–32.

73 Ettie Grenfell to Evelyn de Vesci, 12 March (no year), de Vesci Papers, Somerset Archive and Local Studies Service (South West Heritage Trust): DD/DRU103.

74 Ettie Grenfell to Evelyn de Vesci, 22 June (no year), de Vesci Papers, Somerset Archive and Local Studies: DD/DRU103.

75 Mary Wemyss to Ettie Grenfell, 1917, Desborough Papers, Hertfordshire Archives and Local Studies: D/ERVC477/58.

76 Ettie Grenfell to Evelyn de Vesci, 22 June 1917, de Vesci Papers, Somerset Archives and Local Studies Service (South West Heritage Trust): DD/DRU103.

77 15 January 1918, Cynthia Asquith, *Diaries*, p.396.

78 Raymond Asquith to Ettie Grenfell, 12 August 1915, Desborough Papers, Hertfordshire Archives and Local Studies: DEX789 C60.

79 Mary Wemyss to Evelyn de Vesci, 18 December 1917, de Vesci Papers, Somerset Archives and Local Studies Service (South West Heritage Trust): DD/DRU103.

80 Angela Lambert, p.201.

81 Raymond Asquith to Katharine Asquith, 4 September 1916, in John Joliffe, p.291.

82 Mary Wemyss to Arthur Balfour, 21 January 1917, in Jane Ridley and Clayre Percy (eds), p.343.

83 Angela Lambert, p.221.

84 Mary Wemyss to Ettie Grenfell, 23 October 1931, Desborough Papers,

Hertfordshire Archives and Local Studies: D/ERVC
477/102.

CHAPTER FIVE

1   Paul Cornish, pp.215–16.

2   For a full account of the situation in 1918, see Jeremy Paxman, pp.252–54.

3   Quoted in Paxman, pp.253–54.

4   *The Times*, 18 June 1918, p.9.

5   Judy Middleton, *Hove and Portslade in the Great War* (Pen & Sword, 2014).

6   Niall Ferguson, pp.199–201.

7   Quoted in Niall Ferguson, p.202.

8   'Pathetic Evidence', *Exeter and Plymouth Gazette*, 7 November 1914, p.5.

9   *Exeter and Plymouth Gazette*, 9 November 1914, p.5.

10   *Express and Echo*, 9 November 1914.

11   *Western Times*, 26 January 1917, p.4.

12   *Exeter and Plymouth Gazette*, 13 May 1915, p.4.

13   Adrian Gregory, p.2.

14   *Ibid.*, pp.36–39.

15   *Ibid.*, p.103.

16   *Ibid.*, p.102.

17   *Taunton Courier and Western Advertiser*, 29 November 1916, p.2.

18   David Stevenson, *With Our Backs to the Wall: Victory and Defeat in 1918* (London: Penguin Books, 2012) pp.374–75.

19   'Echo Chamber', the Quaker Arts Network – quakerarts.net.

20   Quoted in Paul Cornish, p.108.

21   Mary Davis, *1914–1918*, TUC History Online.

22   David Stevenson, p.363.

23   29 December 1915. A.J.P. Taylor (ed.) *Lloyd George: A Diary by Frances Stevenson* (London: Hutchinson, 1971) p.86.

24   Niall Ferguson, p.346.

25   *Western Times*, 7 April 1916, p.7.

26   David Parker, *The People of Devon in the First World War* (Stroud: The History Press, 2013).

27   Paul Cornish, p.110.

28   Adrian Gregory, p.7.

29   *Ibid.*, pp.204–05.

30   *Ibid.*, p.202.

31   Niall Ferguson writes that until the Battle of the Somme the British

mainly fought because they wanted to, not because they were made to. However, he adds that not all Britons were equally keen to fight and that it was certainly not true that 'all classes [...] gave equally'. There were many middle-class men, who were potential officer material, who enlisted as privates in their eagerness to see action. Ferguson concludes that the middle class was keener to fight (p.199).

32   For a full discussion of the extent of patriotic fervour, see Niall Ferguson, p.202.

33   Peter Hart, pp.22–24.

34   Norman Stone, *World War One: A Short History* (London: Penguin Books, 2008) p.162.

35   *Legacies of War: Untold Otley Stories*, Otley Museum and Archive Trust (2014) p.23.

36   *Ibid.*

37   *Ibid.*, pp.4–6.

38   *Ibid.*, p.6.

39   *Ibid.*, p.20.

40   David Stevenson, pp.447–49.

41   *Legacies of War: Untold Otley Stories*, p.25.

42   Robert Coles, *History of Beaulieu Airfield* (Lymington: Robert Coles, 1982) pp.9, 18.

43   *Ibid.*, p.30.

44   Robert Coles, p.33.

45   *Ibid.*

46   'The Real New Forest Guide' – newforestguide.co.uk.

47   Quoted in Paul Cornish, p.217.

CHAPTER SIX

1   *The Times*, 4 June 1918, p.9.

2   Lyn MacDonald, *The Roses of No Man's Land* (London: Penguin, 1993) p.244.

3   Katherine MacDonald to Mrs MacDonald, undated. Canadian War Museum Archives. Archive DU MCG 58A 1114.9; Manuscript 19950037-014.

4   'On Night'. Katherine MacDonald's scrapbook. Canadian War Museum Archives. Archive DU MCG; Textual Record 58E 25.2.

5   Dr Fleck Graham to Mrs MacDonald, undated. Canadian War Museum Archives. Archive DU MCG; Manuscript 19950037-019.

6   Captain John Ballantyne to Mrs MacDonald, 28 May 1918. Canadian War

Museum Archives. Archive DU MCG; Manuscript 19950037-013.

7 Katherine MacDonald to Mrs MacDonald and Florence MacDonald, undated. Canadian War Museum Archives. Archive DU MCG; Manuscript 19950037-014.

8 Katherine MacDonald to Mrs MacDonald and Florence MacDonald, undated. Canadian War Museum Archives. Archive DU MCG; Manuscript 19950037-014.

9 Vera Brittain, pp.411–12.

10 Mary Macleod Moore, *Maple Leaf's Red Cross: The War Story of the Canadian Red Cross Overseas* (London: Skiffington, 1919) p.61.

11 *Ibid.*, pp.70–74.

12 *Ibid.*, p.85.

13 'Summary of Inspections and Work Done During the Month Away from HQ', 8 May 1918. The National Archive, Kew: WO95/3990.

14 Vera Brittain, pp.411–12.

15 Katherine MacDonald to Mrs MacDonald and Florence MacDonald, 24 March 1918. Canadian War Museum Archives. Archive DU MCG; Manuscript 19950037-014.

16 Captain Ronald Gordon Cumming, 'The Nursing Sister', in Katherine MacDonald's scrapbook. Canadian War Museum Archives. Archive DU MCG; Textual Record 58 2 5.2.

17 'Summary of Inspections', May 1918. The National Archive, Kew: WO95/3990.

18 Peter Hart, p.263.

19 Katherine MacDonald to Mrs MacDonald and Florence MacDonald, 18 May 1918. Canadian War Museum Archives. Archive DU MCG; Manuscript 19950037-014.

20 *Ibid.*

21 Major S.J.M. Comoton to Captain John Ballantyne, 2 June 1918. Canadian War Museum Archives. Archive DU MCG; Manuscript 1995037-013.

22 Edith Campbell to Miss Dalmage, undated. Canadian War Museum Archives. Archive DU MCG; Manuscript 19950037-019.

23 *Ibid.*

24 Queen Alexandra to Miss McCarthy, undated. Canadian War Museum Archives. Archive DU MCG; Manuscript 19950037-019.

25 Citation for the Award of the Military Medal for Distinguished Service in the Field for Nursing Sisters Helen Elizabeth Hansen and Beatrice McNair. Royal College of Nurses Archive online.

26 'Summary of Inspections and Work Done During the Month Away from HQ', 22 May 1918. The National Archive, Kew: WO95/3990.

27 Roland Hill, *Crag and Canyon* (Banff, Alberta) 13 July 1918.

28   Vera Brittain, p.433.

29   Captain John Ballantyne to Mrs MacDonald, 28 May 1918. Canadian War
      Museum Archives. Archive DU MCG; Manuscript 19950037-013.

30   *Ibid.*

31   *Ibid.*

32   Captain John Ballantyne to Mrs MacDonald, 29 May 1918. Canadian War
      Museum Archives. Archive DU MCG; Manuscript 19950037-013.

33   Captain John Ballantyne to Florence MacDonald, undated. Canadian War
      Museum Archives. Archive DU MCG; Manuscript 19950037-013.

34   Revelations 7: 9–17.

35   E.E. Ridley, Principal Matron Canadians, 'Report of Visit to the Étaples
      Area', 26 May 1918. Canadian War Museum Archives. Archive DU MCG;
      Manuscript 19950037-018.

36   Major S.J.M. Comoton to Captain John Ballantyne, 2 June 1918. Canadian
      War Museum Archives. Archive DU MCG; Manuscript 19950037-013.

37   E.E Ridley, Principal Matron Canadians, 'Report of Visit to the Étaples
      Area', 26 May 1918. Canadian War Museum Archives. Archive DU MCG;
      Manuscript 19950037-018.

38   Vera Brittain, p.417.

39   Mary Macleod Moore, pp.180–81.

40   Lottie M. Borland to Mrs MacDonald, undated. Canadian War Museum
      Archives. Archive DU MCG; Manuscript 19950037-019.

41   Dr Fleck Graham to Mrs MacDonald, undated. Canadian War Museum
      Archives. Archive DU MCG; Manuscript 19950037-019.

42   *Ibid.*

43   Lieutenant Colonel Clifford H. Reason to Mrs Graham. Quoted on
      Brantford Great War Centenary Association's website.

44   'Summary of Inspections and Work Done During the Month Away from
      HQ', 30 May 1918. The National Archive, Kew: WO95/3990.

45   Dr Fleck Graham to Mrs MacDonald, undated. Canadian War Museum
      Archives. Archive DU MCG; Manuscript 19950037-019.

46   *Brantford Expositor*, 24 September 1918.

47   Jennifer Morse, 'Gerald Edward Moira', *Legion Magazine* (1 January 2006).

48   Niall Ferguson, pp.208–09.

49   Lyn MacDonald, *The Roses of No Man's Land*, pp.277–79.

50   Beatriz Chadour-Sampson and Hubert Bari, p.10.

51   COHSE, 'Canadian Nurses World War One', http://cohse-union.blogspot.
      co.uk/2006/10/canadian-nurses-ww1.html.

52   *Brantford Expositor*, 24 May 1918.

CHAPTER SEVEN

1   Lyndsey Jenkins, *Lady Constance Lytton: Aristocrat, Suffragette, Martyr* (London: Biteback Publishing, 2015) p.214.

2   Alfred Harmsworth Northcliffe, pp.126–27.

3   27 March 1918, *Daily Mail*, p.4.

4   D. Chapman-Huston (ed.), *The Private Diaries of Daisy, Princess of Pless. 1873–1914* (London: John Murray, 1950) p.48.

5   *Ibid.*, p.47.

6   Justine Picardie, *Coco Chanel: The Legend and the Life* (London: Harper, 2010) p.145.

7   *Ibid.*, p.144.

8   Leslie Field, *Bendor: The Golden Duke of Westminster* (London: Weidenfeld and Nicolson, 2003) p.83.

9   Russell Harris, 'Princess Daisy of Pless: The Happy Years', Victoria and Albert Museum website (2011).

10 Justine Picardie, pp.148–49.

11 D. Chapman-Huston, p.32.

12 Shelagh, Duchess of Westminster, to Daisy, Princess of Pless, 22 February 1909. Quoted in D. Chapman-Huston, p.213.

13 Shelagh, Duchess of Westminster, to Daisy, Princess of Pless, 15 October 1909. *Ibid.*, p.226.

14 Leslie Field, p.1.

15 *Ibid.*, pp.127–28.

16 Charles S. Myers, *Shell Shock in France 1914–1918* (Cambridge: Cambridge University Press, 1940) p.4.

17 James Mackay, *Sir Thomas Lipton: The Man who Invented Himself* (London: Random House, 2012).

18 Charles S. Myers, p.5.

19 Ben Shepard, *Headhunters: The Search for a Science of the Mind* (London: Random House, 2014).

20 Charles S. Myers, p.4.

21 *Ibid.*, p.5.

22 *Ibid.*, p.6.

23 Leslie Field, pp.131–32.

24 Charles S. Myers, p.7.

25 Arthur Percival Marsh to Adine Waller, 5 July 1915. Leicestershire, Leicester and Rutland Record Office: DE3695/123.

26 The testimony of Lynette Powell appears in full in Lyn MacDonald, *The Roses of No Man's Land*, pp.67–68.

27 D. Chapman-Huston, p.312.

28 *Ibid.*, p.315.

29 Leslie Field, p.144.

30 11 July 1916, *The Daily News*, Perth.

31 Catherine Bailey, p.350.

32 Diana Duff Cooper, pp.117–19.

33 *Ibid.*, p.136.

34 Quoted in William E. Carson, *Northcliffe: Britain's Man of Power* (Cornell, 1918) p.273.

35 Major C.W. Wingrove to M. Oppenheimer in Rangoon, August 1918, *The Singapore Press*.

36 Lucinda Gosling, *Great War Britain: The First World War at Home* (Stroud: The History Press, 2014) p.77.

37 22 May 1918, Cynthia Asquith, *Diaries*, p.440.

38 20 June 1918. *Ibid.*, p.451.

39 Lyn MacDonald, *The Roses of No Man's Land*, p.67.

40 2 February 1915, David Lindsay, Earl of Crawford, *The Crawford Papers: The Journals of David Lindsay, Twenty-Seventh Earl of Crawford and Tenth Earl of Balcarres (1871–1940), During the Years 1892 to 1940* (Manchester: Manchester University Press, 1984) p.349.

41 'The Way of the World', 17 July 1918, *The Sketch*, p.64.

42 Quoted in Lucinda Gosling, p.83.

43 'In France: A Duchess at Her Hospital', *The Sketch*, 20 March 1918.

44 'World War One Nurse Martha's Cheerfulness a Tonic for "Broken Soldiers"', *The Sentinel*, 29 September 2014.

45 Interview with Martha Frost's great nephew Ian Broad, 5 April 2016.

46 'Summary of Work for May 1918', The Joint War Committee Reports, Red Cross Archives.

47 Peter Hart, pp.272–74, 294.

48 Norman Stone, p.169.

49 'Surprise Romance Wedding to Flying Officer', *Motherwell Times*, 30 January 1920.

50 *Ibid.*

51 'The Way of the World', *The Sketch*, 17 July 1918, p.64.

CHAPTER EIGHT

1 Beatriz Chadour-Sampson with Hubert Bari, p.10.

2 'Crown Coronets', *The Sketch*, 15 December 1915, p.236.

3   'Small Talk', *The Sketch*, 13 March 1918, p.224.

4   'The Way of the World', *The Sketch*, 19 June 1918, p.322.

5   Peter Hart, pp.296–98.

6   'The Way of the World', *The Sketch*, 19 June 1918, p.322.

7   Lord Charles Mercer Nairne to Lord Lansdowne, October 1914. Bowood Archive.

8   'Major Lord Charles Mercer Nairne, 1874–1914, M.V.O (1911), Royal Dragoon Guards', Bowood Archive.

9   Lord Lansdowne to Andrew Bonar Law, 2 November 1914. Parliamentary Archive, Bonar Law Papers: BL/35/2/2.

10   Jo Johnston, archivist at Bowood, explains that it is not clear in the letter whether the 'soldier boy' was a toy, a real soldier, or even the scaled down copy of his father's uniform he was given to dress up in.

11   Evelyn, Duchess of Devonshire, to Lady Lansdowne, 2 November 1914, Bowood Archive.

12   Margot Asquith, 19 May 1915. In Michael and Eleanor Brock, p.126.

13   Margot Asquith to Violet Asquith, 7 June 1915. In Mark Pottle. *Champion Redoubtable: The Diaries and Letters of Violet Bonham Carter 1914–45* (London: Weidenfeld and Nicolson, 1998) p.63.

14   Anne de Courcy, *Margot at War: Love and Betrayal in Downing Street 1912–1916* (London: Weidenfeld and Nicolson, 2014) pp.240, 247–48.

15   Lucinda Gosling, pp.53–54, 63.

16   7 June 1916, Cynthia Asquith, pp.172–73.

17   Juliet Nicolson, *The Great Silence: 1918–1920. Living in the Shadow of the Great War* (London: John Murray, 2009) p.31.

18   Lou Taylor, *Mourning Dress: A Costume and Social History* (London and New York: Routledge, 1983) p.229.

19   *Ibid.*, p.267.

20   'Mourning for British Heroes', *The Yorkshire Post*, 29 August 1914, p.6.

21   'Small Talk', *The Sketch*, 23 June 1915, p.238.

22   Lou Taylor, p.269.

23   10 June 1915, Cynthia Asquith, *Diaries*, p.39.

24   Margot Asquith, 3 August 1915. In Michael and Eleanor Brock, p.170.

25   Derek Wilson, *Oxford Dictionary of National Biography*.

26   Lucie Dounay to Violet Astor, 22 June 1916. Philip Astor Letters.

27   Ettie Desborough to Violet Astor, 21 June 1916. Philip Astor Letters.

28   Violet, Duchess of Rutland to Letty Elcho. Wemyss Papers.

29   John L. Renton to Violet Astor, 17 June 1916. Philip Astor Letters.

30   William Waldorf Astor to Violet Astor, 7 June 1916. Philip Astor Letters.

31   Louise Beaufort to Violet Astor, 29 June 1916. Philip Astor Letters.

32   Violet, Duchess of Rutland to Letty Elcho. Wemyss Papers.

33   'Marriage of Captain the Hon. J. Astor and Lady Charles Mercer Nairne',
      Reading Mercury, 2 September 1916.

34   Maurice Bonham Carter to Violet Asquith, 22 June 1915. In Mark Pottle,
      p.69.

35   *Dundee Evening Telegraph*, 26 November 1915.

36   'Wedding Gifts from Members of Parliament', *Newcastle Journal*,
      26 November 1915.

37   'Miss Violet Asquith's Wedding', *Yorkshire Evening Post*, 30 November 1915.

38   Violet Bonham Carter to Eddie Marsh, 17 December 1915. In Mark Pottle,
      pp.88–89.

39   Michael and Eleanor Brock, p.xcvii.

40   Mark Pottle, p.85.

41   7 January 1916, James Munson (ed.), *Echoes of the Great War: The Diary of
      Reverend Andrew Clark 1914–1919* (Oxford: Oxford University Press, 1988)
      p.106.

42   30 November 1915, Cynthia Asquith, *Diaries*, p.106.

43   *Ibid.*, 27 January 1916, p.125.

44   10 February 1916 in A.J.P. Taylor, p.97.

45   Michael and Eleanor Brock, p.xcviii.

46   Lady Violet Astor to Lady Lansdowne, 30 October 1918. Bowood Archive.

CHAPTER NINE

1   'Over 70 Pearls Yesterday', *The Times*, 29 June 1918, p.9.

2   Samuel Hynes, *The Edwardian Turn of Mind* (London: Pimlico, 1968)
     pp.328–30.

3   'The Post Impressionists', *The Times*, 17 November 1910, p.4.

4   Samuel Hynes, p.326.

5   Carter Ratcliff, *John Singer Sargent* (New York, London, Paris: Artabras,
     1982) p.181.

6   Karen Corsano and Daniel Williman, *John Singer Sargent and his Muse:
     Painting Love and Loss* (New York amd London: Rowman and Littlefield,
     2014) p.18.

7   9 June 1916, Cynthia Asquith, *Diaries*, p.174.

8   'Exhibition of the Royal Society of Portrait Painters at the Grafton
     Galleries', *The Scotsman*, 3 June 1916. Quoted in Natasha Wallace, JSS
     Virtual Gallery online.

9   'Exhibition of the Royal Society of Portrait Painters at the Grafton

Galleries', *The Ladies' Field*, 24 June 1916. Quoted in Natasha Wallace, JSS Virtual Gallery online.

10   *The Queen*, 15 June 1918, p.642.

11   'Inspection by Two Queens', *The Times*, 24 June 1918, p.5.

12   Sir Robert Hudson to Lord Northcliffe, 22 June 1918. Northcliffe Papers Vol. XVII (ff.171). The British Library ADD. MS. 62169.

13   'Pearl Exhibition', *The Times*, 21 June 1918, p.9.

14   *Ibid*.

15   *Ibid*.

16   Robert Dixon, *Photography, Early Cinema and Colonial Modernity: Frank Hurley's Synchronized Lecture Entertainments* (London: Anthem Press, 2013) p.44.

17   *Ibid*., p.45.

18   *Ibid*., p.46.

19   Niall Ferguson, p.236.

20   Paul Cornish, p.127.

21   Niall Ferguson, p.236.

22   4 August 1916, in A.J.P. Taylor, p.112.

23   Robert Dixon, p.48.

24   Robert Dixon and Christopher Lee (eds), *The Diaries of Frank Hurley 1912–1941* (London: Anthem Press, 2011) p.xxi.

25   *Ibid*., p.xxii.

26   *Ibid*., p.104.

27   *Ibid*., p.xx.

29   Robert Dixon, p.54.

29   *Ibid*., p.48.

30   'Inspection by Two Queens', *The Times*, 24 June 1918, p.5.

31   'Over 70 Pearls Yesterday', *The Times*, 29 June 1918, p.9.

CHAPTER TEN

1   Maurice Baring, 'Julian Grenfell' Printed Memorial. Desborough Papers, Hertfordshire Archives and Local Studies: DD/DRU103.

2   Nicholas Mosley, p.165.

3   *Ibid*., p.65.

4   Richard Davenport-Hines, p.81.

5   Niall Ferguson, p.229.

6   Julian Grenfell, 'Into Battle'. Quoted in Nicholas Mosley, pp.384–85.

7   Henry James to Ettie Desborough, Hertfordshire Archives and Local

Studies. Quoted in Nicholas Mosley, p.399.

8   Quoted in Cynthia Asquith, *Remember and Be Glad*, p.199.

9   Nicholas Mosley, p.349.

10   Cynthia Asquith, *Remember and Be Glad*, p.199.

11   Israel Gollancz, *Pearl: An English Poem of the Fourteenth Century Re-Set in Modern English* (London: George W. Jones, 1918).

12   'Red Cross Pearls', *The Times*, 10 December 1918, p.11.

13   Israel Gollancz.

14   *Ibid.*

15   Ruth Hibbard, 'Pearls: Piety, Poetry and Pre-Raphaelites – Part One', Victoria and Albert Museum blog (2013).

16   Israel Gollancz.

17   Ruth Hibbard.

18   Israel Gollancz.

19   *Ibid.*

20   Tennyson, quoted in Israel Gollancz.

21   A.N. Wilson, 'Tennyson's In Memoriam: A Farewell to Religious Certainty', *The Guardian*, 4 January 2011.

22   Raymond Asquith to H.T. Baker, 28 December 1897. In John Joliffe, p.33.

23   Raymond Asquith to H.T. Baker, undated. *Ibid.*, p.34.

24   Cynthia Asquith, *Diaries*, pp.136, 148.

25   J.M. Barrie, 'Bron the Gallant', *The Times*, 4 December 1916, p.11.

26   Maurice Baring, *The Puppet Show of Memory* (Boston: Little, Brown & Company, 1922) p.170.

27   Raymond Asquith to Aubrey Herbert, 20 March 1906. In John Joliffe, p.140.

28   Raymond Asquith to Katharine Horner, 20 March 1905. *Ibid.*, pp.123–24.

29   Tessa Boase, *The Housekeeper's Tale: The Women Who Really Ran the English Country House* (Aurum Press, 2014).

30   J.M. Barrie, 'Bron the Gallant', *The Times*, 4 December 1916, p.11.

31   Maurice Baring, *Flying Corps Headquarters 1914–1918* (London: Faber & Faber, 2008) p.12.

32   Anne de Courcy, pp.299–300.

33   Jeanne MacKenzie, *The Children of the Souls: A Tragedy of the First World War* (London: Chatto & Windus, 1986) p.32.

34   Maurice Baring to Ethel Smyth, 25 October 1914. In Ethel Smyth, *Maurice Baring* (London: William Heinemann, 1938) p.314.

35   Mark Pottle, p.10.

36   Maurice Baring, *Flying Corps Headquarters*, p.86.

37   Maurice Baring to Ethel Smyth, 20 September 1916. In Ethel Smyth, p.314.

38   Nicholas Mosley, p.147.

39   Maurice Baring, *Flying Corps Headquarters*, p.194.

40   J.M. Barrie, 'Bron the Gallant', *The Times*, 4 December 1916, p.11.

41   Maurice Baring. *Flying Corps Headquarters*, pp.186–88.

42   Richard Davenport-Hines, p.213.

43   'Crowns, Coronets and Courtiers', *The Sketch*, 13 December 1916, p.230.

44   Maurice Baring. *Flying Corps Headquarters*, p.193.

45   J.M. Barrie, 'Bron the Gallant', *The Times*, 4 December 1916, p.11.

46   Maurice Baring, *The Puppet Show of Memory*, p.396.

47   'Maurice Baring: Obituary', *The Times*, 17 December 1945, p.6.

48   Laura Lovat, *Maurice Baring: A Postscript by Laura Lovat with Some Letters and Verse* (London: Hollis & Carter, 1947) p.12.

49   Maurice Baring, *Darby and Joan* (Thirsk, Yorkshire: House of Stratus, 1935) p.124.

50   Maurice Baring, *In Memoriam: Auberon Herbert, Captain Lord Lucas, Royal Flying Corps, Killed November 3, 1916* (Oxford: B.H. Blackwell, 1917) p.13.

51   Elizabeth Vandiver, *Stand in the Trench, Achilles: Classical Receptions in British Poetry of the First World War* (Oxford: Oxford University Press, 2010), p.360–61.

52   Maurice Baring. *In Memoriam*, p.14.

53   T.E. Shaw to Maurice Baring, 30 October 1928. In Ethel Smyth, p.338.

CHAPTER ELEVEN

1   Paul Cornish, p.218.

2   Lyn MacDonald. *The Roses of No Man's Land*, p.312.

3   Peter Hart, pp.362–64.

4   Sir Robert Hudson to Lord Northcliffe, 22 June 1918, Northcliffe Papers. The British Library: ADD MS 62169 Vol.XVII (ff.171).

5   War Office telegram, 31 October 1914. Lansdowne Papers, Bowood Archive.

6   Henry, 5th Marquess of Lansdowne to his wife Maud, 28 October 1915. Lansdowne Papers, Bowood Archive.

7   Henry, 5th Marquess of Lansdowne to his wife Maud, 8 November 1915. Lansdowne Papers, Bowood Archive.

8   Extracts from the account of Lord Charles Mercer Nairne (1874–1914) written by the 5th Marquess of Lansdowne for his grandson, George. Lansdowne Papers, Bowood Archive.

9   Henry, 5th Marquess of Lansdowne to Lord Edmond, 4 October 1917. Lansdowne Papers, Bowood Archive.

10 Quoted in 'For King and Country: Bowood and the First World War', *Western Daily Press*, 8 March 2014.

11 Jeremy Paxman, p.237.

12 'The Way of the War', *The Graphic*, 8 December 1917, p.4.

13 'Motley Notes', *The Sketch*, 19 December 1917, p.246.

14 Diana Duff Cooper, p.191.

15 Jeremy Paxman, p.237.

16 'Lotteries for War Charities', *The Times*, 29 July 1918, p.7.

17 'Letter to the Editor from Edward Winton, the Bishop of Winchester. The Lotteries Bill', *The Times*, 2 August 1918, p.9.

18 'Bishop of Norwich: The Lotteries Bill', *The Tiimes*, 5 August 1918, p.9.

19 'Common Sense: The Lotteries Bill', *The Times*, 6 August 1918, p.5.

20 Archbishop of Canterbury, 29 July 1918. Lotteries (War Charities) Bill, Hansard.

21 Sir Robert Hudson to Lord Northcliffe, 28 July 1918. Northcliffe Papers, The British Library: ADD MS 62169 (ff.171).

22 Lord Northcliffe to Sir Robert Hudson, undated. *Ibid*.

23 Sir Robert Hudson to Lord Northcliffe, 30 July 1918. *Ibid*.

24 Lord Northcliffe to Sir Robert Hudson, 1 August 1918. *Ibid*.

25 Lady Northcliffe to David Lloyd George, undated. Parliamentary Archive: LG/F/41/8/33.

26 12 February 1916, in A.J.P. Taylor, p.98.

27 29 April 1917. *Ibid.*, p.157.

28 Sir George Cave, 6 August 1918. Lotteries (War Charities) Bill, Hansard.

29 Theodore Taylor, 6 August 1918. *Ibid*.

30 Sir Stephen Collins, 6 August 1918. *Ibid.*

31 Sidney Robinson, 6 August 1918. *Ibid*.

32 Evelyn Cecil. 6 August 1918. *Ibid*.

33 Sir Arthur Stanley, 6 August 1918. *Ibid*.

34 'The Letters of Eve', *Tatler*, 14 August 1918, p.170.

35 'The Lotteries Bill', *The Official Journal of the British Red Cross Society* (September 1918) p.101.

36 'The Vote on the Lotteries Bill', *The Times*, 8 August 1918, p.7.

37 'Letter to the Editor', *The Spectator*, 9 August 1918.

38 'The Pearl Queue', *Daily Mail*, 18 December 1918, p.3.

CHAPTER TWELVE

1 John Pollock, *Kitchener* (London: Robinson, 1998) p.482.

2 Anne de Courcy, p.319.

3 Raymond Asquith to Katharine Asquith, 11 June 1916. In John Joliffe, p.267.

4 Vera Brittain, p.272.

5 'King's Message of Sympathy to Lord Kitchener's Sister', *Gloucester Chronicle*, 10 June 1916, p.5.

6 John Pollock, p.xx.

7 Conversations with Lady Emma Kitchener, 18 January 2016 and October 2016.

8 Letter Referring to Lord Kitchener of Khartoum, 7 November 1916. Imperial War Museum: 6067.

9 *Ibid.*

10 'Lord Kitchener's Sister', *Portsmouth Evening News*, 12 January 1915, p.2.

11 'Kitchener's Sister Dead', *Yorkshire Evening Post*, 10 February 1925, p.9.

12 John Pollock, p.486.

13 Raymond Asquith to Katharine Asquith, 13 June 1916. In John Joliffe, p.268.

14 Millie Parker to Mrs Hankey, 18 July 1916. Imperial War Museum: 89/1295.

15 Millie Parker to Captain Brittain, 9 July 1916. Quoted in 'Pathetic Letter from Kitchener's Sister', *Dundee Courier*, 12 July 1916, p.6.

16 Richard Davenport-Hines, p.101.

17 Ethel Anne Priscilla Grenfell, p.61.

18 Lord Kitchener to Ettie Grenfell, undated. Desborough Papers, Hertfordshire Archives and Local Studies: DE X789-C22, p.4.

19 Richard Davenport-Hines, p.101.

20 John Pollock, p.445.

21 Lord Kitchener to Willie Grenfell, undated. Desborough Papers, Hertfordshire Archives and Local Studies: DEX789/C26.

22 Richard Davenport-Hines, p.199.

23 Lord Kitchener to Ettie Grenfell, 9 August 1915. In Ethel Anne Priscilla Grenfell, pp.617–18.

24 Tom Clarke, p.76.

25 Anne de Courcy, p.277.

26 James Munson, p.106.

27 Margot Asquith, 26 October 1914. In Michael and Eleanor Brock, p.40.

28 Margot Asquith, 4 June 1915. *Ibid.*, pp.148–49.

29   Quoted in J. Lee Thompson, *Northcliffe: Press Baron in Politics 1865–1922* (London: John Murray, 2000) p.254.

30   'Frances Parker Alias Janet Arthur', Scottish Archives for Schools Online.

31   Elizabeth Crawford, *The Women's Suffrage Movement: A Reference Guide 1866–1928* (London: Routledge, 2003) p.526.

32   Lynsey Jenkins, p.210.

33   Elizabeth Crawford, p.526.

34   J. Lee Thompson, p.208.

35   Quoted in Reginald Pound and Geoffrey Harmsworth, p.518.

36   David Stevenson, p.440.

37   Adrian Gregory, p.96.

38   'Lord Kitchener's Sister and Drink', *Hull Daily Mail*, 12 April 1915, p.3.

39   'Lord Kitchener's Sister at Dunfermline', *Dundee Courier*, p.5.

40   Anne de Courcy, p.253.

41   Adrian Gregory, p.109.

42   Anne de Courcy, p.254.

43   'Red Cross Rubies', *Daily Mail*, 29 July 1918, p.4.

44   'Red Cross Pearls', *Daily Mail*, 9 August 1918, p.4.

45   M.W. Daly, *The Sirdar: Sir Reginald Wingate and the British Empire in the Middle East*, Vol. 222 (American Philosophical Society, 1997) p.100.

46   *Ibid.*, pp.166–67.

47   Rudyard Kipling to Lieutenant W.H. Lewis, 5 December 1913. Rudyard Kipling and Thomas Pinney, *The Letters of Rudyard Kipling 1911–1919* (Iowa: University of Iowa Press, 1990).

48   M.W. Daly, pp.251, 319.

49   'Lord Norbury as Factory Worker', *Yorkshire Evening Post*, 15 June 1915, p.6.

50   'Peer as a Fitter to Start Work in an Aeroplane Factory', *Birmingham Gazette*, 16 June 1915, p.5.

51   'War News as seen by our Cartoonist', *Sunday Mirror*, 27 June 1915, p.11.

52   'Peer-Mechanic Hard at Work', *Dundee Evening Telegraph*, 3 September 1915, p.2.

53   Jeremy Paxman, p.238.

CHAPTER THIRTEEN

1   Norman Stone, p.175.

2   Paul Cornish, p.220.

3   *Ibid.*, pp.223–26.

4   Henry Wadsworth Longfellow, 'Santa Filomena', *Birds of Passage: Flight the First*.

5   'Tiffany Windows', www.redcross.org.

6   'Red Cross Pearls', *The Times*, 7 December 1918, p.11.

7   Red Cross Pearl Necklace Auction Catalogue, December 1918, Victoria & Albert Museum, Christie's Archive and Red Cross Archive.

8   'The Red Cross Pearls', *The Times*, 3 December 1918, p.11.

9   Hans Nadelhoffer, *Cartier* (Chronicle Books, 2007) pp.118–20.

10   *Ibid.*, p.120.

11   *Ibid.*

12   *Ibid.*, pp.120–21.

13   H.C. Marillier, *Christie's 1766–1925* (London: Constable & Co., 1926) p.163.

14   'An Ideal New Year's Gift: Sessel Pearls', *The Queen*, 5 January 1918, p.29.

15   'Dress and Fashion', *The Queen*, 2 February 1918, p.146.

16   Arthur J. Rees, *The Hand in the Dark* (London: John Lane, 1920).

CHAPTER FOURTEEN

1   Nicola Beauman, p.241.

2   Mary Wemyss' Diary, 11 November 1918, Wemyss Papers.

3   Ettie Grenfell to Mary Wemyss, 11 November 1918. Quoted in Richard Davenport-Hines, p.229.

4   *Ibid.*, p.228.

5   Ettie Grenfell to Letty Elcho, 15 November 1918. Wemyss Papers: vi.2.042.

6   Mary Wemyss to Ettie Grenfell, 27 November 1918. Desborough Papers, Hertfordshire Archives and Local Studies: D/ERV477/63.

7   Ettie Grenfell to Letty Elcho, 15 November 1918. Wemyss Papers: vi. 2.042.

8   Cynthia Asquith, *Diaries*, 7 October 1918, p.480.

9   'The Red Cross Pearls', *The Times*, 25 November 1918, p.5.

10   *Ibid.*

11   'Pearl Sale Week', *Daily Mail*, 17 December 1918, p.5.

12   'The Sale of the Red Cross Pearls', *The Queen*, 28 December 1918, p.634.

13   'Pearl Sale Week', *Daily Mail*, 17 December 1918, p.5.

14   H.C. Marillier, p.150.

15   'Selling Household Goods for Charity: The Red Cross Auction', *Illustrated London News*, 17 April 1915.

16   *Ibid.*

17 H.C. Marillier, *Christie's 1766–1925* (London: Constable and Co., 1926) pp.152–3.

18 'Small Talk', *The Sketch*, 5 May 1915, p.98.

19 Raleigh Trevelyan, *Grand Dukes and Diamonds: The Wernhers of Luton Hoo* (London: Secker & Warburg, 1991) p.173.

20 F.M.L. Thompson, *English Landed Society in the Nineteenth Century* (London: Routledge, 2013).

21 Raleigh Trevelyan, p.174.

22 For a full description of the Wernhers' lifestyle see Raleigh Trevelyan, *Grand Dukes and Diamonds*.

23 Raleigh Trevelyan, p.254.

24 *Ibid.*, p.266.

25 *Ibid.*, p.267.

26 'Crowns, Coronets, Courtiers', *The Sketch*, 26 January 1916, p.76.

27 'Small Talk', *The Sketch*, 5 May 1915, p.98.

28 *Ibid.*

29 'Crowns, Coronets, Courtiers', *The Sketch*, 26 January 1916, p.76.

30 'Art Treasures for Red Cross Sale', *The Times*, 4 March 1916, p.9.

31 Raleigh Trevelyan, p.266.

32 *Ibid.*, pp.295–96.

33 'Lady Northcliffe Red Cross Sales: Crowns, Coronets, Courtiers', *The Sketch*, 2 February 1916, p.100.

34 'Christie's Sales', 'Report of the Red Cross Society's War Activities. Part III. Sources of Income'. Red Cross Archives (1921) p.36.

35 H.C. Marillier, p.153.

36 'Art Treasures for Red Cross Sale', *The Times*, 4 March 1916, p.9.

37 'Crowns, Coronets, Courtiers', *The Sketch*, 21 April 1915, p.54.

38 H.C. Marillier, p.155.

39 'Crowns, Coronets, Courtiers', *The Sketch*, 24 January 1917, p.78.

40 Raleigh Trevelyan, p.272.

41 'Lady Wernher's Millions', *Sunderland Daily Echo and Shipping Gazette*, 17 January 1917, p.2.

42 'Crowns, Coronets, Courtiers', *The Sketch*, 24 January 1917, p.78.

43 Norma S. Davis, *A Lark Ascends: Florence Kate Upton, Artist and Illustrator* (Scarecrow Press, 1992) p.147.

44 *Ibid.*

45 For a full discussion of this idea see James Fox, *British Art and the First World War 1914–1924* (Cambridge: Cambridge University Press, 2015) p.63.

CHAPTER FIFTEEN

1 'The Welcome to Haig', *Newcastle Journal*, 20 December 1918, p.1.

2 *Ibid*.

3 'The Letters of Eve', *Tatler*, 20 June 1917.

4 'The Woman About Town', *The Sketch*, 20 June 1917, p.vi.

5 Raleigh Trevelyan, pp.xxi–xxii.

6 'Mr Anderson's Speech', Christie's Archive.

7 '£22,000 for the Necklace', *The Times*, 20 December 1918, p.11.

8 Niall Ferguson, p.247.

9 Jeremy Paxman, pp.81–82.

10 'The Kitchener Bowl', *Liverpool Daily Post*, 24 June 1916, p.1.

11 'Red Cross Pearls', *The Times*, 14 December 1918, p.5.

12 'The Necklace Mystery', *New Zealand Herald*, 26 August 1913, p.4.

13 'Crowns, Coronets, Courtiers', *The Sketch*, 21 April 1915, p.54.

14 Lord Rowallan. *Rowallan: The Autobiography of Lord Rowallan, K. T.* (Edinburgh: Paul Harris Publishing, 1976) p.37.

15 'Red Cross Prisoners', *Birmingham Gazette*, 5 January 1916, p.4.

16 Elsie Corbett, *Red Cross in Serbia 1915–1919. A Personal Diary of Experiences* (Banbury: Cheney & Sons, 1964) p.viii.

17 *Ibid*., p.74.

18 *Ibid*., p.111.

19 *Ibid*.

20 *Ibid*., p.vii.

21 Lord Rowallan, *Rowallan: The Autobiography of Lord Rowallan, K. T.* (Edinburgh: Paul Harris Publishing, 1976) p.49.

22 Lord Rowallan, p.47.

23 *Ibid*., p.50.

24 'Popular Wedding at St Andrews', *Dundee Evening Telegraph*, 14 August 1918, p.3.

25 The Rowallan family do not know what happened to the necklace. Elsie had a pearl necklace which she intended to leave to her niece, but when she died in the Priory, London, no one could find her pearl necklace. Her sister-in-law, Lady Rowallan, had a single-strand pearl necklace which was made up of natural pearls, not cultured, but it was stolen from her in the Lansdowne Club in the 1960s. Information from Lady Rowallan's daughter, Fiona Patterson.

26 'This Morning', *Daily Mirror*, 13 April 1915, p.12.

27 The Countess of Carnarvon, *Lady Almina and the Real Downton Abbey: The Lost Legacy of Highclere Castle* (London: Hodder & Stoughton, 2011) p.222.

28 'Memories and Tears', *The Times*, 2 December 1918, p.11.

CHAPTER SIXTEEN

1   '*The Times* Fund', 'Part III – Sources of Income', Red Cross Archives, p.15.

2   '*The Times* Fund', *Red Cross Journal* (15 January 1919) Red Cross Archives.

3   '*The Times* Fund', *Red Cross Journal* (15 May 1918) Red Cross Archives.

4   Reginald Pound and Geoffrey Harmsworth, p.533.

5   J. Lee Thompson, p.361.

6   'Hudson and Northcliffe Friends', *The Sydney Mail*, 8 October 1930.

7   J. Lee Thompson, p.394.

8   J. Lee Thompson, p.1.

9   Reginald Pound and Geoffrey Harmsworth, p.882.

10 'A Love Triangle that Never was Profane', *The Brooklyn Daily Eagle*, 6 May 1923.

11 Paul Ferris, p.271.

12 Cecil H. King, *Strictly Personal: Some Memoirs of Cecil H. King* (London: Weidenfeld and Nicolson, 1969) p.62.

13 'A Love Triangle that Never was Profane', *The Brooklyn Daily Eagle*, 6 May 1923.

14 *Ibid.*

15 Paul Ferris, p.304.

16 'Pearl Necklace Fund', *Reports of the Joint Committee 1919*, Red Cross Archives.

17 'France and Belgium. Convalescent Homes', *Reports of the Joint Committee 1920*, Red Cross Archives.

18 'Hostels for Relatives of Wounded in France and Belgium', *Reports of the Joint Committee 1920*, Red Cross Archives.

19 'Graves Fund', *Reports of the Joint Committee 1920*, Red Cross Archives.

20 'Summaries of Work', October 1918, p.8; December 1918, p.14; December 1918 (no. 106) p.11. 'Rehabilitation after the First World War', redcross.org. uk/WW1.

21 'Star and Garter Home', *The Times*, 11 July 1924, p.11.

22 Laurence Spring, 'Star and Garter Home – Surrey in the Great War', Surrey History Centre, www.surreyinthegreatwar.org.uk.

23 *Ibid.*

24 *Ibid.*

25 'The Royal Star and Garter Homes', starandgarter.org.uk.

26 'Rehabilitation after the First World War', redcross.org.uk/WW1.

27 'Star and Garter Home', *The Times*, 11 July 1924, p.11.

28 'Homes for the Totally Disabled', *The Times*, 3 June 1916, p.9.

29 'Rehabilitation after the First World War', redcross.org.uk/WW1.

30 Alfred Harmsworth Northcliffe, p.25.

31 'Earl of Rothes Sells his Fife Estate', *Dundee Courier*, 21 June 1919.

32 Jeremy Paxman, p.284.

33 Christopher Simon Sykes, *Private Palaces: Life in the Great London House* (London: Chatto & Windus, 1985) pp.322–23.

34 *Ibid.*, p.328.

35 *The Times*, 19 May 1920. Quoted in Christopher Simon Sykes, p.322.

36 Mary Wemyss to Ettie Desborough, 3 December 1916. Desborough Papers, Hertfordshire Archives and Local Studies: D/ERVC477/50.

37 'The Red Cross Pearl Necklace', *Illustrated London News*, 8 March 1919, p.25.

38 Emma Clarke, press and marketing at Mikimoto, London.

39 Beatriz Chadour-Sampson with Hubert Bari, p.28.

40 'A Japanese Pearl Farm', *Yorkshire Evening Post*, 19 June 1914, p.6.

41 Beatriz Chadour-Sampson with Hubert Bari, pp.27–29.

42 'The Pearl Puzzle', *Dundee Evening Telegraph*, 1 August 1921, p.11.

43 'Pearl Cultivation', *Lincolnshire Echo*, 7 May 1921, p.4.

44 Emma Clarke, press and marketing at Mikimoto, London.

45 *Ibid.*

46 Emma Clarke, press and marketing at Mikimoto, London.

47 Jane Mulvagh, p.64.

48 'World Control of Pearls', *Hull Daily Mail*, 25 May 1936, p.5.

49 'A Bonfire of Pearls', *Dundee Evening Telegraph*, 15 April 1937, p.3.

50 Emma Clarke, press and marketing at Mikimoto, London.

51 'Spirit Oysters', *Nottingham Evening Post*, 2 December 1936, p.6.

52 Bronwyn Cosgrave, Vogue *on: Coco Chanel* (London: Quadrille Publishing, 2012) p.54.

53 *Ibid.*, p.56.

54 *Ibid.*, p.58.

55 Justine Picardie, p.163.

56 Bronwyn Cosgrave, p.64.

57 Justine Picardie, p.168.

58 Justine Picardie, p.183.

59 Justine Picardie, p.168.

60 Jane Mulvagh, p.52.

61 Bronwyn Cosgrave, p.69.

SELECT BIBLIOGRAPHY

Alston, Isabella, *Coco Chanel* (London: Bellagio Press, 2014).

Asquith, Cynthia, *Haply I May Remember* (London: James Barrie, 1950).

— *Lady Cynthia Asquith: Diaries 1915–18* (London: Hutchinson, 1968).

— *Remember and Be Glad* (London: James Barrie, 1952).

Bailey, Catherine, *The Secret Rooms: A Castle Filled with Intrigue, a Plotting Duchess and a Mysterious Death* (London: Penguin, 2013).

Barczewski, Stephanie, *Titanic One Hundredth Anniversary Edition: A Night Remembered* (London: A & C Black, 2011).

Baring, Maurice, *Darby and Joan* (Thirsk, Yorkshire: House of Stratus, 1935).

— *Flying Corps Headquarters 1914–1918* (London: Faber & Faber, 2008).

— *In Memoriam: Auberon Herbert, Captain Lord Lucas, Royal Flying Corps, Killed November 3, 1916* (Oxford: B.H. Blackwell, 1917).

— *The Puppet Show of Memory* (Boston: Little, Brown & Company, 1922).

Beauman, Nicola, *Cynthia Asquith* (London: Hamish Hamilton, 1987).

Bivona, Daniel, *British Imperial Literature, 1870–1940: Writing and the Administration of Empire* (Cambridge: Cambridge University Press, 1998).

Boase, Tessa, *The Housekeeper's Tale: The Women Who Really Ran the English Country House* (Aurum Press, 2014).

Brandon, Ruth, *The Spiritualists: The Passion for the Occult in the 19th and 20th Centuries* (New York: Alfred A. Knopf, 1983).

Brittain, Vera, *Testament of Youth: An Autobiographical Study of the Years 1900–1925* (London: Virago, 1978).

Brock, Michael and Eleanor (eds), *Margot Asquith's Great War Diary 1914–16: The View from Downing Street* (Oxford: Oxford University Press, 2014).

Cannadine, David, *The Decline and Fall of the British Aristocracy* (London: Penguin, 1990).

Carnarvon, Countess, *Lady Almina and the Real Downton Abbey: The Lost Legacy of Highclere Castle* (London: Hodder and Stoughton, 2011).

Carson, William E., *Northcliffe: Britain's Man of Power* (Cornell, 1918).

Chadour-Sampson, Beatriz and Hubert Bari, *Pearls* (London: V&A Publishing, 2013).

Chapman-Huston, D. (ed.), *The Private Diaries of Daisy, Princess of Pless 1873–1914* (London: John Murray, 1950).

— *Daisy, Princess of Pless by Herself* (London: John Murray, 1928).

Clarke, Tom, *My Northcliffe Diary* (London: Victor Gollancz, 1931).

Coles, Robert, *History of Beaulieu Airfield* (Lymington: Robert Coles, 1982).

Colson, Percy, *A Story of Christie's* (London: Sampson Low, 1954).

Cooper, Diana Duff, *The Rainbow Comes and Goes* (London: Rupert Hart-Davis, 1958).

Corbett, Elsie, *Red Cross in Serbia 1915–1919: A Personal Diary of Experiences* (Banbury: Cheney & Sons, 1964).

Cornish, Paul, *The First World War Galleries* (London: Imperial War Museum, 2014).

Corsano, Karen and Daniel Williman, *John Singer Sargent and his Muse: Painting Love and Loss* (New York and London: Rowman and Littlefield, 2014).

Cosgrave, Bronwyn, Vogue *on: Coco Chanel* (London: Quadrille Publishing, 2012).

Courcy, Anne de, *Margot at War: Love and Betrayal in Downing Street 1912–1916* (London: Weidenfeld and Nicolson, 2014).

Crawford, Elizabeth, *The Women's Suffrage Movement: A Reference Guide 1866–1928* (London: Routledge, 2003).

Daly, M.W., *The Sirdar: Sir Reginald Wingate and the British Empire in the Middle East*, Vol. 222 (American Philosophical Society, 1997).

Davenport-Hines, Richard, *Ettie: The Intimate Life and Dauntless Spirit of Lady Desborough* (London: Weidenfeld and Nicolson, 2008).

Davis, Norma S., *A Lark Ascends: Florence Kate Upton, Artist and Illustrator* (Scarecrow Press, 1992).

Dimond, Frances, 'Princess Victoria (1868–1935)', *Oxford Dictionary of National Biography* (Oxford: Oxford University Press, 2004–14).

Dixon, Robert, *Photography, Early Cinema and Colonial Modernity: Frank Hurley's Synchronized Lecture Entertainments* (London: Anthem Press, 2013).

Dixon, Robert and Christopher Lee (eds), *The Diaries of Frank Hurley 1912–1941* (London: Anthem Press, 2011).

Farr, Martin and Xavier Guegan (eds), *The British Abroad Since the Eighteenth Century*, Vol. 2 (Palgrave Macmillan, 2013).

Ferguson, Niall, *The Pity of War* (London: Penguin Books, 1999).

Ferris, Paul, *The House of Northcliffe: The Harmsworths of Fleet Street* (London: Weidenfeld and Nicolson, 1971).

Field, Leslie, *Bendor: The Golden Duke of Westminster* (London: Weidenfeld and Nicolson, 1983).

Forbes-Robertson, Diana, *My Aunt Maxine: The Story of Maxine Elliott* (New York: The Viking Press, 1964).

Fox, James, *British Art and the First World War, 1914–1924* (Cambridge: Cambridge University Press, 2015).

Gollancz, Israel, *Pearl: An English Poem of the Fourteenth Century Re-Set in Modern English* (London: George W. Jones, 1918).

Gosling, Lucinda, *Great War Britain: The First World War at Home* (Stroud: The History Press, 2014).

Granstein, J.L. and Norman Hillmer (eds), 'A Nursing Sister Near the Front May 1918', *Battle Lines: Eye-witness Accounts from Canada's Military History*, 490 (Toronto: Thomas Allen Publishers, 2004).

Gregory, Adrian, *The Last Great War: British Society and the First World War* (Cambridge: Cambridge University Press, 2008).

Grenfell, Ethel Anne Priscilla, *Pages from a Family Journal 1888–1915* (Eton College: Privately Printed – Spottiswoode, Ballantyne & Co. Ltd, 1916).

Hall, N. John, *Max Beerbohm Caricatures* (Yale: Yale University Press, 1997).

Harris, Russell, 'Princess Daisy of Pless: The Happy Years', Victoria and Albert Museum website 2011.

Hart, Peter, *1918: A Very British Victory* (London: Weidenfeld and Nicolson, 2008).

Hemmings, Robert, *Modern Nostalgia: Siegfried Sassoon, Trauma and the Second World War* (Edinburgh: Edinburgh University Press, 2008).

Hibbard, Ruth, 'Pearls: Piety, Poetry and Pre-Raphaelites – Part One', Victoria and Albert Museum blog 2013.

Hynes, Samuel, *The Edwardian Turn of Mind* (London: Pimlico, 1968).

Jenkins, Lyndsey, *Lady Constance Lytton: Aristocrat, Suffragette, Martyr* (London: Biteback Publishing, 2015).

Joliffe, John (ed.), *Raymond Asquith: Life and Letters* (London: William Collins, 1980).

King, Cecil H., *Strictly Personal: Some Memoirs of Cecil H. King* (London: Weidenfeld and Nicolson, 1969).

Kipling, Rudyard, and Thomas Pinney, *The Letters of Rudyard Kipling 1911–1919* (Iowa: University of Iowa Press, 1990).

Konody, Paul G., *Art and War* (London: Forgotten Books, 2013).

Lambert, Angela, *Unquiet Souls: The Indian Summer of the British Aristocracy* (London: Macmillan, 1984).

Lamont Brown, Raymond, *Alice Keppel and Agnes Keyser: Edward VII's Last Loves* (Stroud: The History Press, 2011).

Lindsay, David, Earl of Crawford, *The Crawford Papers: The Journals of David Lindsay, Twenty-Seventh Earl of Crawford and Tenth Earl of Balcarres (1871–1940), During the Years 1892 to 1940* (Manchester: Manchester University Press, 1984).

Lodge, Sir Oliver J., *Raymond, or Life and Death: With Examples of the Evidence for Survival of Memory and Affection After Death* (New York: George H. Doran, 1916).

Lovat, Laura, *Maurice Baring: A Postscript by Laura Lovat with some Letters and Verse* (London: Hollis & Carter, 1947).

Lovell, Mary, *The Churchills: A Family at the Heart of History – from the Duke of Marlborough to Winston Churchill* (London: Abacus, 2012).

MacDonald, Lyn, *The Roses of No Man's Land* (London: Penguin, 1993).

— *To the Last Man: Spring 1918* (London: Viking, 1998).

MacKay, James, *Sir Thomas Lipton: The Man Who Invented Himself* (London: Random House, 2012).

MacKenzie, Jeanne, *The Children of the Souls: A Tragedy of the First World War* (London: Chatto & Windus, 1986).

Marillier, H.C., *Christie's 1766–1925* (London: Constable & Co., 1926).

Messinger, Gary S., *British Propaganda and the State in the First World War* (Manchester: Manchester University Press, 1992).

Middleton, Judy, *Hove and Portslade in the Great War* (Pen and Sword, 2014).

Moore, Mary Macleod, *Maple Leaf's Red Cross: The War Story of the Canadian Red Cross Overseas* (London: Skiffington, 1919).

Morse, Jennifer, 'Gerald Edward Moira', *Legion Magazine* (1 January 2006).

Mosley, Nicholas, *Julian Grenfell* (London: Persephone Books, 2014).

Mulvagh, Jane, *Costume Jewellery in* Vogue (London: Thames and Hudson, 1988).

Munson, James (ed.), *Echoes of the Great War: The Diary of Reverend Andrew Clark 1914–1919* (Oxford: Oxford University Press, 1988).

Myers, A. Wallis, *Captain Anthony Wilding* (London: Hodder and Stoughton, 1916).

Myers, Charles S., *Shell Shock in France 1914–1918* (Cambridge: Cambridge University Press, 1940).

Nadelhoffer, Hans, *Cartier* (Chronicle Books, 2007).

Nicolson, Juliet, *The Great Silence: 1918–1920 Living in the Shadow of the Great War* (London: John Murray, 2009).

Northcliffe, Alfred Harmsworth, *Lord Northcliffe's War Book* (New York: George H. Doran, 1916).

Otley Museum, *Legacies of War: Untold Otley Stories* (Otley: Otley Museum, 2014).

Parker, David, *The People of Devon in the First World War* (Stroud: The History Press, 2013).

Paxman, Jeremy, *Great Britain's Great War* (London: Penguin, 2014).

Pearce, Joseph, *Literary Converts: Spiritual Inspiration in an Age of Unbelief* (Ignatius Press, 2006).

Picardie, Justine, *Coco Chanel: The Legend and the Life* (London: Harper, 2010).

Pollock, John, *Kitchener* (London: Robinson, 1998).

Pottle, Mark (ed.), *Champion Redoubtable: The Diaries and Letters of Violet Bonham Carter 1914–45* (London: Weidenfeld and Nicolson, 1998).

Pound, Reginald and Geoffrey Harmsworth, *Northcliffe* (London: Cassell, 1959).

Pugh, R.J.M., *Wingate Pasha: The Life of General Sir Francis Reginald Wingate 1861–1953* (Pen and Sword, 2011).

Ratcliff, Carter, *John Singer Sargent* (New York, London, Paris: Artabras, 1982).

Rees, Arthur J., *The Hand in the Dark* (London: John Lane, 1920).

Renton, Claudia, *Those Wild Wyndhams: Three Sisters at the Heart of Power* (London: William Collins, 2014).

Reynolds, K.D., 'Violet, Duchess of Rutland', *Oxford Dictionary of National Biography* (Oxford: Oxford University Press, 2004–14).

Ridley, Jane and Clayre Percy (eds), *The Letters of Arthur Balfour and Lady Elcho 1885–1917* (London: Hamish Hamilton, 1992).

Rowallan, Lord, *Rowallan: The Autobiography of Lord Rowallan, K.T.* (Edinburgh: Paul Harris Publishing, 1976).

Sebba, Anne, *Battling for News: Women Reporters from the Risorgimento to Tiananmen Square* (London: Faber & Faber, 2013).

Shepard, Ben, *Headhunters: The Search for a Science of the Mind* (London: Random House, 2014).

Smyth, Ethel, *Maurice Baring* (London: William Heinemann, 1938).

Souhami, Diana, *Mrs Keppel and Her Daughter* (London: St Martin's Press/ Hachette, 2013).

Stevenson, David, *With Our Backs to the Wall: Victory and Defeat in 1918* (London: Penguin Books, 2012).

Stewart, Alexander, *A Very Unimportant Officer* (Hachette, 2009).

Stone, Norman, *World War One: A Short History* (London: Penguin Books, 2008).

Sykes, Christopher Simon, *Private Palaces: Life in the Great London Houses* (London: Chatto & Windus, 1985).

Taylor, A.J.P. (ed.), *Lloyd George: A Diary by Frances Stevenson* (London: Hutchinson, 1971).

Taylor, Lou, *Mourning Dress: A Costume and Social History* (London and New York: Routledge, 1983).

Taylor, S.J., *The Great Outsiders: Northcliffe, Rothermere and the* Daily Mail (London: Phoenix Giant Paperback, 1996).

Thompson, F.M.L., *English Landed Society in the Nineteenth Century* (London: Routledge, 2013).

Thompson, J. Lee, *Northcliffe: Press Baron in Politics 1865–1922* (London: John Murray, 2000).

Trevelyan, Raleigh, *Grand Dukes and Diamonds: The Wernhers of Luton Hoo* (London: Secker & Warburg, 1991).

Turner, E.S., *Dear Old Blighty* (London: Faber & Faber, 2012).

Wemyss, Mary, *A Family Record* (London: The Curwen Press, 1932).

Wilson, Derek, 'John Jacob Astor, first Baron Astor of Hever (1886–1971)'. *Oxford Dictionary of National Biography* (Oxford: Oxford University Press, 2004–14).

Wingate, Sir Ronald, *Not in the Limelight* (London: Hutchinson, 1959).

Wrench, John Evelyn, *Uphill: The First Stage in a Strenuous Life* (London: Ivor Nicholson and Watson, 1934).

Vandiver, Elizabeth, *Stand in the Trench, Achilles: Classical Receptions in British Poetry of the First World War* (Oxford: Oxford University Press, 2010).

Young, Angela, 'The Titanic's Secret Saviour', *You* magazine, the *Mail on Sunday* (12 April 2015).

INDEX

If you enjoyed this title from

The History Press …

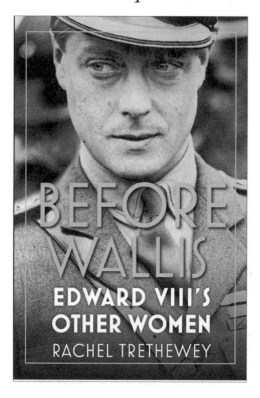

978 0 7509 8560 4